D1554199

FAIRYTALE IN THE ANCIENT WORLD

Did the familiar children's fairytales of today exist in the Ancient World? If so, what did they look like in a world whose societies were often so alien in outlook to our own? Could fairytales have existed in a world without society balls and glass slippers, or are they an invention of storytellers not much earlier than the European Renaissance? And could they have served the same social purposes as the fairytale of today?

Graham Anderson examines texts from the classical period which resemble 'our' Cinderellas, Snow Whites, Red Riding Hoods, Bluebeards, and others, and argues that many familiar fairytales were already well known in antiquity in some form, but are often now to be found in the least accessible corners of classical literature. Examples include a Jewish-Egyptian Cinderella, complete with ashes, whose prince is the biblical Joseph; a Snow White whose enemy is the goddess Artemis; and a Pied Piper at Troy, with King Priam in the role of the little boy who got away. He breaks new ground by putting forward many previously unsuspected candidates as classical variants of the modern fairytale, and argues that the degree of cruelty and violence exhibited in many ancient examples means that such stories must often have been destined for adults.

Fairytale in the Ancient World is the first modern general study of the ancient fairytale. It bridges a major gap between the study of the ancient world and the wider world of oral culture, and will be of immense value and interest to students and scholars of classical and comparative literature, folklore and the social sciences.

Graham Anderson is Professor of Classics at the University of Kent at Canterbury. He has written studies on Lucian and Philostratus, and on fiction in the ancient world, as well as *Holy Men in the Early Roman Empire* (Routledge 1994) and *The Second Sophistic* (Routledge 1993). He is currently assembling the first ever *Anthology of Ancient Fairytales*.

FAIRYTALE IN THE ANCIENT WORLD

Graham Anderson

London and New York

First published 2000
by Routledge
2 Park Square, Milton Park, Abingdon, Oxon, OX14 4RN

Simultaneously published in the USA and Canada
by Routledge
270 Madison Ave, New York NY 10016

Routledge is an imprint of the Taylor & Francis Group

Transferred to Digital Printing 2005

© 2000 Graham Anderson

Typeset in Galliard by Taylor & Francis Books Ltd

British Library Cataloguing in Publication Data
A catalogue record for this book is available from the British Library

Library of Congress Cataloging in Publication Data
Anderson, Graham.
Fairytale in the ancient world/Graham Anderson.
Includes bibliographical references and indexes.
1. Mythology, Roman. 2. Mythology, Greek. 3. Fairy tales–History and criticism.
4. Classical literature–History and criticism. I. Title.

BL805 .A63 2000

292.1'3–dc21

00-029109

ISBN 0–415–23702–5 (hbk)
ISBN 0–415–23703–3 (pbk)

FOR ROGER AND AGNES CARDINAL

CONTENTS

PREFACE

A modern collection of English fairytales begins with an attack dating from as early as 1596 against the pedants who would spend a whole day talking about the origins of *Fe Fi Fo Fum*. By contrast a modern Italian collector of fairytales acknowledges that there were times when he would have exchanged the whole of Proust for just one more variant of the tale he was currently collecting. These two attitudes well describe the conflict represented in searching for earlier and earlier versions of fairytales. There is horror at the triviality of it all (as there was in antiquity itself), and amazement at the mania that sooner or later takes hold of the collector. But there is a great deal more to it than that: by so much as asking whether the ancient world had a *Red Riding Hood* or a *Rumpelstiltskin*, we enter an area of cultural history which has been almost entirely forgotten or ignored.

This author's association with folktale research goes back a long way. In my first appointment I had the privilege of conversations with Sean O'Sullivan and Kevin Danaher, and my classical colleague Tom Williams showed me a rural hero cult in operation in County Kildare on a Sunday afternoon. It was in a classical context, working on *The Golden Ass* of Apuleius, that I realised that a purely literary approach left much territory unexplored, and that popular oral tales had to be taken into account. And it was in a comparative literary context, when I began to teach oral narrative and children's literature, that once more I became conscious of the great gaps in my own knowledge of my own field of Classical Antiquity, and benefited from the immense expertise of the late Vivienne Mylne in eighteenth-century French fairytale.

I have set out to address this study to several different audiences simultaneously: to classicists, for whom, on the whole, fairytale exists only as a kind of degenerate mythology, if it exists at all; to scholars of folktale and children's literature, for whom antiquity exists as a barrier of polite literature through which little popular material is allowed to penetrate; and to comparative literary specialists, for whom the semantics of postmodernism may often mean more than questions as simple as 'How old is Cinderella?'. I have tried, at least some of the time, to spare those outside professional folklore circles some of the rigours of type-indexing and historic-geographic method, and have found the

Opies' book on fairytales a model of clarity and simplicity. But some convolution cannot be kept out of an area where evidence is so sparse and so awkwardly placed between traditionally separate disciplines. Much of the time one feels like the prince hacking away at the undergrowth that surrounds the Sleeping Beauty's enchanted castle. But the delight is commensurate with the task: when the undergrowth is cleared away we have a castle full of Snow White and Cinderella, Rumpelstiltskin, and the rest – all in the same room. Most amazing of all: they have been lying there not for a hundred years, but in some cases for several thousand; and parts of the castle are not medieval, but built of classical columns on even earlier foundations.

It is part of the pleasure of folktale scholarship to try out versions of stories on people and watch for signs of recognition or otherwise. I have tried out materials at various times on Shirley Barlow, Tom Blagg, Ewen Bowie, Christopher Chaffin, John Court, Jim Neville, Bryan Reardon, Michael Reeve, Alex Scobie, Stephanie West, Peter Walsh and Antony Ward. I have also found classes on the traditional tale in the University of Kent a constant stimulus, particularly where mature students were able to compare the versions of tales they heard as children with those they are now encountering. Parts of the book have been delivered as lectures in the Universities of Edinburgh and St Andrews, and as a seminar in the Institute of Classical Studies in London.

I have derived much support, kindness and encouragement from Jack Zipes, and from a second anonymous Routledge reader; their suggestions have prompted an additional chapter and the relegation of some of the more complex cases to footnotes and appendices. Richard Stoneman and his staff have eased the metamorphosis of manuscript into book with an invisible magic appropriate to the subject matter. As copy-editor Mary Warren has duly performed the heroine's impossible tasks.

Most of all, I have benefited from the continued support and toleration of Roger and Agnes Cardinal over the many years that we have taught comparative literature together. And my wife Margaret has listened to the recitation of more tales than all the other victims put together, as our house has turned into a Bluebeard's castle of dismembered narratives.

Graham Anderson
University of Kent at Canterbury

ABBREVIATIONS

.

AEL	*Ancient Egyptian Literature*
ANET	Ancient Near Eastern Texts relating to the Old Testament
AT	Aarne, Antti and Thompson, Stith (1961) *The Types of the Folktale* (2nd edn)
CQ	*Classical Quarterly*
EA	*Egyptian Antiquities*
FGrH	*Die Fragmente der griechischen Historiker*
KUB	*Keilschrifturkunden aus Boghazkoei*
JAOS	*Journal of the American Oriental Society*
JEA	*Journal of Egyptian Archaeology*
LIMC	*Lexicon Iconographicum Mythologiae Classicae*
MGAM	*Modern Greek in Asia Minor*
ML	Reidar Christiansen, *The Migratory Legends* (1958)
MW	*Merkelbach–West*
OCD	*Oxford Classical Dictionary*
SHA	*Scriptores Historiae Augustae*

Latin terms which are routinely abbreviated are:

Met.	*Metamorphoses*
Mor.	*Moralia*
Nub.	*Nubes*

1

INTRODUCTION

In the course of a vulgar dinner party in a Roman novel, the nouveau riche host looks back on his career and announces that 'the man who was once a frog is now king' (*qui fuit rana nunc est rex*). A little earlier in the same dinner party one of his freedmen guests had explained the career of another nouveau riche: 'after he had stolen the goblin's cap, he found the (goblin's) treasure' (*incuboni pilleum rapuisset, thesaurum invenit*).[1] Here then, in the ordinary course of conversation of the less well educated, we have the spontaneous mention of a frog prince and a goblin's treasure, two familiar ingredients of what we might think of as fairytale. In both cases we have brief allusion to material with which the reader is assumed to be familiar. Two questions might naturally arise: were there fairytales in the Ancient World, and if so, were they much different in form, content and function from the stories we should ourselves recognise as fairytales? And if such tales did exist in antiquity, why do we seem to encounter them so seldom?

Fairytales, as we have come to recognise them, are perhaps easier to illustrate than to define: we tend to use the term loosely to mean 'tales like Cinderella or Snow White', and leave it at that. The term itself is as old as the late seventeenth century, appearing as the title of Mme d'Aulnoy's *Contes de fées* in 1698,[2] whereas the broader term folktale does not arrive till the early nineteenth century. A reasonable definition might however ask for 'short, imaginative, traditional tales with a high moral and magical content', essentially the qualities offered by the German term *Maerchen*, with its association with the world of Grimms' fairytales.[3] Such definitions are all too often doomed to admit exceptions: almost the first thing the first acknowledged modern European Cinderella does is murder her stepmother![4] But they are useful, nonetheless, and this one may be allowed to stand. The same vagueness as we might have about the definition of fairytales also tends to provide us with the assumption that they are somehow 'timeless' without actually being 'old'. The assumption, too, that fairytales are somehow the province of children seems somehow to disqualify them from existing in antiquity, precisely because we tend to take it for granted that there *were* no children in antiquity – of the kind we somehow take for granted as the audience, readers or viewers of fairytale.[5]

It has been generally appreciated that *some* evidence exists for *some* fairytales in the Ancient World,[6] but all too often we are left with the feeling that the trail quickly runs out for material of this kind. There are two contradictory assumptions that frustrate efforts to explore any possibility of any ancient genre of the kind. The first is that because popular orally transmitted stories are always changing, ancient fairytales would somehow have to look different from their modern counterparts; and, second, if they were indeed to be so different, it would be very difficult to identify them with their modern counterparts at all.[7] Part of the reason why fairytales seem so elusive is that at least in the Graeco-Roman world wonder tales told for entertainment, and especially those directed at children, were felt to be either beneath notice or, indeed, to be quite seriously discouraged: the sort of things that nurses might tell children could have expected little encouragement outside the nursery (or indeed inside, for that matter). At the same time, there is a hint that whatever the frowns of the educated, such storytelling is still obviously going on, though at a sub-literary level for the most part; this is clearly the situation reflected in Petronius' account with which we began, one of very few contexts in ancient literature where the lower orders seem to have a voice.

Name and repertoire

The general name used to describe folktale, fairytale or myth, as we should understand them, is the considerably flexible term in Greek *mythos* ('tale'). Already this term tends to carry a degree of doubt about the truthfulness of what is being recounted, a nuance paralleled in such English expressions as 'telling stories'. An additional tone of contempt is present in such expressions as *graon* or *titthon mythoi*, 'old women's tales' or 'nurses' tales' respectively;[8] in Latin some variant of *aniles fabulae*, again 'old women's tales'[9] – our 'old wives' tales' – is the regular term. The association of old women with tales can be accounted for by a sideswipe in the Christian polemist Lactantius:[10] 'as old women with time on their hands are accustomed [to tell]' (*sicut otiosae aniculae solent*). Fairytales are not to be encouraged as a serious pursuit of the working population.

We have ancient testimonia to describe in fairytale terms a number of examples: the chorus in Aristophanes' *Lysistrata* claim as children's stories that of Meilanion as a hater of women, and lover of the hunt, and Timon, hater of men.[11] We can certainly recognise both as performing deeds worthy of fairytale, as when Meilanion expends heroic toil in wooing a wayward huntswoman Atalanta, or Timon is favoured by the gods with magical wealth.[12] There is an obvious overlap between fairytale and fable, as when the tale is told of the moon and his mother,[13] or when Aesop's fables are said to consist of 'frogs and donkeys and such nonsense as is swallowed by old women and children'.[14] In his discussion on education in early childhood Quintilian has fables succeeding the *fabulae nutricularum*, 'nursery tales'.[15] Bogeymen and women loom large in the nursery repertoire: Akko, Alphito,[16] Ephialtes, Gorgo, Lamia and Mormo or Mormolyke form a small but recurrent canon of child threateners.[17] Miracles and impossible events are standard fare: Tertullian offers apples growing in the sea and fish in trees (*in mari poma nasci et in arbore pisces*);[18] Minucius Felix offers as an illustration the phenomenon of metamorphosis – men changing into birds and beasts, trees and flowers (*de hominibus aves et feras et de hominibus arbores atque flores*).[19] Other materials we should perhaps loosely classify with myth include: 'That Theseus did wrong and left Ariadne asleep on Naxos you have no doubt heard from your nurse', Philostratus assures a ten-year-old boy;[20] while Ovid presents one of the Getae as telling the story of Orestes and Pylades as a popular tale (*fabula vulgaris narrata*),[21] and one which he attributes to oral tradition in a country close to the Scythians themselves. Or we find the satirist Persius offering fairytale situations as examples of idle prayers: 'let the king and queen wish for this man as their son-in-law; let girls snatch this other fellow away; whatever this fellow tramples, let it turn into a rose' (*Hunc optet generum rex et regina; puellae/hunc rapiant; quidquid calcaverit hic, rosa fiat*).[22] The second of these we might identify as the story of Hylas,[23] while the others might hope to find a place in a variety of fantastic tales.

Tertullian comes perhaps closest to the content of a specific modern tale with an allusion to 'towers of the Lamia [a cannibal ogress] and combs of the sun' (*Lamiae turres et solis pectines*), heard by a child as a cure for sleeplessness (*inter somni difficultates*).[24] In their annotations to the Grimms' fairytales, Bolte and Polivka tentatively suggest an allusion here to the story of Rapunzel: this is certainly a very plausible purpose and context for the ogress's tower, to be scaled by the lover; as Rapunzel often shades into an obstacle-flight story where objects are thrown in the ogress's path by the lovers, the two allusions could indeed belong to the one tale, with the sun's comb as one of the objects.[25]

The circumstances of storytelling

We seem to be given little enough information about what was told by way of fairytale. And our information is equally sparse on when tales might expect to be told. When introducing an unlikely story, the chorus in Aristophanes' *Lysistrata* give their source as 'I want to tell you a story (*mythos*) that I once heard while I was still a child';[26] this is not material to admit to giving credence to as an adult. With similar disapproval Plato mentions tales which children have heard since being nursed by their nurses' or their mothers' milk.[27] The purposes of telling stories to children, in particular, vary within a predictable range of familiar situations. They can be told simply for delight: the emperor Julian highlights the function of the *mythos* of providing delight for children (*psychagogian*), as opposed to the *ainos*, which provides *parainesis* (instruction) as well.[28]

The fairytale could also be used for instruction,[29] and Strabo credits the wisest Persian teachers with making up fanciful material for their advantage.[30] One could also scare children with bogeymen such as Lamia, Mormolyke and the rest:[31] Plutarch notes that Akko and Alphito are used by women (age unspecified) to stop children from getting up to mischief (*kakoscholein*).[32] Encouragement is also marked out as a motive: it emerges from Plutarch's explanation of the telling of stories at the Athenian Oschophoria that this practice commemorates the telling of stories by mothers of children to be sent to Crete to the Minotaur to keep up their spirits[33] – a rare testimony to fairytale within fairytale. This is also the purpose of the famous occasion in which an old woman (*anus*) tells the tale we know as *Cupid and Psyche* to a young girl (not a child) at Apuleius 4.27: 'But I will distract you immediately with soothing old wives' tales' (*Sed ego te narrationibus lepidis anilibusque fabulis protinus avocabo*).[34] With some insight Dio of Prusa offers a variation – the role of tales as peace-offerings: 'as nurses tell children, when they hit them, then to console and win back their favour later on tell them *mythous*'.[35] A natural diversionary role is to be seen in bedtime stories.[36] Overall, Maximus of Tyre neatly sums up the aspect of social control inherent in telling children stories when he speaks of nurses who mind or shepherd children (*boukolousin*) by means of storytelling.[37] A further purpose is whiling away the time in repetitive female tasks: Ovid has the daughters of Minyas tell *Maerchen* as they go about their daily spinning chores.[38] Through the eyes of most ancient writers who deign to mention such tales at all, this section of the population would not have been far removed in intellectual status from children or their nurses.

The formulae of tales

The scholiast on Aristophanes' *Wasps* 1179 says that the formula *houto pote en [mys kai gale]* ('so there was once [a mouse and a weasel]') is used to preface stories, and illustrates with *en houto geron kai graus* 'now there was this old man and woman'. Other less specific openings occur in our very randomly preserved materials: Sotades introduced his tale of Adonis with *Tina ton palaion thelet' akousai* ('do you want to hear one of the olden tales?'); compare Choricius' *akoue de pros touto mala kalou logou* ('hear then besides this a nice story)' (of a mime subject).[39] There are certain mannerisms of delivery, as there still are: ('[nurses?] are good at telling those sorts of stories and weep over them at will').[40] Pliny offers a 'roll up, roll up' call, presumably as of an itinerant story-teller (*Ep.* 2.20.1): *assem para et accipe auream fabulam* ('get your money ready and listen to a really glittering tale') for a suite of three trickster episodes offered as true tales of the disreputable barrister-cum-fortune-teller Regulus.[41] (The *auream* may refer not only to the story's quality, but to the fact that Regulus himself is a gold-digger.)

We are poorly served by such limited references, in comparison with what has been rescued from modern oral cultures. I am aware of no such formulae as occur, for example, in Afanas'ev's Russian collection when a tale ends in a wedding: 'I was there, and some of the beer dripped down my face, but none went into my mouth' (i.e. I cannot vouch for the whole truth of the foregoing account).

As far as actual telling of tales is concerned, we have very limited testimony indeed, though what we have is scarcely open to argument. The following is the start of what is generally acknowledged as our only 'action replay' of a fairytale being told in its natural context:

> *Erant in quadam civitate rex et regina. Hi tres numero filias forma conspicuas habuere.*
>
> In a certain country there were a king and queen. They had three beautiful daughters....
>
> (Apuleius 4.28.1)

Even in this case arguments continue over whether the following tale, the first recognised telling of *Cupid and Psyche*, is a real fairytale as we understand it, or some synthetic product which it has been convenient for the author of *The Golden Ass* to present as a fairytale.[42] But in fact there is a little more evidence, of a slightly different kind, on the subject of telling stories to children. The elder of two Philostrati who describe a series of pictures in the later Empire offers us an imaginary trip around a picture gallery where a ten-year-old child is being asked to look at fairytale, or quasi-fairytale, subjects from art and literature. We find subjects such as: Heracles and Antaeus, an obvious 'giant-killing' theme (1.21); Heracles among the pygmies, an obvious counterpart to the dwarfs of fairytale (1.22); Heracles and Atlas (a 'stupid ogre' story); Palaemon (perhaps a Tom Thumb-type story, 1.16); Perseus (1.29), often regarded in its details as the ultimate fairytale; or the birth of Hermes (Tom Thumb again, 1.26). But such tales are mixed up with a good many other obvious children's or, more specifically, boys' interests – pets, animals, exciting chariot-races and the like, as well as some scenes from Epic and Tragedy, from which 'our' instinct would be to keep children well away, such as the madness of Heracles. Besides the accommodation to children in his subject matter, Philostratus' tales are often quite resourcefully told, with little asides to encourage audience participation:

> As for Antaeus, my boy, I think you are afraid of him; for he looks like some wild beast, nearly as broad as he is tall...No doubt you see (the giant) panting and looking at the ground which is unable to help him...And here is Hermes arriving to put a crown on Heracles.
>
> (2.21.4 ff.)

We also have a still less well-known item from a Christian father in the context of advising parents on how to tell Bible stories. This is John Chrysostom's homily *de inani gloria et de liberis educandis*. Although Chrysostom's object is

5

ironically to *discourage* what we should regard as fairytale, he affords valuable confirmation of the way we should expect children to be introduced to a repertoire of stories:[43]

(38) Therefore let (children) not hear frivolous stories and old wives tales: 'This youth kissed that maiden. The king's son and the younger daughter have done this'. Do not let them hear these stories, but let them hear others simply told with no elaboration. They can hear such from slaves, but not from all...Let those of the servants who are well fitted take part. If there be none, then hire someone who is free, a virtuous man, and entrust the task especially to him, so that he may have a full share in the undertaking.

(39)...But when the boy takes relaxation from his studies – for the soul delights to dwell on stories of old – speak to him, drawing him away from childish folly...Speak to him and tell him this story: 'Once upon a time there were two sons of one father, even two brothers.' Then after a pause continue: 'And they were the children of the same mother, one being the elder, the other the younger son. The elder was a tiller of the ground, the younger a shepherd, and he led out his flocks to woodland and lake.' Make your stories agreeable so that they may give the child pleasure and his soul may not grow weary. 'The other son sowed and planted. And it came to pass that both wished to do honour to God. And the shepherd took the firstlings of his flocks and offered them to God.' Is it not a far better thing to relate this than fairytales about sheep with golden fleeces? Then arouse him – for not a little depends on the telling of the story – introducing nothing that is untrue but only what is related in the Scriptures...And let the child's mother sit by while his soul is being formed by such tales, so that she too may take part and praise the story. 'What happened next? God received the younger son into heaven; having died he is up above...'.

(40) So far is enough for the child. Tell him this story one evening at supper. Let his mother repeat the same tale; then, when he has heard it often, ask him too, saying: 'Tell me the story' so that he may be eager to imitate you. And when he has memorised it you will also tell him how it profits him...Say to him afterwards: 'you see how great is the sin of greed, how great a sin it is to envy a brother...'. (41) This is not all. Go leading him by the hand in church and pay attention particularly when this tale is read aloud. You will see him delighted and leaping with pleasure because he knows what the other children do not know, as he anticipates the story, recognises it, and derives great gain from it. And after this the episode is fixed in his memory. He can profit in other ways from the story. So let him learn from you: 'There is no

reason for grief in adversity. God shows this from the very first in the example of this boy, seeing that He received one who was righteous through death into heaven.'

To the general reader the story of Cain and Abel is just that, a Bible story; in folktale terms it bears a good deal of resemblance to two tales: those of a just and unjust brother, and *The Singing Bone* (*AT* Type 780). The idea that the voice of the murdered Abel cries out to God from the ground offers an example of 'murder will out'. The child is then to be led from one 'two brother' story to a second, that of Jacob and Esau, culminating, from Chrysostom's point of view, in Jacob's Dream.

> (51) Consider how many things he will learn. He will be trained to trust in God, to despise no one though the son of one who is well-born, to feel no shame at simple thrift, to bear misfortune nobly, and all the rest. (Only when he is older should he be told more fearful tales, 52.)

Much of Chrysostom's text, virtually unknown in this connection, confirms, subsumes and enlarges the implications of most of the scattered testimony we have noted from so many other contexts. Stories have a moral potential; and they can and should engage a child's attention; they should also be made interesting, and they require some care as damage may be inflicted by leaving them in the wrong hands. It might be reasonably suggested that the example chosen by Chrysostom is one of the least interesting versions of 'be sure your sins will find you out'; almost any other version of *The Singing Bone* available in antiquity is more memorable and more action-packed than *Cain and Abel*. One suspects that Chrysostom is taking to its conclusions a process begun in a totally classical environment by Plato, and blinding himself to the perils of putting the message before the medium. As an antidote we might quote a story offered to children some three centuries earlier by no less earnest a moralist, Dio of Prusa:

> Would you like me, then, to delight the younger members of the audience with a short tailpiece to my story? For (the Libyans) believe every bit of it and consider that it is true. They say that once later on a group of Greek envoys were on their way to the oracle of Ammon with a heavy guard of cavalry and archers, when one of these creatures appeared to them. They thought they saw a woman lying on the sand, with a sheepskin thrown over her head the way Libyan women wear them; she was exposing her bosom and breasts and had her head thrown back. And they took her for one of the courtesans on their way from one of the neighbouring villages to join their band. So two young lads were smitten by her beauty and went towards her, vying with each other to get there first. But the creature got one and

dragged him off to her lair in the sand and ate him up. The other lad rushed past and saw her and cried out, so that the rest came to help. But the creature lunged at this lad too with its snake part foremost, killed him, and went off with a hiss. And the body was found, rotting and putrefying. And the Libyan guides would not allow anyone to touch the body, or they all would have died.

(*Or.* 5.24–27)

Dio does not quite tell us what age group he has in mind, but shock-horror has an ageless quality which he knows how to exploit.

The storytellers

As storytellers we have already noted children's nurses, working women, and older women who might naturally include grandparents, but there is also the possibility of the professional storyteller.[44] Aristophanes mentions a storyteller, Philepsios, 'who put together charming stories' (*suntitheis mythous charientas*).[45] The suggestion of professional storytellers is implied in Dio of Prusa:

not long ago (*ede pote*) I was going through the hippodrome and saw a good many men doing different things, one playing the flute, one dancing, one performing a marvel, one reading a poem, one singing, one telling a story (*historia*) or a tale (*mythos*).

(Or. 20.10)

Suetonius offers a puzzling mention of *aretalogoi* (*Aug.* 74), tellers of miracle stories or wonder tales at the court of Augustus; the second-century imperial contender Clodius Albinus may have employed the same.[46] In either case, as in the Dio Chrysostom passage, the implication would not be very elevated. It might be seen as exceptional in elevated court circles and hence as the stuff of anecdotal, trivialising biography. Dio himself brackets storytellers with the motley of market-place entertainers, though he is not above suggesting that Diogenes told Alexander the Great a Libyan monster story for its moral value.[47]

But occasionally we come across other instances which are a good deal less easy to categorise. Dio once more happens to give us an account of a woman from whom he claims to have heard an oral story:

Now as I was on my way from Heraea to Pisa beside the river Alpheus, I was able to find the road for part of the way, but in the course of coming on some woodland and rough country and more than one path leading to various herds and flocks, I met no one and was unable to ask the way, so that I was lost and at high noon I was wandering aimlessly. When I saw on some high ground a clump of oaks that looked like a sacred grove, I made for it in the hope of seeing some road or house from there. So I found some stones set together after a fashion, and animal pelts from sacrificed animals hanging and clubs and sticks, offerings from some shepherds, so it appeared; a little further off I saw a woman sitting, big and strong and getting on in years; she had a generally rustic dress and locks of white hair hanging down. I addressed all my questions to her. And she gently and kindly told me (in a Doric dialect) that the place was a grove sacred to Heracles, and about herself, that she had a son who was the shepherd and that often she looked after his flocks. She also claimed to have been endowed with the art of prophecy from the mother of the gods, and that all the shepherds round about made use of it, and the farmers, about how to produce and safeguard harvests and flocks...At some time you will meet a great man, the ruler over a great many lands and peoples; you must not hesitate to tell them this story, even if some people take you for a wandering babbler...listen then to the following tale and pay careful attention so that you recall it clearly and can tell it to the man I say you will meet: it is about the god before whom we are at this moment.[48]

What follows is really a political allegory, but is set in a fantastic landscape. Hermes leads the hero Heracles to a mountain with two peaks: paths lead to a modest regal lady, and to a repulsive tyrannical one, embodying good and bad kingship. What the old lady is telling is a thinly concealed version of a familiar folktale in which a good girl and a bad girl are competing for the attentions of a husband, who naturally opts for the former. The setting is the authentic one for a country fairytale: the old wise woman off the beaten track, telling a wonderful tale at siesta time in a place that no one can really authenticate, and who can convey genuine country wisdom to the passing stranger. Even if Dio has invented the setting, there is no doubt of the veneer of authenticity he is trying to re-create. Here we have the old woman of the genuine *anilis fabula* against her characteristic background.

All in all the evidence mentioned hitherto is a meagre harvest. Often we can identify common enough folktale motifs, but much less often actual fairytales complete. Again, *Cupid and Psyche* tends to be offered as the honorary exception, and even that is frequently explained away as something else. One recurrent problem is that so much of ancient folktale seems submerged under the catch-all label of myth or literature, or both.

The prejudice

The general ethos of such mentions is condescension, condemnation, moral disapproval or the like, as in Tacitus *Dialogus* 29, where a speaker can dismiss the *fabulae* and *errores* of the Greek childmaid. Those concerned broadly with education or morality, or both, in a philosophical context tend to regard such tales at best with suspicion.[49] The tastes of Augustus and of Clodius Albinus for storytelling may be cited as exceptional, eccentric or demeaning: the latter is dismissed by his doubtful biographer in the *SHA* as *neniis quibusdam anilibus occupatus*, as well as with *Milesias Punicas* (presumably tales like Apuleius' *Golden Ass*) and *ludicra litteraria* (*SHA* Albinus 12). But the most revealing testimony comes in the context of Old Comedy, close to the grass roots of Athenian society. In a father-and-son dialogue in the *Wasps* Aristophanes presents the young Bdelycleon trying to 'educate' his uneducated father:

B: Well then, will you know how to tell proper stories (*logous semnous*) in front of educated, sophisticated people?

Ph.:   I will indeed.

B: So what story would you tell?

Ph.:   No end of them. First of all how the Lamia farted when she was caught; then how Cardopion did his mother...

B: None of your *mythous*! But some of the human interest stories, the sort we're used to telling at home.

Ph.:   Alright, one that's very homely. So there was this mouse and this ferret...

B: You ignorant lout, as Theogenes said to the dung-collector, and that was meant as an insult. Are you going to talk about mice and ferrets in the company of grown-ups?

Ph.:   And what sort of stories should I tell?

B: Important ones, like how you were on a state delegation with Androcles and Cleisthenes.

Ph.:   But I've never been on a state delegation to anywhere, except to Paros, and then I only got paid two obols.

B: Well, at least you ought to say, for example, how Ephudion fought well in the free-style event against Ascondas, when he was already getting on and grey-haired but still had his huge ribcage, great arms and flanks, and a marvellous trunk.

Ph.:   Stop, stop, you're talking rubbish. How could he fight free-style carrying his trunk...

B: That's the way the clever people tell stories.[50]

Here we have a revealing contrast in attitudes: the old man draws first of all on two fairytale characters capable of obscene and antisocial actions, which his sophisticated son is bound to regard as infantile; he then moves on to animal fable, evidently no better in adult company; and he has no time for morally uplifting examples unless they are coloured by drunkenness. (He will move on to a lively story of theft, in the first person.) Throughout there is a strong sense of what is expected in polite and sophisticated circles – and of what comes more naturally to those outside them.

We have some prospect of guessing the context of Philocleon's first two stories: the Lamia was widely mentioned in Graeco-Roman antiquity as a child-eating monster;[51] we have in fact more than one complete Lamia-tale from the ancient world. The fart may not have been to confound its pursuers so much as out of panic; it might also be a product of indigestion from child-eating. Kardopion ('Little Kneading-trough?') was one of the *Daktyloi*, a gang of Cretan dwarfs[52] – we are still not far away from the nursery.

The case does however highlight another context for storytelling – the symposium for adults, usually adult males, whose entertainment might be varied by the introduction of either isolated tales or a whole sequence. Plato's *Symposium* includes, among more exclusively philosophical displays, at least two tales with some fairytale association: the nonsense story attributed to Aristophanes himself, in which humans are split in half and go around looking for their other halves, part of which does surface in a fairytale,[53] and Socrates' account of Diotima's speech, in which her gender and occupation as a priestess of Mantinea might again point to a kind of inspired old wives' tale, with its account of Love as the outcast child.[54] Plutarch's *Banquet of the Seven Sages* is of the same order.

It is however when we come to fiction proper, in Petronius, Lucian and Apuleius, that potentially philosophical occasions are used, sometimes facetiously, to contain clearly popular materials. Byrrhaena's banquet in *The Golden Ass* contains a complex ghost-and-necromancy story complete with the apodeictic gestures of the lively narrator Thelyphron.[55] Trimalchio's banquet includes two blood-curdling tales that are *meant* to lower the tone but liven the party: Niceros and the host Trimalchio tell tales that betray the credulity of the uneducated,[56] while Lucian attributes such tales in the *Philopseudes* to a group of eminent philosophers. Here, in a whole dialogue entirely devoted to superstitious tales, we have most of all the sense of 'That reminds me – did you hear the one about...?'. Sometimes the content in all three cases seems to cross from fairytale into realistic novella, but the prevailing atmosphere of magic and ghosts still justifies the former label. It should be emphasised that often enough narrators purport to be telling outrageous stories of supernatural experiences that happened to them in the here and now, and so emphasising what is often taken for granted as an ancient convention of telling fictional stories only under a pretext of enquiry or realism. That any such convention was *only* a pretext is patent enough: Eucrates' philosophical friends in the *Philopseudes* may purport to be exploring the supernatural around their ailing master's bedside, in imitation of the discussion concerning the soul in Plato's *Phaedo*, but anything closer to 'ghost stories around the fireside' would be hard to find.

The modern study of folktale and fairytale

We have seen, then, that there is evidence enough of what we should recognise as folktale and fairytale in antiquity, and of recognisable social contexts through which to diffuse and perpetuate them. All that that amounts to, however, is an invitation to start looking, an apparent indication that there *ought* to be something there. But it has been all too seldom taken up. How can ancient 'old wives' tales' be related to the study of folktale and fairytale on a wider basis? It is unfortunate that most scholars connected with ancient languages and literatures have little interest in, and even less command of, the materials of folktale scholarship, and vice versa. I wish to outline briefly what the study of folktale does and how, in the light of it, folktales can be seen to work.

Much of the work since the end of the nineteenth century has concentrated on collecting the raw materials – the stories gathered orally from people who had themselves heard such stories by word of mouth. The work of the Grimm brothers in the first half of the nineteenth century laid the foundation for the concept of a national archive of folktale, and the massive *Anmerkungen* by Bolte and Polivka on the Grimms' work still forms a starting-point for the serious comparative study of Western traditional tales at least. In fact there are several landmark collections of fairytale before the Grimms, and the short literary collections by Giambattista Basile in his posthumous oeuvre of 1634–6, and of Charles Perrault in 1697 still have a relevance and an influence out of proportion to their scale. But the Grimms mark the transition to the academic study of popular taletelling, although much retouching and even expurgation went on from edition to edition of the *Kinder- und Hausmaerchen*.[57] A further landmark might be said to have been reached by 1893 when the English collector Marian Cox assembled more versions of a single tale than the Grimms had put together in their whole collection.[58]

The emergence at the end of the nineteenth century of the so-called historic-geographic method[59] provided a path for folktale research for some six decades, and, with some modification, is likely to continue to flourish.[60] When a collection of variants of an individual tale reached a respectable total, it became possible to attempt to analyse the similarities and differences between variants, to localise distinctive features of a tale to a particular area, and to try to work out the geographical movement of a tale from one point to another over a period of time – in other words, to attempt to reconstruct the life history of a given tale. One can, for example, divide up a story where a heroine is helped in one group of variants by a dolphin and in another by a donkey. There will be no surprise when a people familiar with the sea tell the first version, while those in an inland mountainous area recount the second. Or let us suppose that a hero has a sword of bronze in one group of texts and of iron in another. The inference might be drawn that the former tradition is earlier than the latter, since Bronze Age metalworking precedes the Iron Age. The weakness of the method is that the oral variants tend to be concentrated in the last two centuries, and the traces of the tale further back in time tend to be scattered, literary, and seldom fully appreciated. Often any given tale may appear to be confined to western Europe, or to have an epicentre in, for example, Scandinavia, for no better reason than that intensive collection has taken place there, and virtually none in the Near East.[61] But the methodology must not be condemned on account of the unfortunate distribution and accessibility of materials; one does not give up on textual research because there are many late manuscript copies and few early papyri.

One issue soon arises: that if we compare isolated motifs in tales (such as, let us say, 'a ring swallowed by a fish') we should expect to get nowhere very quickly. The motif occurs in a number of quite different tales, not just those connected with Herodotus' celebrated story of Polycrates of Samos. From wide distribution a misleading assumption tends to arise: one says 'Fish swallow rings. Fish are caught. Hence tales containing this motif are reinvented all the time in every culture'. That is plausible, but how sound is it? If we apply it to a hero who discovers a wheel, how often do people reinvent the wheel? The answer ought to be: 'as often as it is lost' – but who loses it? One might say that no society can afford to forget it, therefore it is never lost. Can any society afford to forget a story with a fish swallowing a ring? They will not suffer the same economic inconvenience as when they forget the wheel. But if a story is memorable enough, will people not remember it as a good story? If we accept the latter premise, then we can accept the hypothesis of widespread diffusion of folktale, with deviant and misrecollected versions by forgetful or inaccurate storytellers easily corrected by those with better memories. What we should guard against is the idea that tales will be reinvented in more or less identical form by different societies as they proceed through progressive stages of civilisation, a fantasy of nineteenth-century proto-anthropology, or that because a large number of popular tales use a finite number of motifs, then oral story-tellers simply shuffle the motifs around to make new tales. There are indeed instances where two convergent tales can become confused, or where one tale seems to borrow from another, but on the whole hybrids, common as they are, still remain marginal in the process of diffusion of tales. The more examples of any given international tale-type we study, the more clearly we can see the integrity of the structure and logic of the tale. The only really obvious case of a hybrid in Briggs' *Dictionary of British Folktales* involved an instance where half of *Red Riding Hood* and the other half of *The Pied Piper* run together on a faulty tape-recording.

Students of classical literature seem to experience a major stumbling block, I suspect for bibliographical reasons. The Stith Thompson *Motif-Index* is widely accessible in reference libraries and, to confirm that a motif is found 'in folk-tale', one has only to quote a reference from it. But classical scholars too often seem totally unaware of a motif-index of larger units amounting to whole tales and the concept that these combinations of motifs are far more distinctive than their constituent motifs. Too often, too, it is assumed in the most cavalier manner that because a folktale is known to the Grimms, then it is 'universal' (and therefore must occur as a matter of course among the Patagonians or the Australian Aborigines as well). The idea is uncritically accepted of a tale known 'all over the world', a 'universal folk-theme', or the like. In almost the same breath scholars tend to assume a contradictory proposition that most folktales date from relatively recent times – that Ovid's *Metamorphoses* must be hundreds of years older than Snow White (of which, in fact, it even contains a specific named example).

Apart from elementary howlers of this order, the great difficulty surrounding us on venturing into folktale for the first time is that we are faced with widely different and well-defined examples of a folktale which are difficult to relate together. I quote a celebrated case from two distinguished field workers as late as 1948 – Rose and Argenti printed as no. 23 in their collection of folktales from Chios the following tale: a fox attaches himself to a human master and by a series of familiar tricks contrives to make him wealthy. They comment that the tale is of a very common type and note that the fox is feminine, like her counterpart in classical Greek. They do not go on to acknowledge that it is none other than Puss-in-Boots, with nothing more than a natural change of animal appropriate to the area. So familiar, one assumes, is the English stereotype of a cat as hero that anyone confronted with any other animal is blind to the correspondences in the rest of the tale.

As a result of the tale collections and classifications of earlier this century, it has been possible to assemble a type system to attempt to collect together all known instances of particular tale-types. This index is not without its problems, a view shared by even its most enthusiastic proponents, but it is more practical to work with than the 'quick-fix' solution advocated by Vladimir Propp,[62] and as new national tale collections are indexed they have tended to adopt the Aarne–Thompson system. Some may be tempted to try out the system on a particular example of a particular tale and find it does not fit comfortably either in respect of the definition of motifs or movements within a tale. But experience with the system as a whole rapidly confirms its basic strength and integrity, even in respect of culture areas where it has been less frequently applied. I have keyed my examples to it wherever possible.

Over the past few decades professional students of folklore have tended to broaden their base beyond what has been perceived as the aridity of historic-geographic approaches; interest in the underlying social relationships, psychology of gender and storytellers' mannerisms have assumed a much greater degree of interest, and it is those branches of contemporary folkloristics that are much more likely to engage the interest of students of the classics whose interests have begun to diversify in similar directions. I have looked briefly at the implications of such approaches for ancient fairytale in a penultimate chapter. This is not to underrate their importance; it is rather to emphasise that we must first establish whether or not there is an identifiable body of ancient fairytale to study.

The age of stories

How old, then, are folktales?[63] A convenient answer would be: 'old enough for us to be seldom confident that we have found the first example of any given tale'. It is often assumed, again by those outside the field, that a folktale changes every time it is told and hence quickly distorts into something completely different. But one classic recent illustration shows that this will not always happen, provided that the story is clear, logical and naturally stable. A number of variants were recorded in the late 1940s of an Israeli trickster-tale, and these were published. A few years later a text from some two and a half millennia earlier written in Akkadian, the *lingua franca* of the Babylonian empire, was deciphered. The stories were virtually identical, indeed so close that it was possible to elucidate obscurities in the Babylonian text from the folk-tale.[64] That does not prove that *all* tales are stable over long periods, but it does underline that we are never entitled to assume that, because there is a long time gap between surviving examples, the tale has been lost and reinvented, or reintroduced through a printed version to which oral storytellers were unlikely to have had access. Similarly, if a close analogue of a Greek novel turns up in a medieval French prose tale many centuries after the loss of Greek as an educated language in western Europe, we must be content to infer that the tale has survived in oral or sub-literary conditions.

The basic repertoire of surviving tales

Students of classical mythology and of modern folktale alike have arrived at a brief canon of tales which appear to have *some* continuous existence from antiquity to the present time. Such are: 'Jason and the Argonauts', which incorporates the tales of 'six around the world' and 'the obstacle flight'; Phrixus and 'Hop-o'-my-thumb' (execution of the executioner's own children thanks to deft substitution); 'Cupid and Psyche'; 'Master Thief'; 'Odysseus and Polyphemus' and the 'No-man' story (normally transmitted as separate tales); wisdom tales such as the allegory of the belly and the limbs; legends such as that of Tarpeia; birth stories of Romulus and Remus;[65] certain traditions concerning universal or local floods;[66] and the story of Oedipus as a popular tale.[67] Even in these cases however many classicists nurture a suspicion that the sheer popularity of many of these *as classical texts* is enough to account for their survival in a now popular form. Folklorists tend to favour the opposite alternative – that originally oral tales reflect a fixing of early oral versions in their brief appearances in classical literature, and that the oral tradition is then reflected in all its fluidity in the peasant tales recorded in the nineteenth and twentieth centuries. There may be cases where either is right, but the more versions there are, the more the folklorists' explanation is likely to be the more attractive. There is of course always the risk (more in theory than in practice for the experienced) that an oral tradition is influenced by a written form of a tale, or even supplanted by it. This is not really a problem until the end of the nineteenth century: it is only with the mass circulation of children's literature, the mass increase in literacy and the growth of media such as children's cartoons that a 'Disney version' of a fairytale tends to supplant more authentic and less stereo-typical or sanitised versions.

One fact cannot be overemphasised: that there can be only a limited distinction both of genre and content between myth, legend and folk- and fairytale.[68] It is a frequent preliminary to mis-classifying or not classifying a folk- or fairytale to proclaim that it is a myth, and then to find some dubious definition of myth to exclude the material from any other category. Take the following brief paraphrase from Ovid's *Metamorphoses*, long and elaborately told as a cautionary tale in Book 8 and purporting to be yet another instance of metamorphosis, a phenomenon we tend arbitrarily to associate with myth rather than folk- or fairytale:

> Once upon a time in Phrygia there was a pious couple, Philemon and Baucis. Jupiter and Mercury came round to inspect the region and failed to find any hospitality from a thousand homes. Only when they visited the poor but contented pair did they find themselves offered a humble but wholesome meal. They told the couple how to escape the flood that would reward the wickedness of their neighbours, and offered a reward to the overawed pair, who opted to remain inseparable. Both were in due course transformed to trees, while their house was transformed into a temple. The temple precinct with the two trees is still to be seen to this day; the teller, Lelex, saw them still garlanded.[69]

Here now is the same tale with the characteristic decor of an English folktale. The account is short enough to be cited verbatim:

> A long time ago there was a village in the North Riding of Yorkshire called Simmerdale, at one end of which stood a church, and the house of a Quaker woman at the other end. It happened one day that a witch came into the village and, beginning at the house next to the church, asked for food and drink; but her request was refused. And so she went on from house to house, without getting any food or drink, until at last she came to the Quaker woman's house. There, sitting in the porch, she was regaled with bread, meat and beer. Having finished her repast, she rose and waved an ash twig over the village, saying:
>
> > Simmerdale, Simmerdale, Simmerdale, sink,
> > Save the house of the woman who gave me to drink.

> When the witch had said these words the water rose in the valley and covered the village, except the old woman's house. Simmer Water is now a peaceful lake, and on fine clear days people in the neighbour-

16

hood can see down in its placid depths the ruins of the village and the church.[70]

It might be argued that we are looking at two local variants of what might be called a local legend: floods do recur, and are frequently given moral connotations. But what we really seem to have here are two different cultural settings of an identical tale. The pagan Latin catalogue poet has provided two gods and two mortals; the simpler folktale has the basic minimum of one woman and one supernatural power, which in a Christian context could well have been a saint but is here a (neutral rather than evil) witch. The jingle element characteristic of popular fairytale, and storytelling generally, is supplied and is especially appropriate to the witch. Both settings have the element of local observation: the old man Lelex has heard from old men who had nothing to gain by deceiving him; the local Bithynian peasants still pointed to the trees. Interestingly, a religious contrast is underlined in the folktale: the witch finds that it is the simplest Christian – and a woman at that living furthest away from the church, who is truly hospitable. Ovid's element of metamorphosis, not strictly necessary to the logic of the tale, is absent from the popular version. Ovid had included a good deal of social comedy, gently smiling at the clumsiness of the simple peasants; this element is unsurprisingly absent from the less sophisticated folk version.

When the variations have been noted or explained away, one fact stands out: it is less than helpful to classify the two versions as different kinds of story. Ovid's version is not a myth in the sense that his account of creation is a myth, and it helps comparison considerably if we use the Aarne–Thompson numbering for the tale – *AT* Type 750A.

Some problems of method

There is an initial problem which must be faced by any student of orally transmitted tales: no two tellings are alike and variation is inevitable. If differences are minor – if Cinderella has only one sister, and if she herself is the elder rather than the younger – there is really no difficulty. If there is one major difference, as when Cinderella is recognised by a ring rather than a shoe, there is still likely to be no problem. But what if there is *no* recognition test – if the ball is replaced by some equivalent such as a visit to a church or, in a culture where balls are not a normal social institution, a visit to a theatre, and if Cinderella is called by some other name? The basic structure of the tale should still be apparent and should be able to be reflected by comparison with one or several parallel examples. But when is a parallel not a parallel? This question gives special problems to scholars such as classicists who may be used to working with near-verbatim correspondences between texts copied from previous texts in a literary tradition. There is no hard and fast criterion for a convincing rather than unconvincing parallel, but a brief illustration devised by Vladimir Propp may serve to illustrate both problem and solution.[71] Take the following situations:

17 A Tsar gives an eagle to a hero; the eagle carries the hero to another
kingdom.

An old man gives Suvchenko a horse; the horse carries Suvchenko to
another kingdom.

A sorcerer gives Ivan a little boat; the boat carries Ivan to another
kingdom.

A princess gives Ivan a ring; young men appearing out of the ring carry
Ivan to another kingdom.

It is obvious enough that all these situations are parallel, but it is equally
obvious that at its simplest it is the verbs rather than the nouns that guarantee
the parallels; all the agents are performing the same function. It is equally
obvious that a ring is not normally parallel to an eagle, or a horse, or a boat, but
that the context is what determines that in this case it is. In another context it
might be parallel to a shoe, as in the bride tests at the end of *Cinderella*. There
will be times, too, when a princess, a king, a sorcerer, or an old man will similarly have their value as parallel agents determined by their actions. What Propp
does not emphasise here is that in other contexts a particularly memorable
object, apparently used in different ways in two texts, will call attention to some
parallelism that has been obscured or even lost. If a girl is called Cinderella, or if
she is placed among cinders, there is a prima facie case that she is involved in
some episode which ought to belong to the Cinderella story, and it is unlikely
in the first instance that an oral narrator is simply confusing her with Snow
White. Again, if a glass slipper appears in some totally different context, we
should still look carefully at that context to see whether we are looking at some
mutation of the Cinderella story itself.

There are a number of problems of method that arise when attempting to
compare ancient and modern versions of what appears to be the same story. One is
the relative infrequency of specifically named characters in folktale, and the fact
that we do not expect to align names from 'classical mythology' with modern folk
materials. Let us suppose we want to find an ancient Red Riding Hood. We may
look long and hard and not find a girl about to be eaten by a wolf as such (or a bear
or a lion for that matter). But supposing we were to find an example where, for
instance, a king called Lykokles ('wolf-fame') or Lykophron ('wolf-mind') was
about to conduct a human sacrifice? We should still need a context to help us
decide; it would help if the girl was wearing something red, had red of some sort in
her name, or red was present in some other way. But even that will not solve the
problem: we think of names like Pyrrha (fiery red) in tightly compartmented situations – in this case, associated with Deucalion's flood and nothing else. We may
also have a wholly misguided prejudice: 'that's a myth, not a fairytale', etc. Some
realignment of our perceptions may be needed, and we should constantly try to
put ourselves in the place of an uneducated post-classical Christianising storyteller
who may have to make a classical story intelligible by demoting gods into demons

or magicians, turning oracles into magic mirrors, turning a routine visit to Delphi into a quest for the navel of the earth, or suchlike.

Another obvious difficulty is the random distribution of material. We may have a story conventionally regarded as classical myth, where the brief connected narratives are late and sketchy in their detail, as reported by Apollodorus or Pausanias, and where frequent other references are little more than one-line summaries in mythographers' variants up to a thousand years apart. Almost always, too, the emphasis will not be on magical details that constitute so much of the essence of fairytale, but on quasi-historical genealogy. The corresponding modern tale may be fixed in the minds of all readers from a prettified court version in a literary source from seventeenth-century France,[72] bearing only minimal resemblance to what we can piece together from an ancient analogue. There might be a closer variant in a medieval romance or in a modern recording from an Armenian storyteller recorded as late as 1940 in Detroit, or a modern Greek speaker in an Anatolian village in the early 1900s. The tendency for first entrants in either field, or both, is likely to be bewilderment or despair, with an uneasiness as to what we are actually looking for and whether we can hope to find it with materials so disparate in cultural context and character, and with such immense chronological gaps. The answer, as far as it can be said to exist, lies in the resilience of the material itself. If a story is a genuine folktale or fairytale it will maintain most of its structure, intrinsic logic and basic identity for centuries or millennia on end. In the world of traditional storytelling (as opposed to modern literary parody or pastiche), I have yet to encounter a wolf trying on the glass slipper.

This basic stability of tales is already apparent from varieties of *The Poor Man of Nippur*, which do not differ much in modern Palestine from their presentation in Akkadian texts of the first millennium BC that were found *only after the modern oral texts were recorded*. In such cases the modern storytellers could not possibly have been influenced by published versions of the ancient texts. We have some idea as to how tales can survive in this way: if details become sufficiently well fixed, generations of storytellers and listeners in an oral culture will automatically correct them a good deal of the time. A brilliant parody of the mischievous grandfather attempting to tell wrong versions of a well-known fairytale furnishes all the proof that is needed: the child will not tolerate a tale of 'Little Green Riding Hood' going through the wood and meeting a giraffe, or meeting a wolf that asks 'what's ten times eight?'.[73] But that does not prevent, say, a modern Iranian version of the story sounding perfectly natural to an Iranian audience that expects a male Red Riding Hood who wears nothing red and who, at the end, is not even eaten by the wolf.[74] Perhaps the best example is offered by William Hansen: in a puzzling passage of the *Odyssey* (11.121–134), the hero is instructed to take an oar so far from the sea that it is mistaken for a winnowing fan, and there offer sacrifice to Poseidon. Cedric Whitman's chance encounter with an American seaman in a railway compartment went to the heart of the matter: the sailor said he would move as far from the sea to retire as to where people mistook an oar for a shovel. The sub-literate sailor understood the significance of the 'mistaken object' test: it is not entirely clear that Homer or his commentators have done so. Sea-lore is a conservative and highly international affair, and it is easier to regard the practice as a timeless superstition rather than something reinvented from Homer in modern times, when Homer's text itself was not understood till 1990.[75] In this instance, as it happens, we have considerable intermediate tradition to adduce in the form of legends of St Elias. But even without them we should be inclined to see modern folklore as shedding new light on a problem from the very beginning of classical literature.

The form of a fairytale: variation and variant

In a number of instances we shall find that a legendary or quasi-historical tale is threatening to slip over the border into folk- or fairytale. We can see almost imperceptible differences, for example, in the way that the traditional tale of the musician Arion is told. We are most familiar of course with the version from Herodotus I, which might seem a little *ben trovato* but at least in the realm of the possible. Arion comes home to Corinth, is threatened with death by the pirates who wish to steal the famous singer's fortune, jumps from the ship, is rescued by a dolphin, and survives to confront his accusers at Periander's court in Corinth. The version in Hyginus, however, contains a number of embellishments which in effect transform the whole genre of the tale:

> Apollo appears to Arion before his encounter with the pirates. He then sings until the dolphins have gathered. At this point he leaps, to be carried by the dolphin. But he forgets to push the dolphin back to sea after it lands him, and it is stranded and dies. King Periander supplies it with a tomb. When the pirates are caught, the king asks them to take the oath at the dolphin's tomb, and Arion is made to jump from concealment at it.

In one respect this version is actually more logical than that of Herodotus: it gives more reason for the song than just a free concert for the ungrateful pirates. But overall we are in 'Cinderello' country: the man who has made his wealth, helped by a helpful fish which dies in the rescue attempt.

Another example, which tends to be obscured by its more popular rival version, is the story of Gyges in Plato's *Republic*. Now, in Herodotus I, Gyges is a faithful courtier of his master Candaules of Lydia, who wishes to share with Gyges a sight of his wife's naked body, to the servant's shame and embarrassment. Detected in the ill-fated act, he is given the choice by the queen of execution or murdering the king and succeeding him. 'Gyges chose to live', as Herodotus puts it, and the whole tale is entirely possible if not necessarily probable.

By contrast Plato has Gyges falling into an underground chamber, finding a gigantic bronze horse, and taking a ring from the body of a dead giant inside with the magical property of making him invisible. He blames Gyges himself for abusing his magical powers and seducing the queen, then being able to dispose of the king. But the overall ethos of the story has changed with the advent of a wonder element: it seems to have become prima facie an *Arabian Night* before its time. Or rather, it offers something very close to one specific *Arabian Nights* tale, that of Aladdin. The latter begins his rise to fortune by rescuing an article from an underground chamber. One of his *genii* belongs to a ring rather than a lamp; and he too has the capacity to enter a royal bedchamber and dispose of a rival for the princess's hand.

An example which has been partly recognised suggests the extent of the problem and what ought to be done to alter our perceptions of the whole subject. It has long been realised that the central motif of the story of Hop-o'-my-thumb has its essence in a mythical narrative in Hyginus:

> When Athamas, king of Thessaly, thought his wife Ino, the mother of his two sons, had died, he married Themisto, the daughter of a nymph, and had twin sons by her. Afterwards he found out that Ino was in Parnassus, where she had gone for a bacchic rite. He sent for her and had her brought back, then he concealed her. Themisto found out that she had been found, but did not know who she was. She began to want to kill his sons. She took as her partner in crime Ino herself, whom she took to be a prisoner, and told her to clothe her own (Themisto's) sons in white, those of Ino in black. Ino clothed her own in white, Themisto's in dark clothes. Then Themisto, taken in by the trick, killed her own sons; when she found out, she took her own life. As for Athamas, he killed Learchus, his elder son, on a hunt in a fit of madness; but Ino, with her younger son Melicertes, threw herself into the sea and became a goddess.

Those who have studied the story accept that the substitution of the murderer's children for the victims is indeed that of *Hop-o'-my-thumb*, and that therefore this part of the *Hop-o'-my-thumb* story must be as old as Greek mythology. But all too often it is the follow-up that is lacking: the story that Hop-o'-my-thumb and his brothers go hungry, or that he puts on an ogre's seven league boots and escapes with the giant's treasure – all this seems alien to the concepts of classical mythology. But this is only apparent until we re-read the *rest* of the story of Athamas. Here we find that Phrixus, Athamas' son not by Ino but by Nephele, volunteers for sacrifice during a famine and escapes his murderous stepmother on the golden ram. In terms of this back-ground, the golden fleece combines the gold treasure with the seven league boots. At a further point in the story we pick out the information that Phrixus and Helle were wandering in a wood, as the children do in *Hop-o'-my-thumb* (*Petit Poucet*), when their mother told them to mount the golden fleece. Still further examination of the Athamas legend and Tom Thumb, usually thought unrelated to Hop-o'my-thumb, reveals a similar relationship: Melicertes/ Palaemon is thrown into a boiling cauldron; Tom Thumb falls into a pudding. The motif complex can be seen further in a renaissance fairytale, that of Basile's Nenillo and Nenella ('little Dwarf-boy, little Dwarf-girl'). Helle is normally known for falling off the golden ram and drowning; likewise Nenella falls into the water (from a pirate ship) into the mouth of a fish; Nenillo is the courtier of a prince. They are eventually reconciled together. There are surviving antique versions where Phrixus returns to Athamas, and where Helle survives and is rescued by a lover-husband; while Tom Thumb also has an adventure inside a fish:

Athamas story	*Hop-o'-my-thumb*	*Tom Thumb*
Mother's children wander in wood	Mother's children wander in wood	
They are put in bed with murderer's children	They are put in bed with murderer's children	
Identity tags are changed and murderer murders own children	Identity tags are changed and murderer murders own children	
Surviving stepchild given gold and rapid magic transport	Surviving stepchild steals ogre's gold and seven league boots	
Surviving child falls into boiling cauldron		Child falls into pudding

In such cases we at least have the means of recognising that a story *is* a folk- or fairytale. But in a large number of instances in a Graeco-Roman context such materials tend to be read as something else. A good example is the story of Cycnus, readily classified either as myth or as anecdote. It occurs in Ovid (*Met.* 7.371–81) and Antoninus Liberalis 12 as a tale about the bad-tempered boy who is spoiled by his lover and when thwarted turns into a swan. Students of mythology are simply embarrassed: 'it is libel to call this rubbish mythology' (Rose 1928: 124). Independently commenting on the version in Antoninus Liberalis, Celoria notes 'the bitty inconsequentiality of a story that seems to show the marks of being cobbled together by a village storyteller rather than by an editor in antiquity'. But neither attempts to say *what* folktale.[76] However, a Siberian version reported as recently as 1989 presents the material in something like a conventional domestic context:

A beautiful girl Aioga is consequently vain and refuses to do domestic tasks; a neighbour's daughter performs the tasks, going for water in her stead; a scone is given to the neighbour's daughter who did the errand instead, and she gives the scone back to Aioga now in a tantrum. In her anger she sprouts feathers, and 'waved her arms above the girl so violently that her fingers became as white and fluffy as the wind-blown snow; she toppled over the river bank, forgot the Nani tongue, and only her name remained as the swan's cry Ai-oga-ga-ga'.

(Riordan 1989: 69–71)

In the first instance, we note a quite different cultural nuancing: the Graeco-Roman versions both accept a homosexual couple, of whom one performs the task for the other; the Siberian form of the tale actually does acknowledge such a possibility (in the sense that the good girl performs a task on the bad girl's behalf). Although it is not expurgated to any Christian standards, it is obviously culturally tailored to the domestic situation of a younger child. The tasks, too, are much more domestic – drawing water rather than bringing a lion, an eagle or the like. But it would be wrong to suggest that these creatures belong to mythology and not to folktale.

Celoria also notes Athenaeus 9.939e (Boeus' version: Cycnus was changed by Ares into a bird which set off for the river Sybaris and kept company with a crane). A truncated version, without the metamorphosis element, occurs in Conon 16: the Cretan Promachos falls in love with a beautiful youth Leucocomas, who sets dangerous tasks. The task of bringing an important helmet infuriates the devotee and he gives it to someone else (cf. the Siberian tale, where the mother intervenes to play this role); Leucocomas kills himself. In yet another version (Strabo 10.4.12 citing Theophrastus), a Cretan Leucocomas inflicts on Euxynthetus the task of bringing a dog a great distance.[77] There is a strong prejudice that myth operates at the level of the elevated, while folk- and fairytale at the level of the trivial, but we must keep an open mind, and bear in mind the cultural context of each individual case.

We are able, then, to see that the opportunities, the social framework, and the purpose for folk- and fairytale existed in antiquity, and that prevailing habits of thought tend to ignore or disregard them, much as sophisticated literature in antiquity itself tended to do. But there is enough to go on to make a start at recognising that major folk- and fairytales known to us are less unlikely to be found in antiquity than has been supposed. If the ancient world knew *Hop-o'-my-thumb* and *Cupid and Psyche*, did it know *Cinderella* and *Snow White*? In this author's view the student is constant labouring under the bias that *Red Riding Hood*, *Cinderella*, *The Frog Prince*, *Snow White*, and the rest, somehow should not have had any right to exist in antiquity. The extent to which we have to delve to find traces of them emphasises just how wide such a prejudice there must have been in antiquity itself. To anyone accustomed to reading folktales in quantity it will come as no surprise to encounter a male Cinderella, an angel as fairy godfather, a Cinderella without a slipper test, and many more such deviations from the endlessly repeated stereotypes of Perrault or the Grimms.

2

THE CINDERELLA STORY IN ANTIQUITY

Cinderella can fairly be claimed as the best known of fairytales in modern times, as well as the first tale to be subjected to attempts at the 'exhaustive' collecting of its variants. It was long assumed that the story, or rather group of stories, did not date much further back than the early seventeenth century, when a recognisable form of it appeared as Basile's *La Gatta Cenerentola*.[1] But from time to time throughout this century discoveries have been made to show that the tale must be much older, and few who have seriously examined the evidence would be tempted to measure the tale as a whole by the yardstick of its most famous example, the version published by Charles Perrault in 1697.[2] It can now be seen that a number of the Perrault features such as glass slipper, pumpkin coach, clock striking midnight, and others, are not essential, or even necessarily characteristic, of the orally transmitted story. Taken as a whole, the hundreds of versions known present the heroine under a variety of names: Cinderella, Ashiepattle and Popelutschka are the most obvious European variations; sometimes she has sisters (often less beautiful, rather than ugly), sometimes not; sometimes she has a fairy godmother helper, sometimes a helpful animal or plant, sometimes even a fairy godfather, or some combination of such forces. The basic framework for the story printed by Aarne–Thompson can be slightly abridged as follows:[3]

I   The persecuted heroine   ΤΤ ς ιϑ

    (a1) The heroine is abused by her stepmother and stepsisters; she stays on the hearth and ashes; and

    (a2) is dressed in rough clothing – cap of rushes, wooden cloak, etc.

    (b) She flees in disguise from her father who wants to marry her; or

    (c) is to be killed by a servant.

II Magic help
    While she is acting as servant (at home or among strangers) she is advised, provided for, and fed

(a) by her dead mother; or
(b) by a tree on the mother's grave; or
(c) by a supernatural being, or
(d) by birds; or
(e) by a goat, a sheep, or a cow.
(f) When the goat (or other helpful animal) is killed, there springs up from her remains a magic tree.

III Meeting the prince

(a) She dances in beautiful clothing several times with a prince who seeks in vain to keep her, or she is seen by him in church;
(b) she gives hints of the abuse she has endured as a servant girl; or
(c) she is seen in beautiful clothing in her room or in the church.

IV Proof of identity

(a) She is discovered through the slipper test; or
(b) through a ring which she throws into the prince's drink or bakes in his bread.
(c) She alone is able to pluck the apple desired by the prince.

V Marriage with the prince

All readers will recognise that this framework will describe a recognisable Cinderella – or rather a large number of combinations of Cinderella variants. In fact, the possibilities should be extended quite considerably; the scheme does not take into account variants where the prince never sees the heroine at all before the token test, but only receives a recognition token. This will tend to happen in social situations where strict segregation between the sexes is practised, and so can be expected as a matter of course in some oriental variants. Nor does the scheme recognise situations where the heroine is seen naked rather than clothed, a mainly southern and eastern trait for obvious reasons – it is only likely where naked bathing outdoors is easily feasible. Nor does it take account of such obvious corollaries as the possible punishment of the rival sisters at or after the marriage of Cinderella. But on the whole the headings present a reasonable test of what will constitute a version of the tale.

There are a number of easily distinguishable sub-types of the overall outline. The two latest of the three major analysts, Rooth[4] and Aarne–Thompson, distinguish no fewer than five major varieties in the transmission of the story. There is what we usually see as the most 'proper' version, Cinderella itself, characterised by the motifs of hearth cat, father's mission, treasure tree, shoe test (Basile, Grimm). This requires rival sisters and the inevitable cinders, and entails a preliminary motif (*not* in Perrault) of the father bringing presents to the girls and so establishing their contrasting attitudes of goodness and greed.

A considerably more grotesque variant is offered by the Grimms' 'One-eye, two-eyes, three-eyes': here the characteristic motif is that the sisters spy on the heroine and helpful animal; it usually entails the motifs of a tree, often raised from the bones of the helpful animal, and a fruit-picking test (*AT* Type 511).[5] Both these variants can be combined to form a third, often including an underground test by a supernatural agent (this merges into Aarne–Thompson Type 480, *The Kind and Unkind Girls*).

Two rather different forms are set clearly apart from the standard Cinderella complex: in the *Cap-O'-Rushes* sub-type we expect an incest motif, with the incestuous father required to provide his daughter with some sort of sun, moon and star dress or dresses, and some sort of demeaning camouflage for the heroine to hide the dresses, performing a similar function to the more familiar ashes. Dresses of animal pelts, wood or even lice are found. There are regularly no sisters, and a lovesick prince with the token placed in his food by the heroine employed as a kitchen maid (*AT* Type 510B).[6] And finally, in a male Cinderella type, 'The Little Ox', the hero is saved by a self-sacrificing ox or bull and fed by an 'ear cornucopia' or similar device, often with the secondary motif of a journey through woods of gold, silver and jewels, before the 'normal' events of recognition and marriage take place (*AT* Type 511A). It is an easy matter to go through the summaries of Marian Cox of over 300 versions assigning each one at least approximately to one of these types;[7] though not unexpectedly in a sample of this size, a number of versions, especially literary ones, seem to defy easy or absolute classification.

Nor, it must be stressed, is the evidence static. As new examples are identified, type indexing requires more or less continual expansion and modification, and it is useful to suggest some brief criteria. We should be prepared to admit material as belonging to the cycle if it is closely related to examples in the collections of Rooth or Cox, or if it contains one or more names related to Aschenputtel, Cinderella, Maria Wood, or the like. Where major deviations occur, a tale is not necessarily excluded, but we do have to attempt to explain the oddity; often it may simply be the result of conflation or confusion, but just as readily it may be the result of different social or literary convention, or a different view of family relationships. It would not be particularly disqualifying if a Muslim version of Cinderella were to entail the prince's marriage to a second wife, for example. It is also possible to accept new Cinderellas if they appear to contain a compelling juxtaposition of elements whose conjunction is not otherwise associated in standard folktale repertoire: if a tale were to contain a pumpkin coach and a glass slipper, neither of which is obligatory or even characteristic of the mainstream of Cinderellas but which are not associated with such tales as Rumpelstiltskin, Snow White, or the Assman – or indeed any other tale generally known except Cinderella – then it is once more wise to look carefully to see if the tales containing them belong to one of the basic patterns for the story after all.

Earlier versions

Relatively recently two versions have been identified which place the origins of the tale well outside the boundaries of Renaissance Europe: these are a Chinese version from the ninth century AD,[8] and a much less well-publicised Sanskrit version underlying Kalidasa's drama *Sakuntala* of the fifth century AD,[9] and also known as early as an allusion in the *Mahabharata* of some two centuries earlier. The known age of the tale, then, has been advancing steadily to late antiquity, though not in Europe. It is time to look at classical versions in their own right.

A classical Cinderella I: Rhodopis

Attempts to place any version of the tale in Classical Antiquity have been limited, incidental and neither widespread nor complete. Anna Rooth made a fugitive suggestion of an element of the tale in the *Argonautica* legend and the story of Io,[10] but otherwise the only contender has been a reference in the Greek geographer Strabo (first century BC/AD) to a tale about a girl called Rhodopis:

> They tell the fabulous story (*mytheuousi*) that while she was bathing, an eagle seized one of her shoes from her maid and brought it to Memphis, and while the king was dispensing justice in the open air, the eagle arrived over his head and threw the shoe into his lap. The king was aroused by the *rythmos* of the sandal and the strangeness of the event, and sent all around the country in search of the woman who wore it. When she was found in Naucratis she was brought up country to Memphis and became the king's wife.[11]

This example has no problem in supplying three of the five essential steps as it stands: Rhodopis has the help of an animal, which might also be classed as 'supernatural intervention'; the operation of the slipper test motif could not be clearer, nor could 'marriage to the prince'. On the other hand, there are no rivals and no actual sight of the bride before the slipper test, neither omission unexampled within the modern tale tradition, but there seems to have been no attempt to look at any further details that might be available on Rhodopis herself. These can be found in a long notice on the very same girl in Herodotus (2.134f.) some five centuries before Strabo:

> (Rhodopis) came from Thrace, and she was a slave of Iadmon son of Hephaestopolis, a man from Samos; she was a fellow slave of Aesop the writer of fable...(she) arrived in Egypt, brought by Xantheus of Samos, and when she got there she was freed for a large sum by Charaxus of Mytilene, son of Scamandronymus, brother of Sappho the lyric poet. Having obtained her freedom, she actually stayed in Egypt and became

so popular with lovers that she obtained a huge fortune for a person in her profession...she wanted to leave a memorial of herself in Greece by doing something that no one else should have thought of and putting it in a temple, and laying it up at Delphi as her memorial. So having made a great many iron roasting-spits for oxen for a tenth part of her wealth, she sent them to Delphi.

This Rhodopis is clearly the same one as was in due course to be mentioned by Strabo. The latter noted that Charaxus was in love with her, and both writers comment on the fact that she is claimed to have built one of the pyramids, a claim Herodotus emphatically rejects and Strabo accepts without discussion, Indeed, that is the only reason why either writer sees fit to mention her at all. Herodotus provides all the essential information except for the marriage to the Pharaoh and the identification by means of the slipper.

Several details in Herodotus' account point to a legendary quality. It is not a matter of historical confidence that she was a slave in the same household as Aesop, a figure whose own existence is either legendary or would claim legendary elements. Moreover Sappho writes of a girl called Doricha, not Rhodopis, and other writers disagree as to whether the two were one and the same character. Sayce long ago noted that 'Hephaestopolis' ('Firegodville') is an odd name for the *father* of her owner – a place name rather than a personal name. What has not been done is to see what the story looks like once Herodotus' and Strabo's testimonia are put together as information available about one and the same Rhodopis by Strabo's time:

> A girl called Rhodopis was a slave in the household of Iadmon son of Hephaestopolis ('Firegodville') in Samos. She was taken to Egypt by Xantheus ('Goldman') where she was given her freedom by Charaxus ('Seabream'/'Vinepole') of Mytilene. There she worked as a courtesan and while she was bathing in Naucratis an eagle carried her shoe to the Pharaoh; after finding it was hers by testing it on all the women in the country, he married her. As a thank-offering she gifted a collection of iron ox-roasting spits to Delphi.

We have already noted the Cinderella element in Strabo. Do Herodotus' details amplify this aspect of the story? They tell us that she was a slave, and concurrently and/or subsequently a courtesan. This indicates a 'persecuted heroine' – a slave status and a despised profession. But the names add something as well. Cinderellas in the Balkans often have the heroine allege on her three encounters with the prince that she comes from places connected with the hearth ('Tongstown', 'Ashborough', 'Scuttleforth', or the like). Here we have a connection with 'firegodville', a place name with similar associations.[12]

Still more cogently, the offerings at Delphi are of a kind one makes when able to give up a trade or profession: gladiators dedicate their swords, sailors their oars, and so on. Someone who dedicates ox spits would reasonably be implying service in the hearth as a kitchen maid. The name Charaxus is significant for a Cinderella tale: it is the name for a fish, the sea-bream, and for a vine pole (we are also told by Strabo that he was a wine-importer). This gives her some more helpers: we have noted that trees and fish, separately or in combination, help Cinderella, or that she may be expected to deal with a killed ox. All these elements are hinted at here. The story may have the 'feel' of historical anecdote, but the characters have names reminiscent of the talking trees and animals that routinely advance the fairytale heroine's career. Moreover, the offering, attributed with perhaps selfish motives by Herodotus, might be seen as an act of piety: the great Egyptian queen as she now is thanks the Greek god and shows herself not unmindful of her rags-to-riches past. The implication of combining the testimonies of Herodotus and Strabo on the same heroine is that at least by the latter's time of writing in the first century BC/AD the wherewithal for a 'full' Cinderella based on a quasi-historical Rhodopis was clearly available. It might of course have been available long before: Herodotus might have rejected information about the slipper test and the eagle as fanciful, if indeed he knew it; he certainly has an extensive repertoire of folktales told almost incidentally for their own sake.[13]

Here, then, we have a recognisable overlap of stories concerning the same girl, both of which are consistent with a basic pattern of Cinderella. We should perhaps be asking ourselves already why it is that the Strabo version is so much more readily recognisable than that of Herodotus. Whatever our answer, Rhodopis is our most readily identifiable classical Cinderella.

Aspasia of Phocaea: an early literary Cinderella in Aelian

Rhodopis is not by any means the only ancient candidate for the fairytale princess in the Graeco-Roman world. The name of the heroine is no more standardised in antiquity than in the modern tale. Aelian's story from the second/third century AD about Aspasia of Phocaea presents an important missing link between fairytale and Romance. It is told as an extended moral exemplum in the *Varia Historia* (12.1), a miscellany of curious facts, diverting anecdotes, and the like: in the handling of individual details the author could scarcely make it clearer that this is a story of virtue and modesty rewarded. But some almost incidental characteristics point towards a classification of the story as a Cinderella. A summary will best bring out the Cinderella characteristics:

> Aspasia of Phocaea loses her mother at birth and her father brings her up in poverty. She dreams however that she will be with a noble man. But she is disfigured by a growth on her face. In a dream a dove appears and changes into a woman; Aspasia is instructed to treat the growth with Aphrodite's roses; her beauty returns. She is now compelled to attend at a banquet of Cyrus the Younger with three

other girls. The others are dressed and behave as courtesans; Aspasia modestly repels the prince's advances and so attracts him all the more; he rejects the others and forms an exclusive and two-sided relationship with her. She rewards Aphrodite with a golden statue and a jewelled dove, and looks after her father; when Cyrus the Younger offers her a precious necklace fit for a queen, she proves her nobility by offering it to his mother instead. In a short sequel she is taken over by Artaxerxes after Cyrus' own death; she gratifies him by wearing the eunuch Timagenes' clothes over her own black mourning garb.

The relationships and dynamics of this story bring it close to Cinderella tradition even when details and outcomes are opposite. The Aphrodite figure and the dove discharge the function of fairy godmother and helpful animal respectively. The heroine's disfigurement is not due to poverty or to malice from sisters, but it is solved by a supernatural helper and her own obedience to instructions. This time, in contrast to the case of Rhodopis, we do actually have something resembling a ball, insofar as the girl is presented at what is clearly designed as a formal (and competitive) social occasion at court. She does not receive clothes or jewellery directly from the fairy godmother, but the animal helper-cum-fairy godmother – Aphrodite herself, it appears – is still responsible for the restoration of her superlative natural beauty; she would presumably not have been chosen to appear before Cyrus with her clear disfigurement. What is particularly characteristic of the tale-type is the mixture of beautiful attire and reticence: normally Cinderella goes out of her way to be seen as little as possible in her magically acquired finery, and continually tries to revert to her original humble state, testing the resolve of her suitor and requiring to be loved for herself rather than her finery. In this version, this reticence is carried so far that at the point where we expect the token test, the heroine actually refuses to put on the precious necklace that serves the function of a token. This is a stage further, in effect, than the instances where she hides from the test of her own accord as opposed to being hidden by her rivals. Aspasia secures the proof of her beautiful nature and her eligibility for royal favour by *not* wearing the token. In other words, the token test is adapted to a court etiquette where a powerful mother-in-law figure has to be won over. The motif of refusing a token is on occasions found in 'normal' Cinderellas: sometimes in cases where Cinderella has been insulted by the prince on some previous occasion, she refuses to accept the slipper – or accept it back (though she usually relents in the end). It should be noted, however, that a number of Cinderellas lack the test altogether: the prince may simply be able to prevent the girl from leaving the ball and able to marry her straight away.

The unusual feature here is that ball and bride tests are in effect conflated. Some Cinderellas have the prince's overtures rebuffed (running away from the ball is itself often able to be read as such an act); it is unusual, if not unique, to have the sensuous detail provided here of the King fondling the heroine's breast. A very few examples have the hiding of the prince's gift instead of a token test. I have found only one other where the competitors are three and not one or two,[14] and it is unusual to have them as simply rivals and not specifically sibling rivals.

The name of the heroine raises a problem: in Greek it means 'welcomed', from *aspazein*, but it is close enough to the sequence of names for the modern heroine Aschenputtel, Ashiepattle, and suchlike, normally connected with ashes (and sometimes obscenely so). It may be that an original of the latter in some non-Greek language has been Hellenised into the nearest Greek name available, but further evidence is needed before any conclusion can be drawn.

Once more it is significant to see a complete Cinderella so early, though both the Rhodopis texts and one of the Asenath ones discussed below are actually earlier still. What is more striking is the feel of a developed psychological romance and rags-to-riches fairytale side by side in a story with a specific historical setting. Here is a Cinderella, or a very near approach to one, placed in a specific historical setting and treated as the heroine of a romantic novella. It ought to give the lie to B.E. Perry's dogmatic assertion that novella could not develop into romance:[15] it would be easy enough to multiply every page by ten by *ecphrasis* and other kinds of expansion.

The relationship between historiography and folktale is also raised: Plutarch clearly regarded the *chreia* at Cyrus' banquet as having actually taken place, and can pause in more than one strictly historical context to remark on it.[16] But history and folklore are clearly convergent in a 'bride-show' tale, and, irrespective of its Aarne–Thompson tale-type, Aelian's presentation could be argued to have the flavour of fairytale in its own right, and fairytale with seventeenth- to nineteenth-century human values at that. This is a tender and well-told 'art tale' of a kind that the lady storytellers of a French court, such as Madame D'Aulnoy or Madame LePrince de Beaumont, would readily have expanded. Here then are the essential 'movements' of Aelian's Aspasia:

Aspasia the daughter of Hermotimus came from Phocaea and was brought up as an orphan; her mother had died in childbirth. Afterwards Aspasia was brought up in poverty, but she was taught modesty and self-control. She had a recurrent dream which offered her the prophecy of good fortune and gave a hint of good luck in the future – that she would live with a fine and noble partner. While she was still a child, she had a growth below her face, just underneath her chin. It was unsightly to look at and distressed father and daughter alike. So her father showed her to a doctor, who undertook to cure her for a fee of three staters. Her father said he did not have the money, and the doctor said that he for his part did not have enough of the medicine. Aspasia naturally was distressed at this and went out to cry. As she put a mirror on her lap and saw herself in it she was very upset. She took nothing to eat in her misery, but at just the right moment she fell asleep, and as she slept she dreamt that a dove arrived, turned into a woman, and said: 'Never fear, and have done with doctors and drugs alike. But take all Aphrodite's withered garlands of roses, grind them up and put the powder on the growth.' When she heard this the girl did as she was told and the growth disappeared. And once more Aspasia was the most beautiful girl of her time, and had regained her beauty from the most beautiful goddess.

Once Aspasia visited Cyrus son of Darius and Parysatis, the brother of Artaxerxes. She had been reluctant to go and her father had been reluctant to send her, but she went of necessity, as often happens when cities are taken or tyrants or satraps have their way. At any rate it was one of Cyrus' satraps who had brought her to him together with other girls...When she first came to Cyrus, he just happened to have come from dinner, and was on the point of having drinks according to Persian custom – for the Persians, after filling themselves with food, spend a long time in their cups and toasts; they prepare for drinking as [Greeks] do for a wrestling bout. While they were in the midst of the drinking, then, four young Greek girls were brought to Cyrus, including Aspasia, the girl from Phocaea. They were most beautifully turned out. The other three had been groomed by their serving women, who had come with them. Their hair had been done and their faces were made up with face powders and cosmetics. And they had been schooled in how to win Cyrus' attention, and how to flatter him and not turn away if he approached them, and not to be annoyed if he touched them, and to let themselves be kissed – in fact the skills of courtesans and the techniques of women who traffic in their beauty. So each vied with the others to outdo the rest in beauty. But Aspasia did not want to put on an expensive dress, nor did she like the idea of an embroidered wrap; she could not even bring herself to take a bath...But she was beaten into submission, and obeyed her instruction, although it caused her distress to be forced to act the part of a courtesan rather than a modest girl. Now the others arrived and looked directly at Cyrus and smiled and put on a facade of pleasantness. But Aspasia looked down; her face was covered in fiery blushes, her eyes were filled with tears, and she was obviously embarrassed at the whole performance. And when he told the girls to sit beside him, they complied in a docile manner, but she took no account of the order until the satrap took hold of her and forced her to. And when Cyrus touched them and looked over their eyes and cheeks and fingers, the rest allowed him, but she would not; when he so much as touched her with the tip of his finger she gave a yell and told him that if he did so he would be sorry. Cyrus was delighted at this. And when she got up and tried to run off because he had touched her breasts, the son of Darius, contrary to Persian custom, was greatly impressed by her noble behaviour, and said to the trafficker, 'This is the only girl you have brought who is free and unspoilt. The others behave like courtesans, in their looks and even more in their manner'. From this moment Cyrus loved her more than any woman he ever had to do with. And later his love for her deepened, and she loved him in turn; the pair fell so much in love that they were close to equals and did not fall short of a Greek marriage in their harmony and unselfish devotion...

Once a necklace was brought to Cyrus from Thessaly, sent by Scopas the younger; he had obtained the gift from Sicily. The necklace seemed to have been worked with amazing skill and ornament. So everyone Cyrus showed it to was amazed, and delighted beyond measure with his treasure; he at once went to Aspasia in the middle of the day. He took the necklace out of its box and showed it to her, making the remark that this necklace was worthy of a king's mother or daughter. She agreed and he said: 'So I am giving it to you as a present; put it on just as you are and show me how it looks on your neck.' She was not overwhelmed by the gift but gave him a clever and civilised reply: 'And how can I presume to put on a gift worthy of your own mother: rather send this to her, Cyrus; I will show you the beauty of my neck even without it.'

Many moralising asides in the quoted portion, and others outside it, suggest the personality of Aelian himself, both sentimental and Hellenising. The story obviously appealed to him, as he confines most of his anecdotes in the *Varia Historia* to the scale of a paragraph: this is clearly a 'luxury version' on which the author has expended a certain amount of relatively discreet rhetorical presentation. However, there is no doubt that he has not only transmitted the essential details of the story, but the basic moral assumptions as well: modesty, virtue, and simple piety are to be rewarded; forwardness and self-seeking will get a girl nowhere. This is as socially conformist a Cinderella as we are likely to find. It is worth remarking that Aelian also relates an only slightly different version of Strabo's Cinderella story in the next book of the *Varia Historia* (13.33); he is the only ancient author we know to have included two Cinderella candidates in a single work.

Two Jewish Cinderellas: the tale of Asenath

A number of further Cinderellas can be noted where the materials configure clearly enough to one Cinderella or another. Most important, to my mind, in the Graeco-Roman area are two complementary Cinderellas which emerge around the character of the biblical Asenath, wife of Joseph. One of these is Hellenistic and has been recognised for nearly three decades as related to the ancient novel;[17] the other has had a more fugitive existence, considerably later, in medieval rabbinical commentary.[18] The earlier has the ashes, the sighting of the bride at a home/church, the supernatural helper, and the marriage (but, again, a rather unusual variant of the bride test, without an actual slipper); the other has decidely more persecution and death threat, an animal helper similar to that in Strabo's example, and a ring form of the token test. The two have different strategies for explaining how the Hebrew Joseph can marry the Egyptian Asenath: in the first, she has to convert to Judaism; in the second, she is shown to have been Joseph's niece and so a Hebrew all along. The token test, as rarely, is to establish parentage and marital eligibility rather than identity. The two versions can be conveniently placed in synopsis:

Joseph and Asenath	Medieval Asenath traditions
Asenath is the daughter of the priest of Heliopolis, Pentephres (= Heliodorus)	Asenath, cousin of Joseph, is the child of a rape, taken with her mother into the wilderness; kidnapped by an eagle and deposited on the altar of Potiphar, priest of On
Asenath covers her face with cinders (10.26–20)	
A man comes from heaven (14) and tells her to change her clothes and her name, and wear a royal girdle	
Asenath dresses in beautiful bridal dress	
She insists on washing Joseph's feet, as befits his future wife	She throws inscribed ring (birth token) to Joseph; he falls in love with the owner of the ring
They marry	They marry

The importance of these two largely complementary versions of the story of the same girl is this: either can be recognised as a Cinderella-type narrative as it stands. The girl on the left sees and is seen by Joseph from afar; he is now classed as Egyptian royalty, and so plays the role of 'the prince'; after the sighting she casts off her finery and rolls in the cinders; an angel acts the role of supernatural helper/fairy godmother; she is given a change of name, an important secondary characteristic in the folktale versions, but the token test is replaced by a different act concerning the foot. We should be prepared to ask why so characteristic a motif should be different. The reason is perhaps not far to seek. The Cinderella story has been cast here as a Jewish religious tale with Asenath required to renounce idolatry and become a Jew. This motif provides the tension of separation between the couple (apart from the fact also that they have not been close enough together for the normal conditions of communicating a token to be met), and contemporary Jewish practice would have expected the wife to wash the husband's feet, not the husband the wife's.

The second 'composite' version draws on a much fuller range of traditions about Asenath: as merely the foster child of Pentephres/Potiphar she is given a connection already with the family of Joseph (as daughter of his sister Dinah she is in fact his niece); this means that Joseph can thus be made once more not to marry a non-Jew by another route. Here we have the persecuted heroine and one of the two standard tokens, a ring which is among the *gnorismata* (recognition tokens) given to the unborn child when her mother was driven into the desert. But we also see a use of the unusual motif used in Strabo's version of the Rhodopis story. Not just the sandal is transported to the Pharaoh by an eagle, the baby and her token are transported to Egypt en bloc by this same bird.[19] When the two traditions are conflated, the Asenath–Cinderella complex looks like this:

> Asenath is exposed with her mother Dinah in the desert after the latter was raped. She was carried by an eagle to the altar of the priest of On. She grows up as a beautiful girl, outshining her seven handmaidens. Her stepmother falls in love with Joseph and so acts as a rival. She sees Joseph from her room, which is also a shrine, and is herself seen in beautiful clothes, but having previously rejected him she covers her face with cinders and lies in ashes for seven days. However, a man from heaven persuades her to dress in bridal garments. She throws her ring with Hebrew characters inscribed on it to Joseph; she is his long-lost niece and can marry him, which she does; she also undertakes to wash his feet, as his future bride.[20]

Here, then, we have a girl who acquires distinctive characteristics of Cinderella, complete with real cinders, not just the implied ones in the tale of Rhodopis. We also have another detail. In the popular version Joseph acquires a talisman which at one moment assumes the form of a golden branch.[21] This is often a part of *male* Cinderella stories, where the hero sometimes travels through a wood with trees of bronze, silver and gold, off all of which he takes a twig.[22] We also have Joseph, traditionally a persecuted hero in his own right, here at one point despised as simply the son of a shepherd and, of course, initially a slave of Pharaoh. In the popular version he has *gnorismata* of his own. Although the emphasis is always on Asenath, we have at least the hint of a 'double' Cinderella, where the male is himself a 'Cinderello' figure.

It is time, then, to look at the key portion of the first complete Cinderella text to have survived antiquity:

> (*Joseph and Asenath* 10.2) And Asenath was left alone with her hand-maids; she was in a listless state and wept till sunset. She neither ate bread nor drank water, and she alone stayed awake when everyone else was asleep. And she opened the door, and went down to the gate and found the doorkeeper asleep with her children. And Asenath quickly took the leather curtain down from the door and filled it with ashes. She brought it back up to her room and put it on the floor. And she closed the door firmly and put the iron latch across, and she wept and wailed aloud...(10.9) And Asenath got up and quietly opened the door and went into her second room, where she had the chests with her clothes, and opened her chest and brought out a black and

mournful tunic (this was the one she wore when her firstborn brother died). And Asenath took off her royal attire and put on the black tunic and undid the gold girdle and tied a rope round her waist and put off the headdress and diadem from her head and took the bracelets from her hands...(10.16) And she took sackcloth and put it round her waist and took the ribbon from her hair and sprinkled it with ashes...(10.18) And when she got up early in the morning she was amazed to see that her tears had turned the ashes underneath her to mud. And Asenath fell once more on her face on the ashes till sunset. And she did this for seven days without food or drink. (11–13: In her anguish she prays to God.)

(14) And when Asenath had finished her confession to God she was excited to see the morning star rise from the Eastern sky and when she saw it she rejoiced and said: 'The Lord God has heard my prayer, for this star is the herald and messenger of the great day'. And amazingly the heavens were rent near the morning star and an indescribable light appeared. And Asenath fell on her face on the ashes and a man came out of heaven towards her. And he stood over her head and called her: 'Asenath'. And she said: 'Who is calling me, since my chamber door is shut and the tower is high; and how has he come into my chamber?' And the man called her a second time: 'Asenath, Asenath.' And she said, here I am, sir, tell me who you are. And the man said: I am the commander of the Lord's House and the commander-in-chief of the whole host of the Most High. Stand up and I will talk to you.' And she raised her eyes and looked and there was a man who looked just like Joseph in his dress, his crown and royal sceptre, but his face was like lightning, and his eyes were like the light of the sun, and the hair of his head was like flames of fire and his hands and feet were like molten iron. And Asenath saw him and fell on her face at his feet in great fear and trembling. And the man said to her: 'Take courage, Asenath, and do not be afraid, but stand up and I will speak to you.' And Asenath stood and the man said to her: 'Take off the tunic you have put on, the black one, and the sackcloth from your waist, and shake the cinders from your hair and wash your face with living water. And put on a brand new robe and shining girdle, the double girdle of a virgin. And come again to me and I will tell you the words sent to you.' And Asenath went into her chamber where the chests of clothing were and opened the chest and took off her black robe and took a new resplendent dress and put it on...(15) And she went to the man and when he saw her he said, 'Take the veil from your head, for today you are a holy virgin and your head is like that of a young man.' And she took it from her head, and the man said to her: 'Take courage, Asenath: look, the Lord has given you Joseph for a husband and you will be his bride. And you will not be called Asenath but City of Refuge'...(15.9) 'And

look: I am going to Joseph and I will talk to him about you, and he will come to you tomorrow and will see you and be delighted with you and will be your husband. And listen to me, Asenath, and put on your bridal dress, the ancient robe, the first robe stored in your chamber, and put on all your favourite jewellery, and adorn yourself as a bride and get ready to meet him. For he will come to you tomorrow and see you and be delighted with you.' And when the man had finished speaking to Asenath, she was full of joy and fell at his feet...(19) And a little slave came and said to Asenath: 'Joseph is at the gate of our house.' And Asenath came down with her seven handmaidens to meet him. When he saw her Joseph said to her: 'Come to me, holy virgin, because I have received a message from heaven telling me all about you.' And Joseph stretched out his hands and they had a long embrace, and were revived by each other's breath. (20) And she said to him, 'Come into my house', and she took his right hand and brought him into the house. And Joseph sat down on her father Pentephres' seat, and she brought water to wash his feet, and he said to her: 'Let one of your maidens come and wash my feet.' And Asenath said to him: 'No, sir, for my hands are your hands, and my feet are your feet, and no one else but me shall wash your feet.' And she insisted on washing his feet, and Joseph took her by the right hand and kissed her, and Asenath kissed Joseph's head. (They marry the next day.)

Here we have the necessary sequence of familiar motifs – ashes and general wallowing; a fairy godperson so officious that the cinder-girl has no need to turn up at any ball; and an unusual interpretation of the 'slipper test' situation. The central focus is exactly right: the need for supernatural intervention before the extreme and self-abasing modesty of the girl will cause her to dress in the resplendent attire of the bride, who somehow proves herself to the prospective husband in the face of any opposition. There is just the faintest hint of 'sibling rivals' about the handmaidens: our cinder-girl is not taking any chances with them, and we have already been told that they are seven maids born on the same day as Asenath, and sharing her own private rooms: they are her servants, not her sisters. Overall the piety and simplicity of the narrative is very clearly brought out in the extract (even after Asenath's prayer of confession has been cut). The writer relies heavily on a naive paratactic style, a standard symptom of 'popular' narrative. Taking both these aspects together we might almost describe our text as a 'Sunday School Cinderella' which would not have looked out of place in a Victorian milieu. But a Cinderella it is, and Asenath herself continued to be a Cinderella in its medieval successor.

Some mythological treatments: Pherecydes and the Io myth

Cinderella need not be confined to historical anecdote, novella or romance. We seem to have hints of versions of the fairytale in the received body of Greek myth as well. The first Greek prose writer, Pherecydes of Syrus (sixth century BC), yields fragments of a cosmological narrative about a wedding of Zas (Zeus). We are told that on the third day of this wedding Zas gives his bride Chthonie (underground-girl) a great and beautiful robe, and on it are embroidered earth and ocean and the dwellings of ocean. In relation to the same event we have further reference to 'the winged oak and the embroidered robe on it'. And as the result of the wedding gift of Earth Chthonie now becomes Ge (Earth).[23] M.L. West suspected a close connection between the tree and the recipient of the robe, Chthonie/Ge.[24]

Some of the most persistent among Cinderella variants will explain much about this tantalising complex of fragments. Many of these heroines spend a prolonged period incarcerated underground; many ask for a clothing of sun, moon and stars, or for some variant combination, including some kind of sea-robe; the request for such attire is usually either answered by a tree, or allied to a request for a tree-robe, which is itself mobile or even winged (normally to effect a flight from a threat of incest). A frequent concomitant of all this is a change of name: a nickname like Aschenputtel or Cinderella will be replaced by a 'true' name – Maria or the like. And the usual end is of course marriage to a prince. It seems to me that the Pherecydes fragments are intelligible within the parameters of Cinderella stories; I know of no other narrative framework (as opposed to cosmological cliché) within which they make sense. We might not have been surprised to find Ge as the daughter of Zas and flying from him in the winged tree. But this latter object seems at all events to be the 'trousseau-tree' feature that somehow brings about the royal marriage. The description of the robe ties the myth firmly to the Cinderella legend, as does the change of name.

In Pherecydes' narrative, folktale and cosmic allegory seem to converge: we might 'read' it as implying that Earth is no more than underworld till it receives its coating of green earth, sea and sky, justifying its change of name. One notes the significance of change of name in Cinderella: in Basile's seventeenth-century version the Cinderella heroine 'Jujube girl' (Zezolla) can only revert to this her true name Zezolla once she has put on the jewels and clothes supplied by the date tree, when she can discard her mere nickname *Gatta Cenerentola* ('Cat Cinderella'). A combination of several characteristic elements of the cycle seems to have existed, then, in the very first known prose text in Greek.[25]

Conclusion

The overall consequences of these links are very considerable. They show us that there were versions of Cinderella worked as fairytale and as romance, and perhaps even as myth as well, and that the tale seems well established in fairytale and romance before the end of antiquity, and in myth perhaps a good deal earlier. We shall examine two much larger-scale romantic versions in due course.[26] The fact that a Cinderella pattern underlies versions of Rhodopis, Aspasia and Asenath gives the tale as such a strong foundation across a range of genres and cultural contexts at an early stage. Here is a tale whose transmissibility and adaptability are already well attested. But we are not entitled to conclude that these classical versions represent more than a part of the early history of the tale. They can hardly be claimed as its origins. I conclude this initial chapter with two appendixes: a brief pointer to a still earlier mythological setting of the story in our very earliest Near Eastern literature, that of the Mesopotamian civilisation of Sumer. The Sumerian version comes close to the earliest modern European version, that of Basile, in the distinctive detail of the trousseau tree. No such link has to my knowledge been previously noted. Nor, it should immediately be added, can Basile's version be the first post-classical European Cinderella in any case. The second appendix draws attention to a medieval verse version in Marie de France's *lai* of *Le Fresne*. Both these cases should serve as a reminder that the history of this resilient tale is still far from complete.

A Sumerian Cinderella: aspects of the Inanna cycle

We have already seen that there is a good case for arguing that the earliest Greek prose text contained a mythological handling of a Cinderella variant. We should now be prepared to push back the history of the tale still further, to the earliest extant literature of any kind. We have a small but increasing stock of mythological texts from the Mesopotamian civilisation of Sumer. The Sumerians themselves were subsumed into the Babylonian empire, and the Sumerian language itself ceased to be used for copying texts as early as around 1700 BC; the surviving texts stretch backwards through over two millennia.[27] The texts that concern us deal with the fortunes of the love-and-sex goddess Inanna and her relationship with her future consort, the shepherd-king Dumuzi.[28] The story has not been found so far in any single continuous text, but can be pieced together from a number of separate texts concerning the goddess's prospective marriage. Inanna's Cinderella credentials can be set out most conveniently as follows:

She complains to her father Enki that she is expected to look after the spinning of flax and the management of sheep, while her sisters enjoy more elegant and prestigious occupations.[29]
But her brother Utu, the sun, undertakes the management of the flax, with a view to helping her marriage.[30]
She has planted a tree, after her father's ship has been caught in a storm.

She nurtures it carefully, and its trunk provides her marriage bed and domestic objects.[31]

She also receives presents of jewels and clothes from the keeper of a date tree, to provide her wedding trousseau.[32]

She meets her shepherd-prince Dumuzi by moonlight and dances with him, but still returns home safely afterwards to her parental home.[33]

She is able to celebrate her marriage to him.

Her attributes also include the element of clothing of heaven and earth, comparable to the characteristic sun, moon and star dress usually associated with *AT* Type 510B.[34]

The following synopsis shows a sequence of separate but overlapping Inanna texts side by side with Basile's celebrated Neapolitan literary version and a nineteenth century oral version from Palermo:

Inanna-texts	Basile, *La Gatta Cenerentola*	*Grattula-Baedatula*
Rival sisters	Six rival stepsisters	Two rival sisters
Daughter Inanna	Daughter Zezolla (Jujube)	Daughter Ninetta
[text damaged]	Daughters request presents from father's journey	Daughters request presents from father's journey
Father Enki's ship is caught in storm [text damaged]	His ship is stopped till he gets daughter's date tree	His ship is stopped till he gets daughter's date palm
Inanna receives huluppu tree to provide wedding objects, which she looks after	Heroine receives magic tree from fairies, which she looks after	Heroine receives magic palm tree from father, which she looks after
Date tree/date-tree gatherer produces jewels	Tree produces jewels	Tree produces fairies carrying jewels and dresses
Inanna dances with Dumuzi, but runs off	Heroine dances with prince, and twice eludes him at end of dance	Heroine dances with prince, and twice eludes him at end of dance
–	–	Is summoned by king
–	Slipper test	–
Married to Dumuzi	Married to prince	Married to prince

Basile's Cinderella has the distinctive feature that a girl receives jewels from a date tree, a tradition replicated in modern Italian oral tradition (as in Grattula-Baedatula, 'fair date'). This feature has a bearing on the very early history of the tale as it corresponds to a distinctive feature in the Sumerian material – the motif that Inanna seems to be getting jewels from a date-gatherer or from the tree itself. The differences are minimal: our Inanna texts do not cover the whole tale (slipper or ring test is missing, as it is in Grattula-Baedatula). Inanna looks after a huluppu-tree to provide a different set of marriage objects, and the jewel-providing date tree is presented from a fragment of a different text. But in terms of narrative function the two trees are obvious variants on the 'trousseau tree': both provide for Inanna's marriage, at least one of the two as a result of her own efforts. The relationships are close enough to enable us to clarify an obscurity in the Sumerian text by reference to the complete folktale in Basile: Kramer had been unable to construe any context for the apparently jewel-bearing tree on its own.[35] Other Sumerian texts clarify the picture still further. One includes Inanna complaining that tasks are necessary before her marriage; her brother Utu completes them for her. This gives us the 'supernatural helper' motif so characteristic of those who help Cinderella herself. A tailpiece to a creation text that is really about Inanna's father Enki provides the first evidence that Inanna has rival sisters with much more privileged occupations – although they are not much in evidence in the classical texts we have noted, the 'ugly sisters' have been there since as near the beginning as we can go.

An unnoticed Old French Cinderella: *Le Fresne* (Ash-tree girl)

The *lai* entitled *Le Fresne* in Marie de France (twelfth/thirteenth century AD) purports to be a Breton tale and represents an important signpost in the European history of Cinderella. The girl is exposed in infancy by a mother of twins to avoid the accusation of illegitimacy. She has a brocade and a ring as tokens, and is left in an ash tree beside a nunnery, to be discovered by the porter and suckled by his widowed nursing daughter. She lives at the nunnery till a distinguished nobleman sees her when she is grown to womanhood and becomes her lover. Forced in due course to marry, he has to put away his mistress and wed a well-born lady. Fresne accepts this and is in the chamber at the wedding night as a handmaid. She uses her own brocade to cover the bed; the mother recognises it, and she herself can now marry the nobleman. The sister is married to a rich man. We can set out the Cinderella features of the story as follows:

I   Persecuted heroine: she is threatened with death and in humble circumstances.
II Supernatural help: the ash-tree itself acts as shelter; the abbess allows her to be brought up as her own niece.

III The hero sees her 'at a church' (no repeated pattern of balls, but the lord gives endowments to the abbey as a pretext for his visits).
IV Ring and brocade as token; competition with sibling rival (hazel/ash); cruel mother does not want the hero to marry his mistress.
V Token recognition and marriage to hero.

The significance of this version is not just that it is the earliest West European example to survive in the vernacular, but it also shows adjustments to the world of romance rather than folktale. It also has a good many affinities with both *Sakuntala* and *Daphnis and Chloe*:[36] the form of token test is not to find the heroine's identity, but to determine that her parentage is 'correct' for marriage; and the trappings of courtly medieval society are as distinctive as the seventeenth-century trappings of Perrault. We should note the connection with ash; this is not the ash of the fireplace, but the ash *tree*; the two are, however, liable to confusion throughout Germanically-related languages and in that context a confusion may have arisen. We should note that one genealogy of the Greek Io gives her an ancestor Melie ('Ash Tree'); this should serve to strengthen her own Cinderella credentials in turn.

We have seen, then, that the Cinderella story existed in a more or less recognisable form in antiquity, and so at least one fairytale has survived almost unnoticed. In several cases we have had to join different versions or facets of the story, both in combining Strabo and Herodotus on Rhodopis, the Sumerian texts on Inanna, and the medieval tradition of *Joseph and Asenath*, but in the Hellenistic version of *Joseph and Asenath* and Aelian's story of Aspasia we have complete texts. Neither, as it happens, uses the slipper test so clear in Strabo, but both have substitutes which fulfil the criteria for a different kind of 'bride show'. Fairy godpersons vary through the texts from Aphrodite herself in Aelian to an angel in *Joseph and Asenath*, or a divine brother, the son-god Utu, in a Sumerian text. The close association with trees is present as early as the trousseau date tree or Io's ancestor Melie.[37] The connection with hearth or ashes occurs in *Joseph and Asenath* and more obliquely in Herodotus, through the roasting spit and the name Hephaestopolis. From having half a Cinderella sporadically acknowledged in Strabo, we have been able to point to two complete classical Cinderellas, two newly recognised medieval versions, and substantial suspicion of analogues in three classical myths, not to mention the Sumerian fragments.

Even if we had only this one story, we have a strong confirmation, as we had long ago in the first Chinese Cinderella Yeh-Hsien, that fairytales seem at least capable of surviving – for the most part doubtless submerged in oral tradition – over very long periods. But we must now ask: if Cinderella could have survived in this way, what of Snow White and the rest?

3

SNOW WHITE AND RELATED TALES

The question 'How old is Snow White?' is asked less often than 'How old is Cinderella?' One reason is that there are markedly fewer modern texts, and there has been little study, of tales which overlap with the *Snow White* tale itself (*AT* Type 709). Nonetheless, the evidence is just as clear that the tale and some of its close relatives have an ancient pedigree as distinguished as that of *Cinderella* itself.

One obstacle, as with *Cinderella*, is that scholars outside the field of folklore have a stereotype of the tale as inappropriate as is Perrault's *Cinderella* to define its own type. A Brothers Grimm version supplies what is usually recognised as the classic form:[1]

> A queen wishes for a child as white as snow, as red as blood, as black as ebony, and dies when such a child is born. The girl's stepmother has a magic mirror which declares the princess to be the fairer of the two. The jealous queen sends the child into the wood with a huntsman who has instructions to kill her; instead he sets Snow White free and takes the lungs and liver of a boar back to the stepmother. Snow White comes on a house with seven tiny sets of household articles, uses its amenities in turn and sleeps in the seventh bed. Seven dwarfs find her and agree to keep her there; she keeps house for them, and must not open the door to strangers. The magic mirror informs the queen, who attempts three times to kill her stepdaughter, first by tacking her dress too tightly, then by combing her hair with a poisoned comb. The dwarfs twice revive her, but on a third occasion, when the stepmother produces an apple with one side poisoned, fail to do so. They lay Snow White on a bier encased in glass and mourn her on top of a hill. A prince comes by; they refuse to seal the coffin, but give it up on entreaty. In the movement of the coffin the apple fragment is dislodged from Snow White's throat, and she can marry the prince. The stepmother is forced to dance in red hot shoes till dead.

43

Here, as in the Perrault *Cinderella*, we have just those details most likely to be familiar to western European readers: snow-white-rose-red, the queen and her magic mirror, exposure in the forest, seven dwarfs, a poisoned apple, and the glass case with the unburied and ever-fragrant princess. There seems the obvious connection in the first instance of snow with the girl's name. But even that is not guaranteed, especially in areas where snow is less prominent than in some parts of Europe: a modern Jewish-Egyptian version has the heroine going through quite obviously Snow White-type adventures under the name Pomegranate.[2] From the repertoire of over seventy oral versions collected by Ernst Boeklen up to 1915,[3] we can note the following trends in the European/West Asiatic versions as a whole, and these will be important when we come to consider a Snow White romance. The mainspring of the story is the avenging jealousy of another woman.[4] Usually she is the avenging stepmother, but sometimes a jealous sister or some other associate. In one French version reported by Paul Delarue, the heroine is the servant of her rival.[5] Several Snow Whites have a beginning where the heroine is accidentally worshipped, or gossip makes her the equal of a goddess.[6] The 'magic mirror on the wall' is the standard version to establish Snow White's beauty and survival, but it is far from being the only one: the rival may consult the sun, the moon, or some other agent as an oracle.[7] This is consistent with the role of Apollo and Artemis in the mythical forms of the tale; Artemis need only ask her oracle-giving brother about Snow White's beauty, which he has himself experienced.

The rival gives orders for Snow White's exposure, usually in a wood, but sometimes on a mountain, and she is taken in to live, not always by seven dwarfs or indeed by dwarfs at all; sometimes it is simply a case of one or more dwarfs, robbers, or the like.[8] Usually Snow White finds the rustic dwelling by herself and ingratiates herself by keeping house for her master(s). One thinks of a Portuguese version where the heroine lives with a single swineherd;[9] an Italian version from Abruzzi has her enclosed in a hut by the sea, and fed on bread and water;[10] or when the faithful servant refuses to go through with the killing, she eventually falls in with robbers in the wood.[11] Sometimes there is an adventure where she meets a tormented soul or suchlike.[12] In a Breton version she hides in the dog's stall, and in others dire consequences are to follow if she does not feed dogs.[13] A number of variants have the finder of the coffin taking it home and subjecting it to unending devotion; in a small number of cases the coffin is put to sea and found by fishermen.[14] There are even Kabyle and Arabic versions where Snow White, still in her coffin or equivalent, is carried by a camel.[15] In some versions, the heroine is supplanted after marriage by a bizarre rival bride.[16] One German variant has the hero-prince as a pilgrim.[17] Many of these incidental deviations from our 'expected' version will assume a good deal of importance when we come to look at an extended ancient version.

There is a great degree of flexibility in Snow White's protectors – most obviously in the nature of the dwarfs, who can just as readily be giants, or supernatural beings of some kind, or simply a peasant or peasants, especially where the whole handling of the tale is more realistic. The glass case sometimes has adventures of its own, as when it is a chest found by a fisherman, but again deposited in the custody of the prince; the jealous rival need not always be the stereotypical stepmother either. And the 'oracle mirror' can be some other kind of informant. What we also notice however is that the simple tale as illustrated by the Grimms omits certain fairly common episodes recurrent elsewhere in this tale-type: one is the presence of a dog or dogs which the heroine must feed, often with no immediately obvious motivation. Another is the appearance of a 'substitute bride' motif: the prince may forget the heroine, who can be turned by a rival into something else, most often a bird; and he must be reminded of his obligations, most often by some magical means.

When we take these variations into account we tend to find a rather different looking structure, which produces examples like the following:

> A young girl called Pomegranate is persecuted by a sister/stepmother; she flees and falls among forty robbers, for whom she keeps house. A magician is sent to kill her with a bracelet and a ring; a prince rescues her from the glass case, but then the magician turns her into a dove by sticking a pin in her head, while the prince marries her servant; only by means of a ribbon round the dove's neck does the deception come to light.[18]

The story is still recognisable, even without the Snow White name. But there may also be an odd feature, of a Snow White 'colour code' encoded in the text. In the celebrated Grimm version, her mother wishes for a child white as snow, red as blood and black as the black windowsill. In this case we have a competition between the two girls over washing: the heroine is told not to wash till a river is not black or red but white; her rival disobeys the instruction.

We can look also at an obviously recognisable Snow White from Abruzzi in Italy where very few of these features are directly in evidence, but where the tale itself is still quite clearly part of a Snow White group nonetheless:[19]

> A mother and daughter keep an inn, where the mother asks the guests if they have seen anyone lovelier than herself. When one says 'her daughter', she has the girl enclosed in a hut by the sea, to be looked after by the kitchen-boy; the beautiful girl is still detected and reported, so that the mother bribes the kitchen boy with marriage if he will kill the daughter. He brings back the eyes and blood of an animal instead; he allows the girl to flee to twelve robbers in a wood; and she is treated as a sister and keeps house for the robbers. A robber accidentally betrays her to the mother, who hires a witch to kill her with a pin; she is buried in a hollow tree trunk by the robbers, found by a prince's dogs, revived by the removal of the pin and marries the prince.[20]

The tale is still quite recognisable despite the substitution of robbers for dwarfs, a much more ordinary background, a mother rather than stepmother as the persecutor, and the absence of any miraculous means of divination, the absence of any glass coffin, and only two rather than the usual four attempts to kill the heroine (one by means of the compassionate executioner, a run of three by the rival directly). What it usefully shows is how far the tale has to change to accommodate a realistic background.

What, then, is the essence of the Snow White story? We need a persecuted heroine, some kind of prophetic or oracular function for her female persecutor, a series of attempts on the heroine's life, usually involving animal substitution and a compassionate executioner. We should look for some context in which the heroine is transplanted into an alien environment where she nonetheless finds protection, friendship and loyalty in some kind of otherworldly or outside alternative community. We might also look for at least one failed resuscitation attempt, followed by a successful one, as well as at least a gesture towards petrification of some sort (enclosure in glass case).[21]

The Snow White version of the story – by whatever name – has been collected from Europe, North Africa and Western Asia (and corresponding colonial areas). But there are a number of overlapping tales which should be noted as well, and are likely to be useful in investigating ancient versions. The most obvious of these is *Sleeping Beauty*: this time there is only one attempt on the heroine's life, and no seven dwarfs or other protectors; and the maleficent rival is usually a supernatural agent slighted at the heroine's birth; again the question of the false rival can be found after the encounter with the prince. And again there is room for surprisingly 'un-fairytale-like' material: the first modern European Sleeping Beauty, that of Basile, has the prince rape the heroine while she is still asleep – then forget the girl he has thus presented with twins, before his legitimate wedded wife is cast as the false bride.[22] Other related tales, those involving a girl with Snow White characteristics in search of lost relatives or being searched for by them, are postponed for the sake of clarity to the end of this chapter and to Chapter 13.

Some ancient Snow Whites

Are there, then, any ancient Snow Whites? There certainly are a number of mythical or semi-mythical heroines whose names are Chione ('Snowgirl', 'Snowey').[23] The few scraps we have seem to do rather more than reflect the properties of the name itself. We find a Chione, daughter of the Nile and Ocean's daughter Callirhoe, maltreated on earth and evidently raped by a peasant (the text is defective at the critical point) and brought by Hermes into the Clouds, to give her name to snow.[24] This offers us more than meets the eye. One of the associations of the Nile is with *pecheis*, dwarfs depicted or described as children, and sometimes implied to be the offspring of the river itself.[25] This would give any such Snowgirl either a set of dwarf brothers or at least a supporting cast of dwarfs.[26] A second such tradition makes Chione daughter of Boreas and Oreithuia (Northwind and Mountainmaid).[27] This again is a suggestive parentage for 'our' Snow White, since this couple also are credited with two sons Zetes and Calais who change into birds, thus providing the given material for type *AT* 451, 'the search for lost brothers (changed into birds)', as we shall see below. A third has the girl as daughter of Arcturus (North Star) raped by Boreas (Northwind) and reaching a mountain Niphantes ('Snowfall').[28] All three traditions are clearly aetiological in character; they account for two obviously observable facts about weather: that snow is connected with water and falls from the sky, and that snow is blown by fierce winds onto mountain tops. Moreover, two of the three are just long enough to contain the notion of a suffering heroine, in one case at least supposedly 'rewarded in heaven'. But a fourth version has at last the pattern of a detailed episodic story: Chione, daughter of Daedalion, has a thousand suitors; Apollo and Hermes rape her in a single day and night; Hermes puts the girl into a magic sleep; Apollo, the latter of the two, comes disguised as an old woman; Chione has twins Autolycus and Philammon; their mother antagonises Artemis with her boasting, and the latter kills her with an arrow.[29]

There is a further variant, in which a Chione is among the daughters of Niobe: one Manto ('prophetess') commands the latter to acknowledge the superiority of Apollo and Artemis, which Niobe refuses to do. Her own boasting on behalf of her children antagonises Artemis, who again shoots the girl with an arrow. According to this story Zeus changes all the inhabitants of Thebes, presumably including Chione, to stone.[30] This is as far as the language of myth can be seen to take us on present evidence, but it is clear enough to suggest materials for a folktale or a romance about a persecuted heroine. The considerable variety of genealogies may conceal a common identity, at least for some of them; brothers turned into birds and a company of dwarfs are at least implied for good measure. In some cases the connection of the name is quite directly with reference to the creation of snow, but in one case quite conspicuously we have very much more. Where we have a Snow White name and an obvious Snow White motif or motifs we are entitled to claim that we are looking at a genuine version of *Snow White* and that the tale itself is at least as old as our example. We should note, too, a certain difference in the balance of forces in the tale. Normally we expect the magic mirror on the wall (or its equivalent) to tell Snow White's rival that Snow White is the fairest of them all; in the Niobe story we have one Manto ('prophetess', and reasonable equivalent to the mirror) warning Chione's mother not to boast about her daughter's beauty for fear of offending the gods. It is as if the magic mirror in the Grimm tale were being used here not to tell the queen that Snow White is the fairest of them all, but instead to tell Snow White that she must not boast of being fairest of them all for fear of offending the queen! But the clearest view we are offered so far is of the Chione who appears in Ovid's *Metamorphoses*.

[Chione's father Daedalion, son of Lucifer] subdued kings and their peoples by his prowess...He had a daughter Chione. She had reached the age of fourteen and was ready for marriage; and endowed as she was with exceptional beauty, she had a thousand suitors. It so happened that Phoebus and Maia's son Mercury were returning, the one from his favourite haunt of Delphi, and the other from the summit of Mount Cyllene. Both of them saw the girl at the same time and both, at the very same moment, fell in love with her. Apollo (Phoebus) put off his hopes of making love to her till night, but Mercury did not put up with any delay: he touched the girl's cheek with his sleep-inducing wand. At that powerful touch, she lay there, and suffered the god's violent act. When night had scattered the sky with its stars, Phoebus took the form of an old woman, and enjoyed the same pleasures that Mercury had stolen earlier. When her pregnancy had taken its full course, Chione gave birth to twins: to Mercury with his winged feet a cunning child, Autolycus, who would turn white to black and black to white; and to Phoebus, a son Philammon, famed for his singing and the music of the lyre...

But glory is an obstacle to many, and certainly to her: she had the audacity to think herself more beautiful than Diana, and found fault with the goddess's appearance. This provoked the goddess to savage anger: 'You will not find fault with my actions!' she cried, and without delay she bent her bow, shot her arrow from the string, and sent her shaft through the tongue which had brought it on herself. Her tongue fell silent; and the words she was trying to voice failed; her life-blood left her as she was still trying to speak...But her father...bitterly lamented the loss of his daughter. And when he saw her body burning, four times he tried to rush into the heart of the funeral pyre; four times he was driven back. Then he abandoned his limbs to a frenzy of flight (and became turned into a hawk).[31]

Here, then, we have Snow White in a mythical form. Artemis (Diana) is the persecutor, but it is Chione's boasting that is punished – an outrageous injustice to twentieth-century sensibilities. But Chione's sufferings and fate are scarcely exceptional in classical myth, where the gods may not be consistently immoral but are certainly not accountable to humans; and where, as implied in Ovid's version, the attention of gods has been construed as a privilege rather than a degradation by the victim. Of the three encounters only one is a murder; but the *means* of carrying out the rape – disguise as an old woman (Apollo) and putting the victim to sleep (Hermes) – have a role to play in the modern tale, which can be discreetly expurgated without losing its three-fold central action. The disguises for the rapes are in effect recycled in the modern tale into additional murder attempts, thus providing much needed expurgation if the story is to serve as a nursery tale. The fire need not surprise us: it occurs as an alternative to the heroine's coma in *AT* Type 451, and as a threat to the girl in the related Sleeping Beauty type as well.[32] It is not too difficult to see that a version in which Chione is daughter of Niobe will have something in common with this version: here it is the mother, not the daughter herself, who boasts and offends Artemis, and the result is death from an arrow; not enclosure in a glass case, but a different sort of immobility, petrifaction, when Niobe and all her family are turned to stone, Chione presumably included.

We have already seen that Chione, daughter of Nile, has an assured connection with dwarfs, the commonplace associates of the river. And Chione, daughter of Daedalion, indeed has a father with dwarf implications in the diminutive force of his name ('little craftsman'); we can now look for any other girls with dwarf connections and see whether their stories tally at any point with Chione's or with those of modern Snow Whites. We have the report of a Hellenistic treatment of a girl connected with dwarfs (Athenaeus 9.393ef):

> And concerning the crane Boios says that there was a woman of consequence among the Pygmies, and her name was Gerana. This woman was worshipped as a god by the citizens (of the Pygmies), and had a low opinion of the real gods, especially Hera and Artemis. Hera was therefore indignant and changed her into a bird unsightly to look at and made her an enemy hated by her former worshippers the Pygmies; it is said that she and Nikodamas were the parents of a land tortoise.

We have a similar presentation of this information in Antoninus Liberalis 16, where the central figure who is obviously the same girl is called Oenoe ('Winey', which of course might indicate wine-red or wine-white). This adds little, and has Mopsus, the musician, as child of Oenoe, as well as making her the cause of the war between pygmies and cranes. But both texts converge in making a girl an object of worship on the part of pygmies, and in making her undergo metamorphosis. But we also have a girl surrounded by dwarfs, and the same arrogance towards Artemis as we found in the case of Chione herself. Her giving birth to a tortoise actually fits better than it promises: Philammon, offspring of Chione daughter of Daedalion, is a musician; the tortoiseshell is associated with the origins of the lyre as early as the *Homeric Hymn to Hermes.*

Another case of a dwarf context for the heroine of a tale is that of King Pygmalion: this Cypriot king worships the stone statue he creates himself, and, thanks to the pity of the gods, the statue comes to life. He himself by his very name is connected with pygmies ('king little-dwarf'), and that in turn encourages us to view the change from statue to woman as corresponding to the coming alive of Snow White.[33]

How, then, do all these mythological scraps relate to the familiar folktale of Snow White? We can note a considerable collection of recurrent motifs between the versions which suggest the form in which motifs are likely to present themselves in the classical variants. We can point to snow in the name and connections with water, a vindictive rival very often in the person of Artemis, a death that seems to entail some kind of resurrection or transformation, hints of dwarfs, hints of military rivalry and zoomorphic elements in the Gerana stories, and hints that the glass coffin may be expressed in different terms, such as a stone statue. There is also an element of sexual threat or even rape that is far more explicitly developed than in the modern tale.

Chione in the romances

These cases, then, will serve to show that there was *a* varied Chione tradition in the classical world; and that other types related to *AT* Type 709 were already known (*AT* Types 451, 884). But there is another recourse, for we do have at least one surviving and one fragmentary romance connected with the outlines discussed above. First, the fragments: three certain and one probable fragments survive from a romance containing a character called Chione ('Snowgirl').[34]

One of the Chione fragments seems to be pointing in a Snow White direction:

> (fr. 3) These men were determined to deliberate. Quickly the rumour went right round the city about the wedding and nobody talked about anything else. All were anxious at the thought of their barbarous threats and especially since the parties in the Panionion were all to choose a husband for Chione. But no one dared ask the girl after them. But Chione, hearing this from her mother, no longer...

Someone is expecting the hand of Snow White, and threatening to have it under duress. But this beginning is found in a medieval Western Snow White known since the late nineteenth century. Marie de France's old French *Lai of Eliduc* opens what is quite obviously a mainline Snow White tale (*AT* Type 709) with this motif as well:[35]

> The Breton hero Eliduc comes to the rescue of lady Guilliadun when her father, the king of Exeter in England, is being forced to give her to a bullying local suitor, whom Eliduc is able to kill. She later faints (on finding him already married to the 'wrong' woman), and is laid out and worshipped by him in a chapel in a wood, until revived and enabled to marry him by the resignation of his original wife to a nunnery.

Moreover, the last Chione fragment, assigned as simply 'likely' to the *Chione* text,[36] does actually correspond so far as we can construe its context to the most conventional of Snow Whites, that of the Grimms. The expression *tei zonei* ('with a girdle') occurs at the end of one column: in the next some sort of panic is going on: people are forcing in a door, and someone is lying there. In a

Snow White context, *so far as we can infer from so little,* this would be at the point in the action where the rival has attacked the heroine with a tight-fitting bodice, leaving her to suffocate, usually as the first or second murder attempt; she would now be found by her friends and protectors, be they brothers, dwarfs, herdsmen, or the like.[37] There is really no obstacle that I can see to regarding the Chione text as a narration of the fairy-tale Snow White. The name should have suggested this in the first place; and the *Lai of Eliduc* is our guarantee that a 'political' beginning concerning a forced marriage does occur in this tale-type.

In another case we have a complete specimen of a romance for consideration either as a complete Snow White or as strongly 'Snow White related'. The plot of Xenophon of Ephesus' *Ephesiaca* ('An Ephesian Tale') can be summarised as follows:

> A girl called Flower (Anthia) is so beautiful that she outshines Artemis. She has attendants White (Leucon) and Rose (Rhode); her parents send her and her husband abroad in response to an oracle of the sun-god. Captured by pirates, the girl falls into the hands of the jealous rival Manto ('prophetess'); she is sent to live with a peasant (who respects her); called on to execute her, he lets her go. She falls in with robbers, who eventually help her. She takes poison from a visiting beggar which she intends to use to kill herself; it only makes her sleep, and she comes round alive in the tomb. Eventually a fisherman shows the rich husband who is searching for her the corpse of a woman mummified, who reminds the seeker of his lost wife. He then goes on to be reunited with his wife at Rhodes: the event is anticipated by a children's oracle.[38]

It might be tempting simply to regard this as a free fantasia on some Snow White names and motifs. But the coincidence of these names is very cogent. The heroine Anthia ('Flower') has its equivalent in Snow White tradition (Fluorita in a modern Rumanian version); but the names of her servants Leucon and Rhode ('White and Rose') seem to give the game away. It is not very easy to arrange in a realistic narrative for ice mountains and a glass-encased heroine who will revive; but an otherwise unmotivated digression where a wife is subjected to some form of mummification serves to include an equivalent of this motif without actually subjecting the heroine herself to an unacceptable magic world. The robbers serve as protectors (eventually – their previous designs are either murderous or erotic); while the single peasant doubles as humble host (together with the robbers themselves) and compassionate executioner. The oracle delivered by children might also be construed as an interpretation of the role of the dwarfs in the story.

This text is the lynchpin for suggesting connection between the ancient novel and Euripides because of the motif of the peasant who respects the

51

heroine's chastity, which also occurs in Euripides' *Electra*; but since we shall have occasion to notice the connection of the Electra/Iphigenia complex with the Snow White complex anyway, we now have an alternative explanation: that the 'considerate peasant' is a rare but normal equivalent of the heroine's living with male company in the wilds, and who helps her rather than poses a sexual threat. In effect, one single peasant can play the essential role of seven dwarfs without any other consequence to the story. Xenophon's novel has often enough been connected with folktale; we should now identify it as a Snow White in its own right.[39]

The relationship of Snow White with Xenophon's *Ephesiaca* is best seen in the first instance in tabular form. The following discussion then attempts to account not only for the similarities between Xenophon and the folktale tradition, but also the kind of adjustments necessary to make such a tradition conform to the tastes and conventions of romance. Here, then, is Snow White Xenophon-style:

Snow White tales (various)	Xenophon, *Ephesian Tale*
Heroine Fluorita (Roumanian)	Heroine Anthia
Snow white, Rose red	Companions Leucon (white), Rhode (rose)
Antagonises jealous rival by outdoing her beauty	Outdoes the beauty of Artemis herself (without antagonising the goddess)
Rival consults magic mirror	Rival is called diviner (Manto)
She flees to live with menial in wood/ by the sea	She is made to live with menial in countryside by the sea
She falls in with robbers or dwarfs	She falls in with robbers
She is given a sleeping-draught by doctor	She is given a sleeping draught by doctor
Her coffin is decked with silver and gold	Heroine taken for dead and laid in gold coffin
She is transported by camel	She is transported by camel
She is told to feed dangerous dogs	She is shut up with dangerous dogs which have to be fed
She encounters a spirit	She claims to have been possessed by a spirit
She is laid in glass coffin found by fishermen	Hero is shown mummified corpse by fisherman (*not* the heroine's)
Conclusion assisted by cry from children's game[40]	Conclusion anticipated by children's oracle

There seems little doubt that Xenophon's story does indeed correspond to a number of features of mainly European Snow Whites, and indeed it seems fair to regard Xenophon's version as one of them in its own right. It had long been noted as having the feel of a folktale, but so far as I am aware no attempt has hitherto been made to identify it as any folktale in particular.[41] The identity of Leucon and Rhode immediately points to the actual tale,[42] and the correspondence obviously extends beyond the points of contact one might have inferred from the Grimm version. A number of rare modern variants in the oral tradition now appear as integral parts of the ancient tradition of Snow White itself.

Nonetheless, it seems equally clear that Xenophon's choice of details and variants has been dictated at least in some measure by the more limited constraints of romance as a genre. Seven dwarfs may well have been at his disposal in ancient tradition,[43] but if they could have had a place in myth, it is more difficult to accommodate them within the realistic and bourgeois notions of romance. Yet they probably emerge in the children who cluster round just before the final recognition scene and foresee the meeting of the protagonists. We can now study Xenophon's options and the ways in which he has used them.

In the first place, the name Anthia: this may well be an authentic name within the folktale tradition. The one modern occurrence turns up close to the geographical area of the Greek world, i.e. the Balkans.[44] The choice is convenient for a romantic heroine. The choice of Chione might have entailed the long explanation of the original mother's wishes; Xenophon goes for a simple explanation of the name as indicating the bloom of youth (*anthei de autes to soma ep' eumorphiai*) (cf. the name Chloe in Longus).[45] The tell-tale labels white and red are applied to the couple's servants, who are introduced late only after the pair are married.

The next feature of the folktale is another matter. The heroine is the most beautiful girl in the world: we are told that Anthia *polu tas allas hypereballeto parthenous*.[46] The heroine in a Norwegian version is proclaimed most beautiful by three poor youths to whom the heroine has been kind; in Ephesus, as conventionally in the romances, it is the urban crowd as a whole who performs the ecstatic recognition.[47] This is in the heroine's fifteenth year, as it is in the Polish version.[48] A Greek variant has her as beautiful as a hunting dog; Anthia has two such dogs in her retinue, and indeed dogs play a far more significant role in the story than in any other romance except Longus.[49] People wonder that she has not got angels' wings in the third Greek version: Anthia's spectators see her as the goddess Artemis herself.[50] Note, however, that Xenophon makes her blonde; the canonic Grimm version prefers black hair (as ebony).

The normal rival of Snow White is her stepmother or her mother (the latter perhaps the earlier, as Boeklen suspected).[51] Xenophon avoids any suggestion of this, and not unexpectedly. Close family tensions tend to be toned down in the romances, and their role supplied by external rivals instead. Hence Nape in Longus is the tamest of taskmistresses. It should however be noticed that in

Apollonius of Tyre, where folktale reflexes are well to the fore, the rival is a foster-mother and her child;[52] while in Euripides' *Electra*, as we shall see in due course, it is the heroine's mother.

The south-east European versions tend to assign the role of the magic mirror to the sun: this is the case for the Balkan, Chian, South Italian, and second Roumanian versions.[53] So in Xenophon, Anthia's parents correspondingly consult an oracle of the sun-god Apollo at Colophon.[54] But at this stage there is no rival, so that the oracle is not concerned with Anthia's beauty, which is already established in any case. What turns up here, instead, is a rather ineptly garbled oracle about the couple's future sufferings.[55] Where the sun is used in the folktale, it usually gives the rival her continuous news that the heroine is still alive; in one variant this role is supplied by a witch instead.[56] There may be a trace of such a motif in Xenophon: an old woman called Chrysion turns up and informs Habrocomes that Anthia is still alive.[57]

A small number of versions have some preliminary attempt by the rival to spoil the heroine's beauty by some menial occupation: in an Italian version from Abruzzi she is enclosed in a hut by the sea and fed on bread and water, but accordingly becomes more beautiful; other romance versions vary this motif.[58] The detail of the hut by the sea may be significant: Xenophon's text embodies an apparent reference to the sea in relation to Lampon's house, perhaps a careless reminiscence of such a variant.[59]

There is considerable flexibility in the tradition as to how the cruel rival will arrange to dispose of Snow White. Usually the servant's instructions are to kill her in a wood, and to bring back her heart, liver, or the like, and those of an animal are then substituted as a ruse.[60] Xenophon omits this detail (by no means uniquely): it belongs to a rural, hunting culture and does not accord comfortably with the values and tastes even of 'cheap' urban romance. The persistence of such a motif in the popular tradition points rather to a primitive rural ruse of great antiquity.

There are other subterfuges en route: the queen can contrive that Snow White will be lost in the wood, knowing that the seven dwarfs kill any maiden who comes near them; Snow White may be bound to a tree and eaten by wolves, or relegated to the garden of a wild man, a return once more to the abandonment to a peasant in Xenophon's version.[61] An Albanian variant has each of the rival sisters receiving a visit from the Moerae, the Fates, prophesying their fate: Anthia receives a visit in the wild from her rival's husband, Moeris – characteristically turned into an erotic temptation scene for its new context in romance.[62]

The reception by a kindly but humble or unlikely host or hosts is also accorded considerable latitude in the versions. We should forget at times about seven dwarfs: they can be giants, robbers, cannibals, Draks, hunters, fairies, accursed souls, or the like;[63] and their lair varies accordingly – they may live in a glass mountain, a feature which obviously accords very well indeed with the theme of Snow White and which fits very well with the genealogies in the

Chione myth.[64] There are considerable variations in the number: two dwarfs in Icelandic or Finnish versions, an indeterminate number in Ligurian and some Portuguese versions, and the single swineherd in the third Portuguese version. In a few zoomorphic variants the hosts are bears by day, princesses by night: note the ambiguous status of Xenophon's robber Hippothous and his band – aristocrat turned brigand, and reverting finally to his original privileged status.[65]

Sometimes Snow White meets a tormented soul or the like. This motif actually occurs in Xenophon as part of the brothel scene when she makes the (false) excuse that her (pretended) epilepsy was caused by the assault of a departed spirit. Anthia makes these excuses at Tarentum. It is noteworthy that Snow White variants of such an encounter occur as near as Sicily.[66]

Snow White usually reaches the robbers' or dwarfs' den in their absence and cooks and tidies the house for them. Of course Anthia will presumably have done all this for her peasant 'husband' – and nothing more, but there is no indication of her co-operating with the robbers in this way. In neither case is her initiative in question: Greek aristocrats are not expected to volunteer to do menial work, and that is reflected in the proprieties of the novel. Hence we simply find Hippothous capturing Anthia among a party wandering in a wood.[67]

Some other features of the stay with the robbers are presented in Xenophon. When she is put in a trench with two wild dogs, one of the robbers, an admirer, is careful to feed them, so that they do her no harm. In a Breton version we find Snow White hiding in the dog's stall, and in others dire consequences follow if she fails to feed dogs.[68] The usual tradition is that the robbers or dwarfs take their new guest as a sister. Lampis treats his guest in this way in Xenophon, as does Hippothous, who respects her chastity when at last he comes round to merely trying to assault it, rather than to killing her.[69] In one Russian version she is already a prince's bride, and she is already married to the aristocratic Habrocomes in Xenophon.[70] In some versions, Snow White marries the equivalent character to Hippothous, who is accordingly promoted.[71]

The person who administers the poison to Snow White is sometimes a beggar. In the nearest version to Xenophon, the second German, it is a Jewish doctor Sambul, who corresponds to Xenophon's doctor Eudoxus: he poisons half the apple, but only with a sleeping drug.[72] Xenophon's sleeping draught, the method found in several versions and widely spread, is also the 'correct' version for an urban novel with its *Scheintod* scene, where the heroine will be left unguarded in a normal Greek burial vault and will simply wake up.[73] Many of the other Snow White methods, such as a poisoned needle or an apple stuck in the throat, will require some additional intervention to wake the heroine.[74]

The Snow White versions use a variety of methods to preserve and encase the girl's corpse in her suspended animation, most often a transparent glass case. But gold, silver, and even iron coffins are found.[75] A number of variants also have the finder of the coffin taking it home and applying unending devotion to it. In a small number of different cases the coffin is put to sea and found by fishermen.[76] It is in the context of these versions that we have to consider the most distinctive episode in Xenophon:[77] Habrocomes meets a poor fisherman in Sicily (really a Spartan nobleman fallen on hard times), who keeps his dead wife Thelxinoe embalmed in Egyptian style in the inner room of his house.

This bizarre exhibit has rightly puzzled students of the novel: why should Xenophon introduce the fisherman and his bizarrely preserved wife at all? As far as he is concerned it provides only another opportunity to remind us that Anthia is still missing. But it makes little sense as it stands. Why preserve the corpse of an old woman, and how did he learn Egyptian embalming in Sparta or Sicily? It seems difficult to escape the suspicion that what Xenophon is really handling is a common variant, or combination of variants, of the glass coffin scene itself. It should not be the fisherman's wife Thelxinoe, but Anthia who should be in the coffin, having been preserved alive in glass. She should then awaken and recognise the long-lost lover there and then. But Xenophon wants to keep the plot running and opts for the grand reunion at Rhodes. So he relegates the alternative to a very unsatisfactory subplot. In any case, it is not physically possible to keep real people alive in enclosed mummy cases or the like for long periods.

Various other fragments of the tradition turn up in Xenophon. Anthia finds herself sold to an Indian prince who takes her on a camel, before she is rescued by Hippothous and his men.[78] There may be a hint of this in the North African Kabyle and second Arabic version, where Snow White, still in her coffin or equivalent, is being carried on a camel, usually prior to her discovery by the prince.[79] This in itself might be due to coincidence, since the camel is such a standard mode of long-distance transport in the Near East. But against that should be balanced its rarity, even in Greek novels dealing with Egypt.

In some versions of Snow White the heroine is supplanted after marriage by a bizarre rival bride, and has to torment the prince while metamorphosed into a bird.[80] The latter detail is of course impossible in a quasi-realistic romance. But Xenophon may have included a clumsily detailed treatment of the motif of the rival wife. Habrocomes is subjected to the unhealthy attentions of an ugly old woman called Kyno ('Bitch').[81] Much more distinctive, however, within Xenophon is the fact that the robbers incarcerate Anthia with two wild dogs, which however a friendly robber contrives to feed.[82]

Several hints of such an episode do occur in the Snow White tradition. In one Breton version the heroine hides in a kennel and feeds the dogs just prior to her discovery by the robbers/dwarfs. A number of Knidian Snow Whites have a much more extended presentation: while staying with the dwarfs/robbers the heroine must feed the dog/cat or a giant will come and get her.[83] In Xenophon this is cut down to realistic size: the dogs will simply eat her if they are not fed. But again Xenophon may retain a hint of some monster or other. She is rescued from the trench by one Polyeidos ('many form'):[84] in a true folktale version one should expect some kind of Protean shape shifter here.

So much, then, for a fairly complete rendering of the folktale into romance.

It seems clear enough that Xenophon has adapted a folktale, and that the surviving version of Xenophon's tale did not develop into the folktale: it is difficult to distinguish the outlines of the folktale from the additional overlay of romantic melodrama, and a stripped down summary of Xenophon would scarcely produce a version like that of the Grimms. But we do find incorporated into Xenophon the essential mainspring of Snow White – the motif of white-and-red, and two versions of the motif of divination; the heroine's jealous female rival; two different versions of the kindly protectors (the peasant and the robbers); the deathly sleep produced by poison (but differently motivated), and even a hint of the glass coffin, now relegated to a subplot. And it is worth stressing that nothing like this collocation of motifs occurs in any of the extant romances related to different folktale plots.

There is also a stray connection between Xenophon and the Chione fragments: the relatively rare name Megamedes, who appears here either as Chione's father, or less likely as some importunate suitor.[85] As it happens Megamedes is the father of Anthia in Xenophon's version. In etymological terms the name might serve also as an equivalent to Daedalion ('of great skill' or the like), and thus duplicate the father of the Ovidian Chione.[86]

At this point there is just one more addition to the Snow White repertoire. In 1922 Lavagnini published two short papyrus excerpts in which the names Anthia and Euxinos occur.[87] The latter is the name of a pirate in Xenophon's romance, and these fragments could well be from some other form of it. Lavagnini spotted the resemblance, but not a third factor – the presence of the word *pharmakos* in one of the fragments. This episode ought to be sited at the point where Anthia receives the sleeping draught. Other names occur in this new text: Thalassia, which might turn out to be Anthia's mother (if we bear in mind the genealogy of Chione),[88] and Thraseas, who might at this point in the story be a new name for Perilaus, whom Anthia does not wish to marry. None of this offers enough to go on, and all of it must remain provisional guesswork.

What then, can now be said about Snow White in antiquity? We should feel entitled to conclude that there was already a diversity of versions, and that the dwarfs could be represented in some form in the story. We shall see below and in Chapter 12 that the relationship between a form of Snow White and 'the search for the lost brothers' already existed, inter alia in the *Iphigenia* complex. The outline of the folktale is provisionally implied in at least one of the mythical versions, that of Ovid, and regional variations of the folktale offer the foundation of at least the kernel and some of the less conventional episodes of more than one romance. As in the case of Cinderella we must expect to come to the conclusion that myth, folktale and novel represent different presentations of the same basic material. Nor is this the last case of such common ground we shall find.

The search for the lost husband (*AT* Type 451)

So far we have concentrated our attention on the normal 'Snow White', *AT* Type 709. But there is substantial overlap in the modern repertoire between this type and one other in particular, *AT* Type 451. Here the heroine finds that for some reason connected with her birth and prospects of inheriting the kingdom, her brothers have been driven out of it by their father; she goes in search of them, but they are changed into birds or animals. However, she survives, as in *Snow White* texts, in the custody of giants or dwarfs, and may have some feature parallel to the Snow White glass case – such as going into a mountain of ice, or experiencing a long period of silence – before saving the brothers by disenchantment. This type may be prosecuted without any 'marriage to the prince' at all, but where it contains the presence of dwarfs and/or some equivalent of the glass case, its cognates are clear enough and marriage to the prince can also be included.[89] The type may be illustrated from one of several Grimm versions side by side with an English example:[90]

The Twelve Brothers (Grimm no. 9)	*The Seven Brothers* (Briggs 1.1.477)
A king has twelve sons; they leave home to safeguard the inheritance of his daughter	A king has seven sons; they leave home before a daughter is born
The princess goes in search of them and finds their cottage	The princess goes in search of them and keeps house for them in magic house in wood
	They warn her against a neighbouring wicked wizard and his magic
	The wizard bites her finger when she goes to borrow fire, and she becomes ugly
She turns her brothers into ravens by accident (by plucking twelve flowers)	She turns her brothers into bullocks by means of comb bought from wizard disguised as peddler
She marries	She marries
She is to be burned through the slanders of a jealous mother-in-law, but keeps silence even when threatened with burning	She is left down a well by false bride, who tries to have the bullocks killed
Brothers come to her rescue	Brothers come to her rescue
Her silence ensures that the brothers are restored to human form	Grandmother disenchants bullocks
They kill her evil mother-in-law	False bride thrown down well

We can see in this instance how obviously the second version shades into 'our' Snow White; a West Asian variant in Dawkins shows this even more clearly by including the girl's coma and rescue through the removal of the object causing it, though other details are confused.[91] We have already noted that a likely mythological treatment of this tale lies behind the story of Chione, daughter of Boreas: as she has brothers Zetes and Calais, who are changed into birds, there is the possibility that she was able in some form of the story to search for them and disenchant them, but testimony in the mythographers is lacking. We have another tantalising pointer in the same direction, but from a different angle: the first fragment of the *Chione*-romance is about the assignment of a kingdom which a girl and her husband stand to inherit. The speaker exhorts another person or persons to action:

> The kingdom goes to her and her future consort, and so it is necessary for us to take counsel now in order to reach an irrevocable decision. We have thirty days to make up our mind, which to this end from them...[rest unintelligible without context].

As far as it goes this would fit the idea that Chione, finding that her brothers have had to go to clear her claim to the kingdom, should follow them into the *Snow White*-related adventures of *AT* Type 451. But without being sure that the speakers are her brothers, we can only suspect.

We should also note a strong resemblance to the lost brother type of tale in at least some treatments of the story of Iphigenia, Orestes and Electra. Iphigenia's name does not help us ('princess noble'), but the arrangement of motifs is telling. She is a girl promised to a prince (Achilles). She is threatened with sacrifice at the behest of a prophet Calchas, though at the last moment a hind is substituted; she now appears in a hostile far-away land where there are bull-men (Taurians), who offer human sacrifice to their goddess. Along comes a brother and friend, who take her away, *together with a statue of Artemis*. This combines the idea of taking the girl away from her other-worldly environment and the idea of the hero taking away a statue; the Snow White prince often carts off the body of the benumbed girl worshipped by the dwarfs. In addition, Orestes and Pylades, according to Lucian (*Toxaris* 7) were celebrated by the Scythians as *Korakoi*, a title either cognate with, or easily misunderstood as *Korakes* (ravens).

If we see this simply as a puzzling series of mythological footnotes to the legend of Orestes and Iphigenia, it remains one of the peculiar dead ends of myth, so frequent when the principal characters find themselves beyond the familiar pale of the Greek world. But if we attempt to translate the sequence into terms of Snow White motifs we get the following:

> A noble princess is the victim of the envy of Artemis because of an offence by her father; an oracle orders her sacrifice; Artemis has a hind

substituted on the altar, and the girl disappears, to be found among the
wild Bull-men; she finds her brother and his friends there as Raven-
men (?); they steal the holy image worshipped by the Bull-men. (By
implication) the raven men lose their bird identity when they escape
from the land of the bull-men.

We should stress the provisional nature of such an outline, cobbled together
from very disparate strata of mythological information; we should stress, too,
the oddities it offers as a folktale variant. We notice the compassionate executioner motif, here discharged by Artemis herself; the fatal oracle, functioning
rather differently from the modern magic mirror; the prince's taking away of
the statue, *not* identical with the heroine. But after all the reservations have
been made, such a version is still clearly recognisable as belonging to *AT* Type
451, though it leaves a good many questions unanswered.

It is difficult to detach another branch of the family of Agamemnon from the
Chione-complex as well: Iphigenia's sister, Electra, is persecuted by her mother
and stepfather; she is put out in the wild to live with a peasant, who serves the
same purpose as the wild bull-men in relation to her sister, the role of unlikely
protectors in a wild but hostile environment; she shows concern for her brother
Orestes ('mountain-man'), and eventually will be married to his companion
Pylades. She and the ignoble sister Chrysothemis have the same kind of colour
contrast in their names (Amber and Gold-law) as found in some parts in the
Snow White complex (Pomegranate and Lemon in the Jewish–Egyptian
version). If, as seems likely, Electra was persecuted by the Erinyes, then we
might have the possibility of a madness scene of some sort, or a hostile
encounter with bird creatures. Before marriage to Pylades we have no scene of
an ice mountain, glass coffin or any such thing, but her name Electra ought to
mean 'amber-girl', i.e. transparent preserving substance.[92] This again suggests a
hint of the preserving glass case so prominent in the modern Snow White tale,
and unexplained in the parts of Electra's story that we actually know from the
Tragedians and the mythographic record.[93]

Again, we must ask at this stage, as in the case of Cinderella, whether there is
a case for an ancient Near Eastern predecessor of our classical examples. It is of
particular interest and consequence that the same Sumerian goddess who offers
a proto-Cinderella can offer us a proto-Snow White as well. In *Inanna and the
Nether World*, which exists in both Sumerian and Akkadian recensions, Inanna
wanders down to the underworld, where she is strung up as a naked corpse by
her sister Ereshkigal. Only by courtesy of the Annunaki, seven inhuman, sexless
creatures, who act as judges of the dead, is she allowed back to life (in the
Akkadian version). Here we have the jealousy of a close female relative and
murder attempt that form the basis of Snow Whites; in the Annunaki we may
well be looking at yet another perspective on the Seven Dwarfs – as underground personnel out of the normal sphere of human activity. It may be worth
recalling that the Grimm dwarfs spend their day in a mine.

4

CUPID AND PSYCHE (AT 425A)
AND *BEAUTY AND THE BEAST*
(AT 425C)

While Cinderella and Snow White have never yielded complete folktale versions from antiquity until now, Apuleius' *Cupid and Psyche*, on the other hand, is advanced even by its narrator in *The Golden Ass* as an *anilis fabula*, an 'old wives' tale', as early as the mid-second century AD.[1] There has been a long drawn-out controversy as to whether it really does have its origins in a popular fairytale, or whether instead it can be regarded as something completely different or supposedly so, such as a sacred tale or cult myth;[2] or whether again it might be a literary confection from which a folktale has in the course of time been extrapolated. The presence of versions of *Cinderella* and *Snow White* in antiquity may change the climate and balance of probability to some extent, but the case for *Cupid and Psyche* as a popular fairytale has still to be made.

Modern folktale versions of the story there undoubtedly are: Swahn was able to study an assemblage of well into four figures in the same manner as Rooth had studied versions of Cinderella.[3] Something of the range of the tale as classified (*AT* Type 425A) can be seen from such examples as the following:

A princess is shown her way home by a mysterious voice inside an iron stove; she is to return, release and marry him; after two false substitutes are offered he threatens to destroy her father's kingdom if she is not sent. She comes, and finds a handsome prince inside the stove. She is not to speak more than three words to her father, or her prince will be carried off. She does, and has to search for the flying stove: crossing mountains and lakes, but helped by a family of frogs; she finds him about to marry a witch's daughter, but jogs his memory just in time. All is disenchanted.

(Grimm 1992: 127, *Der Eisenofen*)

The tale has a wide distribution over Europe, Western Asia and limited parts of Africa.[4] It is generally assumed by classicists that no adequate ancient analogue has been found, other than Apuleius' famous version itself. But this is not so. Swahn recognised that at least part of the myth of Zeus and Semele is also a variant of *AT* Type 425, a fact which only really becomes clear when we examine the full account in the very late version in the seventh book of Nonnos' *Dionysiaca*:

> Harmonia has four daughters, the youngest of whom, Semele, is seen while bathing by Zeus. The latter appears as an eagle, becomes inflamed with passion, and visits her on the following night. He comes 'with a horned head on human limbs, lowing with the voice of a bull'. Then he appears in 'a shaggy lion's form or he was a panther...A writhing serpent crawled over the limbs of the trembling bride and licked her rosy neck with gentle lips, then slipping into her bosom girdled the circuit of her firm breasts, hissing a wedding tune...'. Zeus tells her who he is, she becomes pregnant, and Dionysus dances in her womb when he hears the sound of pipes. Hera, who hears of the matter, disguises herself as a 'honey-voiced old dame', visits Semele and wants to know who has 'ravished her maidenhood': people will begin to talk ill of her if she gives birth to an ordinary bastard. But, she says, if everyone knows it is Zeus who visits her then no one will take exception. Semele should, therefore, ask Zeus to come in all his glory with thunder and lightning so that people can say 'Hera and Semele both have thunders in waiting for the bedchamber'. Semele begs Zeus to do this and when he is finally persuaded she is killed by lightning. The child Dionysus is saved, however, when the womb 'is withered by the mother-murdering flash'.[5] (In other versions it is Semele's sisters who bring misfortune on her.)

We could argue that this only represents the first half of the tale, since the death of Semele precludes the essential material of the action, namely the 'search for the lost husband', which is the point of the whole exercise. But it is worth noting that in the earliest Renaissance version of *Cupid and Psyche*, Basile's story of Parmetella (*Pentamerone* 5.4), the girl's forbidden bridegroom is actually *called* 'thunder-and-lightning', as clear an allusion as possible to the 'facts' of the Semele story. Swahn did not probe the full extent of mythographers' variants, but from Pindar onwards it is accepted that total incineration was indeed not the end for Semele, and longer later accounts such as those of Diodorus and Apollodorus have her enjoying some manner of heavenly resurrection, the only female mortal in Greek mythology to enjoy such a privilege.[6] In some accounts it is not until Dionysus can go down to Hades for her that she is rescued.[7] But this is consistent with the variants of the story where the search for the husband does not entail actual tasks but rather a long wait (seven years is the favourite period). We should also note the bizarre variant in Hyginus 167: the heart of Dionysus/Zagreus, torn to pieces by the Titans, is ground down by (Zeus) and swallowed by Semele, who then becomes pregnant by Dionysus in the normal way. In this way Semele imbibes the *cor*, the heart of Dionysus, and so arguably his *psyche* in some sense.

Once this story is recognised as a full-blown mythological variant of *Cupid and Psyche*, largely available from materials earlier than Apuleius, it becomes even more impossible to insist that the whole tale is the creation of the author of *The Golden Ass*, mediated to the medieval and modern worlds by the late mythographer Fulgentius.[8] But the proof of the tale's still more ancient ancestry has still to be established.

We can present the *Cupid and Psyche* type, labelled by Aarne–Thompson as 425A, in the following terms, following the analysis of Swahn, based on some 1,100 variants collected up to 1955:[9]

I   The supernatural husband
II   The marriage
III The breaking of the taboo
IV The search for the husband
V   The reunion
VI Final motifs

Most of our early comparative materials relate to the latter part of the tale. If we take the tale from the point when the taboo has just been broken, when Apuleius' Cupid is actually awakened by the drop of oil, we find that he is annoyed with Psyche for breaking his command and seeing him, and that he flies away to heaven where he takes up residence in his mother's quarters. As a result no legitimate and proper relationships and sexual activity are seen by people to be possible among mankind. The facts, including the god's whereabouts, are reported to Venus by a tern.[10] She sends for Psyche and forces the girl to sort a heap of grain, to fetch wool from sheep crazed by the sun, to bring waters (of life?) from the Styx, and finally to obtain a box of beauty ointment from the underworld.[11] When all are applied to Cupid he supplicates Jupiter and obtains Psyche. At an assembly of the gods Jupiter declares that Cupid's days of youthful impulse and mischief are over.[12]

From here we can turn to texts from an unexpected quarter: a series of Hittite texts relating to the anger of the god Telepinus from the second millennium BC.[13] The god is annoyed at something (the first third of the tablet, which must have narrated the cause, is missing), and he wanders off in high dudgeon to a meadow. As a result no sexual activity is possible among mankind. A bee is commissioned to find him and bring him back to his mother, the mother-goddess herself. She commissions the healing goddess Kamrusepas to heal him by soothing him with wheat, with wool from the sheep of the sun-god, and with olive oil, (a well-established folklore equivalent of the waters of life). His anger is then earthed in jars in the underworld. At an assembly the god Telepinus' father declares that his anger is over and fertility returns.[14]

There are two differences between the Latin and Hittite versions, one major, one minor. Kamrusepas' operations are quite clearly presented as rituals for the healing, or rather the exorcism, of Telepinus; Psyche's tasks are prescribed by

Venus pointlessly, or in the hope of punishing Psyche.[15] The second discrepancy concerns the tasks themselves. The Hittite version of the fourth task is more satisfactory: instead of a rather pointless near-doublet of the third, we have a quite different interpretation of Cupid's placing the deadly contents in a box belonging to the underworld.[16]

It seems clear enough to this author that the Hittite myth covers enough of the material of *Cupid and Psyche* to amount to identity rather than similarity. This is moreover reinforced by the genealogy of Telepinus himself. He seems to be a temperamental god concerned *inter alia* with human sexual intercourse, and his mother is the Hittite mother-goddess whose husband is the storm-god. This pairing corresponds correctly to Aphrodite and Ares, the mother of Eros/Cupid and her lover. We should note, too, that the myth was popular in Western Asia, where a number of fragmentary analogues are found. Moreover, one of these has protagonists Anzili and *Zukki*; the latter name ought to raise the suspicion that Psyche's name has not been chosen to embody playful allegory in the first instance, but as an attempt to Hellenise a genuine oriental name.[17] It is a pity that the Hittite version of this myth is too damaged to secure the identification absolutely. In addition, we seem also to have a second Telepinus myth which corresponds to the *beginning* of *Cupid and Psyche* as well. Telepinus is able to threaten the sea-god into giving him his daughter as a wife; this would correspond to the enforced marriage of a king's daughter with a powerful and threatening deity which results in Psyche's encounter in the first place.[18]

We can now examine in more detail the correspondences with Apuleius' text as it stands. The most detailed Hittite version begins as follows:

> Telepinus [...screamed]: 'let here be no intimidating language'. [Then] he drew [on the right shoe] on his left foot, and the left [shoe on his right foot].[19]

The corresponding scene of Cupid's anger in the Latin text merely has Cupid react to the pain of burning, realising that his prohibition has been broken. He perches on a tree long enough to announce that he must leave Psyche before flying off to an undisclosed destination.[20] This is consistent with the charming reticence and sensitivity with which Apuleius treats the couple's relationship. But both texts allow a moment of comic incongruity at this point, despite their totally different details: Telepinus is so angry that he puts his shoes on the wrong feet, while Psyche clasps Cupid's legs and looks oddly attached to him till she drops off from exhaustion.[21] Telepinus now goes off to the steppe, and the land suffers accordingly:

> Mist seized the windows. Smoke [seized the house]. In the fireplace the logs were stifled; [at the altars] the gods were stifled, in the sheep pen the sheep were stifled, in the cattle barns the cattle were stifled.

Therefore barley (and) wheat no longer ripen. Cattle, sheep, and humans no longer become pregnant. And those (already) pregnant cannot give birth.[22]

In Apuleius, the tern reports a similar state of affairs to Venus following the departure of Cupid:

(5.28.5) And so there is no pleasure, no Grace, no Wit, but everything is ugly, unkempt, and repulsive. There are no conjugal relations, and no friendships, and nobody even caresses his children. Everything is in disorder, and people have a hateful aversion for their squalid relationships.[23]

The agricultural element so insistent in oriental myths of this type is cut out: Apuleius insists at this point only on the human consequences of Cupid's disappearance, with typically Hellenistic personnel (Pleasure, Grace, Wit). But in fact Apuleius will take it up also: when Telepinus departs, he takes grain with him as well, thus denying it to mankind. When Cupid is out of circulation, Ceres refuses to shelter Psyche from Venus; in both cases denial of love also means denial of corn.[24]

In the Hittite version Telepinus is sought out by his anxious mother Hannahannas; after a futile search by the eagle, it is the bee who finds him and brings him back. Apuleius, on the other hand, has a white tern, simply to report malicious rumours of what has happened.[25] Clearly, in both cases, all that is required is some quite trivial creature. In the Latin version, Cupid has not actually been reported missing so that nothing is made of the motif of any search by Venus; rather, it is Psyche who is doing the searching.

In the Hittite version there is a double 'cure' for Telepinus: someone, perhaps the sun-god, declares:

[Summon] the mortal. [Let him...] the ...[on] mount Ammuna. Let him move him. [Let] the eagle [approach and] move [him] with a wing. Let the mortal make [him] arise. The eagle [moved?] him with its wing.

Then, after a gap in the text, the healing-goddess Kamrusepas is commissioned to heal Telepinus with soothing cures.[26] Apuleius on the other hand has Psyche ('Human Soul') commissioned to bring waters from the Styx, a task ultimately accomplished by the agency of an eagle acting on Psyche's behalf.[27]

But in one of the characteristic loose ends in Apuleius, we are told that Venus decides:

Should I go for help to my enemy, the lady I've offended so often because of this boy's over-indulgence? But I shudder at the very thought of talking to that filthy yokel of a woman...But she'll give that so-and-so a real telling-off; empty his quiver, blunt his arrows, take the string from this bow and put out his torch...then I'll feel I've had my revenge when she's shaved off the hair which I've so often stroked with my own hands and made it shine like gold.[28]

These desperate measures are not followed up, but they supply clearly enough the notion that Cupid must somehow be cured. The first measure corresponds to Psyche's third task, performed by 'men' rather than by 'soul'; the second may correspond to the role of Kamrusepas as a healing-goddess.

The Hittite myth goes on to describe the rituals performed by Kamrusepas. Several of these correspond with, and indeed help to explain, Psyche's tasks:

> Here lies wheat for you. Just as (this) wheat is pure, let Telepinus' [heart and soul] become pure again in the same way.[29]

> (6.10.1f.)Venus took wheat, barley, millet, poppy seed, chickpeas, lentils and beans, and mixed them together and shuffled them into a single hillock, and told her, 'You are so ugly, a serving wench, that I think you deserve to earn your lovers by no other means than this time-consuming task and this alone: so now I will test your ability in person: separate the confused heap of these seeds into duly-sorted and separated grains'.[30]

Here Venus produces what she sees as merely an obstacle task. But Kamrusepas' healing operations suggest that Apuleius' motivation is not the original one. There is no point in Venus' tasks as set – other than to frustrate Psyche. The grains were already sorted and are now scrambled. But the Hittite version is well-motivated: chaff is separated like the heart and soul of Telepinus. Psyche's first task has the makings of a ritual healing operation, just right for her wounded husband's condition.

A similar healing ritual underlies the second task:

> Kamrusepas says to the gods: 'Go, O gods, now tend the sun-god's sheep for Hapantali, and cut out twelve rams, so that I may treat Telepinus' karas grains. I have taken for myself a basket (with) a thousand small holes. And upon it I have poured *karas* grains, the "rams of Kamrusepas".'[31]

Once again Apuleius seems to present a different view of the same task. Psyche is to bring wool back from the fleeces of golden sheep which are crazed by the heat of the sun: she is warned by a friendly reed to collect it only after the heat of the sun has subsided.[32] The task is once more pointless other than to assure Venus of Psyche's good intentions – or to kill her. Once more the Hittite version is better motivated: to assuage Telepinus' anger and bring him back into circulation.

The third task is to bring back the water of the Styx. In the Hittite there is an injunction that man is to take the spring Hattara on mount Ammuna – with the eagle's wing.[33] The ritual significance of this seems to be explained at the end of the rituals: just as this fire of Telepinus' wrath is quenched, even so let Telepinus' rage, anger and fury be quenched too! And 'Just as water in a pipe flows not upward, even so let Telepinus' rage, anger and fury not come back'.

Apuleius' version drops the motivation: water is necessary to soothe the god and sink his anger.[34] But it very carefully explains how the eagle fits into the operation. It snatches the jar from Psyche's hand and collects the Styx water in defiance of the guardian serpents, repaying a favour of Cupid over Ganymede.

It is Psyche's fourth task that has caused the most difficulty. She is to go down to the underworld and bring back a box which contains a deadly sleep. Impelled by curiosity she opens the box and falls asleep. Cupid himself now appears, puts the sleep back into the box, and so wakens Psyche.[35]

The task is presented rather differently in the Hittite version. There are jars in the underworld from which nothing can escape. Telepinus' deadly wrath has to be put into them.[36] It might reasonably be suggested that this is not really analogous: the box comes from the underworld and is brought by Psyche to Venus; it does not return to the underworld. On the other hand, Cupid has put the deadly contents inside and sealed them safely. That latter motive is the essence of the Hittite version and once more explains the point better: the god's wrath is to be earthed for good: there is no real point in duplicating Psyche's curiosity.

A celestial council drives home the point in both texts: the gods are gathered in assembly under the hawthorn tree. All the gods are present (nine different deities or classes of deity are specified):

> (A god speaks?) '[I have taken] evil from Telepinus' body, I have taken his [anger, I have taken away his] wrath.'[37]

So in Apuleius:

> (Jupiter) commanded Mercury at once to call all the gods to counsel, and proclaim that the fine for absence from the celestial assembly is set at ten thousand. Fearful at the prospect, they filled the celestial theatre before his lofty throne at once, and Jupiter sitting in majesty made this pronouncement: 'Conscript gods, registered in the book of the Muses, you all know no doubt this young man...whose hot-blooded impulses of early youth I have seen fit to restrain.'[38]

It follows once more that this is part of the story, and that only incidental colouring of the council scene can be safely attributed to Apuleius.[39]

So far we have looked only at the end of the myth as presented in the Telepinus texts. But we have Cupid and Psyche complete, and its beginning is certainly no less bizarre. Psyche has been condemned by an oracle to marry – a snake, to all appearances.[40] This she accepts, and she awaits his coming as a bridegroom. After she breaks a taboo he departs and fertility suffers. She searches for him, going round deity after deity. But he recovers from his own wounds in time to cure her from sleep. Folklorists have identified the snake element as a variant on a subtype of 425, namely *Beauty and the Beast*.[41] The girl accepts a monstrous husband, but loses him; she must seek him out and with the final confiscation of his bestial outfit or the like they can live happily ever after. We shall note below at least fugitive traces of this subtype in the mythographic tradition.

It is difficult in the light of the foregoing evidence to do other than acknowledge that *Cupid and Psyche* cannot possibly be an original tale by Apuleius, and it is equally clear that the text most closely resembling it is an engaging text incorporating myth in action, purveying sympathetic folk remedy as we should be tempted to regard it, to appease the wrath of a departed deity.

But the best is perhaps still to come. The Hittite mythological corpus also has a myth about the human soul on its journey. It is searching for something, sought out for it by bees and the animal world in general; the mother-goddess is distressed; the soul has to go down to the underworld, and is terrified:

Why must I a mortal, go into the pit(?)?...I would rather fall into the river. [I would rather fall] into the pond.

Such a text fits Psyche's experience at the moment she is facing her underworld journey to fetch the waters of life.[42] It also seems clear that the whole of nature is helping the soul in its search. This soul-search myth is not directly joined to the Telepinus texts, but so many of the texts printed by Hoffner are clearly myths of lost and returning gods, mostly storm-gods although other deities are mentioned, that it is not difficult to envisage some junction between the two myths. And, indeed, in the second Telepinus myth the god does marry the daughter of the sea from which he also rescues the sun-god; while in the text of the soul-myth allusion is made to the soul of the sun-goddess, the soul of the mother, in a context where it may be equated with the human soul.[43] We are very close to being able to equate Telepinus' bride or partner with Psyche.

Of course none of this excludes a double reference in which the Platonist Apuleius' readers would be expected to see Platonic references encoded in his text as well. But the suspicion that one of the characters in this myth was already called Zukki anyway should be a major consideration: we may have a Platonic-sounding myth by accident. It is also important to acknowledge that the emergence of *Cupid and Psyche* as an oral folktale type will not have depended on Apuleius or his derivatives since a whole myth complex around the subject was clearly long available in Asia Minor.

It is useful to note the degree of speculation by Apuleian scholars as to what is his own contribution to the folktale material with which he was clearly working. It is often treacherous to assume that a motif or treatment is 'literary' just because it is thinly represented in the repertoire of one particular folktale: for Wright (1971), 'The similarity between the exposure of Psyche and that of Andromeda is a reminder of the latter's role in the Dragon-Slayer fairytale, rather than decorative mythological allusion.'[44] We might say the same about the personification of the lamp, the device of the riddling oracle, the amatory troubles of the river, and a good many more details of the kind.[45] It has to be emphasised that the distinction between myth and folktale is modern, and that the distinction between 'literary' and 'popular' far too often is allowed to rest upon it.[46] Wright suggests that the snake is played down to give a more literary feel to the text (275) and to facilitate the verse riddle. But we should also underline that throughout the tale's transmission it is toned down even in popular contexts to fit its environment. In the English variants known to Philip the supernatural practically disappears altogether: instead of going to hell, the girl takes service as a menial below stairs in a country house.

Wright repeats Swahn's insistence that the motif of the heroine's pregnancy in the fairytale is confined to the Balkans.[47] But the purpose of the Hittite text was as a birthing-charm against prolonged pregnancy, which is precisely the punishment imposed on Psyche by Venus in Apuleius,[48] so that the pregnancy must have figured in pre-Turkish Asia Minor. As for the name *Voluptas*, allegorisers may make what they will of its name,[49] but they should take account of the character of the child Dionysus in the Semele version who even dances in the womb when he hears the pipes in Nonnus. And again, the burlesque of the gods' relationships, while 'Alexandrian' to us, is just as comic in some of the Hittite touches: Telepinus putting his shoes on the wrong feet, for example.

We should emphasise how much the Hittite text and the extended myth of Semele show us about the convergence of myth, ritual and fairytale. A great deal of the supposed distinction rests on our own perspective. If the myth of Telepinus is being told to a Hittite prospective mother in prolonged labour, we can see the text as the narrative contents of a birthing ritual involving genuine gods and genuine belief; but we can also see it as midwives telling a mother a story to divert her from the business on hand. Male observers might well see it as an *anilis fabula*, just as Apuleius did. We might usefully bridge the gap by seeing it as 'The Midwife's Tale'.

Beauty and the Beast

This tale (*AT* Type 425C) is generally felt to be of literary origin in more recent times:

Beauty is forced to go to the Beast by a fault of her father, who has trespassed on the Beast's territory and has stolen a rose at Beauty's request, an offence for which the Beast has condemned her father to death; the Beast treats Beauty courteously and allows visits home; her jealous sisters detain her to annoy the Beast, with near-tragic consequences; but the Beast's spell is broken by Beauty's devotions and he inevitably becomes a handsome prince.

Swahn took this quite seriously to suggest that this type owes its existence to the literary tradition represented by Madame LePrince de Beaumont's adaptation of Madame Villeneuve's very long literary version. But these relationships are to some extent academic, since we have not one but two brief versions of essential components of the modern fairytale in the ancient mythographical tradition. These indeed serve as a very good illustration of the mutual blindness of classical and folklore scholars to the identification of one another's materials. At its very simplest we can break down *Beauty and the Beast* to the following:

A girl called Beauty;
trespass in the garden of the Beast;
the Beast is loved by Beauty;
he becomes human, and so she marries a handsome prince.

What the classical texts give us is the following:

(a) A girl picks flowers in a beautiful meadow;
    she is attracted by a god in animal form;
    he takes her away and becomes human;
    she is married to a star king (Asterion).

(b) A girl is called 'Most Beautiful' (Kallisto);
    she mates with a god and *herself turns into an animal*;
    she is to be killed for trespassing in her divine lover's sacred precinct;
    she is turned into a constellation.

These myths are of course the tales of 'Europa and Zeus' and 'Kallisto and Zeus' respectively. The latter as it stands is *Beauty the Beast* rather than *Beauty and the Beast*. It would only take a single attempt (conscious or otherwise) to conflate these two celebrated love affairs of one and the same Zeus and we should have 'our' *Beauty and the Beast*. Moreover, it is easy enough to see how this might happen. If the identity of Zeus becomes less specific and he is simply seen as 'a handsome prince' or 'a great king' who has taken on animal form, the well-defined stories of two of Zeus' mistresses would readily be allowed to merge – if indeed they were not one in the beginning – with the celebrated flower meadow as somehow within the normal purview of Zeus. And, in any case, it would be a relatively simple matter to confuse a girl called 'Beauty' or 'most Beautiful' with the normal heroine of a fairytale. At any rate, the idea of a trespass in a sacred precinct would certainly help us justify the origin of the 'rose in the garden' motif in *Beauty and the Beast*: the Beast seems to overreact somewhat when he wants the death of Beauty or her father for his trespass in a purely fairytale context. The breaking of an original religious taboo would add weight and conviction to the offence. It seems unlikely, then, that a French post-Renaissance *précieuse* invented *Beauty and the Beast*, though, as often, we do not have enough evidence to trace any evolution of this form of the tale with precision.

The Girl and the Bull (Europa and *AT* Type 425B)

There is also a B form of *AT* Type 425, best illustrated in the Scottish tale *The Black Bull of Norroway*:

> The third of three daughters gets a bull as her husband; she rides off on it; and receives jewels in a receptacle for her hour of need. The bull has to fight, and wins; but she loses him somehow and has to find him; she uses a magic jewel-obtaining apple to obtain one night with her lost husband.

We should certainly note that the Europa story contained a motif in which Europa receives a necklace which she uses to bribe a second girl; as early as Hesiod fr. 141 MW it is quite clear that something made by Hephaestus is given by Zeus to Europa after their arrival in Crete. The papyrus is too heavily damaged to give us any certainty as to how it might have been used, but in any case the Greek author is preoccupied, as so often, with genealogy rather than with narrative content. But this would seem to fit the circumstances in the fairy-tale where the girl must reclaim her husband from a rival female suitor (up to three times). One notes that Europa's necklace passes by Kadmus to Harmonia (so Pherekydes 3F89). A modern form of the animal bridegroom from Pharasa (Dawkins 1916: 555) has a snake demanding the king's daughter; it has a magic signet ring needed to build the palace the king has demanded.

We can see, then, that the Ancient World possessed a representation of the first three branches of *AT* Type 425, and that its roots at least are pre-classical. We shall find a no less impressive length of ancestry for our next tale, the even more celebrated *Girl helper in the hero's flight*.

5

THE OBSTACLE FLIGHT
(*AT 313*)

The so-called *Obstacle Flight* or 'Girl as Helper in the Hero's Flight' presents a rather different profile from those tales discussed so far: it is not the modern analogues in fairytale repertoire that tend to be well known, but the ancient tale itself, which corresponds with what we might crudely label 'Jason and the Argonauts' and 'Jason and Medea'. In fact there is an abundance of modern oral materials as well belonging to the same tale-complex. We might paraphrase in terms of an outline that will fit a blend of modern versions:

> A hero sets out on a quest with the help of a range of specialised companions with separate human skills, and/or a marvellous ship; or is tricked into the power of a mysterious other-worldly figure whose domain he must reach, sometimes with the help of aged informants and/or after viewing a battle of birds. He acquires a king's/ogre's daughter after the performance of three tasks with her help. On the return voyage the girl eludes her father's pursuit by creating a series of magic obstacles to the pursuers. But on return to her new husband's kingdom he forgets her, and she leaves him for a sequence of suitors whom she ingeniously prevents from spending the night with her; she finally returns to her husband.

The idea that a persecutor's daughter helps a fleeing hero to gain an object or objects, and delays the pursuit with diversions, is clearly embodied in the handling of the Jason story in classical antiquity itself. The story is already referred to as 'a concern to all men' as early as the *Odyssey*, though its fullest exposition had to wait till the Hellenistic romantic epic by Apollonius of Rhodes.[1]

As regards this tale-type we are particularly fortunate in that myth, folktale and romance preserve recognisable outlines of the story from widely different epochs. We already have a Sumerian version of at least a recognisable element in the type's structure; we have a kind of 'Jason vulgate' already containing many variants in classical antiquity, and we have a folk-epic treatment from medieval

Turkey in the *Book of Dede Korkut*. Much of the modern folktale is well represented in Basile and Grimm, as well as in the usual proliferation of oral variants.

The story at its fullest extent takes in the whole history of the hero: earlier incidents in his adventures may be included, and a main episode-complex consists of the (generally three) tasks set by the persecutor for the hero which require the heroine's help, followed by (typically three) obstacles left in the flight of the pursuer. The 'false bride' motif offers a conclusion to the complete tale in more modern versions with a happy ending. The whole narrative is spread over two type numbers in Aarne–Thompson – Types 513 and 313. This recognises the fact that the overall tale tends to survive in oral tradition as either an outward voyage or a return.

An obviously mythological version is found in the Sumerian tale of *Inanna and Enki*. Inanna, the sex-goddess, visits her father Enki, a kind of trickster creator god, in his water kingdom, the Abzu. During hospitable entertainment she gets him to part with a whole collection of decrees or blueprints for civilisation, which she brings with her on her ship to her own city of Eridu. Her father comes out of his drunken stupor and sends his messenger and sea monsters to fob off the threat; at each of seven stages in the journey Inanna relies on her servant Ninshubur to keep the pursuers at bay until she can reach harbour safely.[2] This tale is at least recognisable as covering the skeleton of the 'obstacle flight' episode itself. There are no hero's tasks (and indeed no hero as such, if we insist on the subordinate role of Ninshubur, but at least there is a male helper, if not a lover, playing an active part in the tale). We are looking at either the original myth or, perhaps more likely, the adaptation of part of it to serve as a charter myth ('How the benefits of civilisation came to (Inanna's city of) Eridu'). In other words this is not so much 'Jason and Medea' as 'how Medea brought the golden fleece to Iolcus'. And in fact there are not three episodes but seven, so that the formula of suspense is already part of the tale ('will Inanna reach Eridu safely or will she somehow fall at the last hurdle?'). We should already feel entitled to conclude that the obstacle flight as such is much older than the story of Jason and Medea, whatever the relationship of Inanna to the character of Medea herself.

The classical materials relating to Jason and Medea show considerable variation:[3] the last book of Apollonius of Rhodes' *Argonautica* concentrates on the flight itself with only one real obstacle left behind, rather than the usual three, in the form of the corpse of Medea's brother Absyrtus. The early handling in Pherecydes (3F52) has the pieces of the corpse thrown into the river from the Argo under sail, and this is much more obviously in the spirit of the folktale. It is from the continuation of the Medea story already known from Euripides' *Medea* that we have the gruesomely tragic business of the hero's forgetting his rescuer and wife, resolved only by the murder of the new prospective wife and Medea's own children by Jason. Medea escapes, but there is no reconciliation or 'happy ending'.

A folk-epic version in medieval Turkish (*The Book of Dede Korkut*)[4]

It is not in fact till the late medieval Turkish *Book of Dede Korkut* that we find a complete version of the whole story of any scale actually extant in the space of a single self-contained text. In the sixth tale, Kan Turali's son Kanli Koja wishes to marry the king of Trebizond's daughter – a princess placed in a corner of the Black Sea notably close to the ancient Colchis itself. It is totally improbable that this version was inspired by any awareness of Apollonius Rhodius: here we have a chance instead to see what the story might look like in the folk memory of a people rather closer to the Colchians than the Greeks. We have a prosimetric narrative in which the hero, dissatisfied with the local girls, sets out with forty followers to woo the daughter of the King of Trebizond. Three tasks must be accomplished before the daughter will be made over: the hero must tame a bull, a lion and, worst of all, a camel. The King's daughter, Princess Saljan, falls in love with Kan Turali on sight, and gives him essential advice for the successful completion of the third task. She then becomes his wife, and her father goes back on the bargain, as Aietes goes back on the return of the fleece.[5] Some will complain that this is not 'our' Jason and the Argonauts: there is no golden fleece; Medea was not really the object of the expedition; ten of our Argonauts are missing; and the forty are not really Argonauts at all, since ships and oars are unknown to the Oghuz Turks who have preserved the tradition. But that is precisely the point: the story can automatically expect to look different from the point of view of a people whose geographical environment is totally different from that of the Greeks.

It is the essential flavour of 'primary epic' that gives this form of the tale its momentum. If we think of the critical moment in the Medea story where Jason needs advice from Medea on the completion of the tasks, he hears the advice without reaction, and the conversation steers immediately towards the future of Jason and Medea themselves. The hero reacts as follows:

> In the meantime Jason remembered Medea's advice: he melted the drug and sprinkled it over his shield and his stout spear and sword.

And we are told that as for his companions,

> The heroes shouted for joy at the prospect of the contest.[6]

But in *Dede Korkut*

> Kan Turali rose to his feet and said 'Now if I grab this camel's nose they'll say I did so because the girl told me to; tomorrow the news will reach the Oghuz land: "There he was, at the camel's mercy, and the girl saved him", they'll say.'[7]

He is having none of this, so he gets his warriors to cheer him; then

> Kan Turali spoke a blessing on Muhammed of the beautiful name and
> gave the camel a kick. The camel screamed, he kicked it again, and the
> camel could not stand on its feet but toppled over. He jumped on it
> and cut its throat in two places.[8]

When the heroine sees the hero and experiences true love, Apollonius' expression of Medea's tender feelings is justly celebrated for its idiosyncrasy as well as
its sensitive perception:

> And many lover's cares assailed her heart; and every detail was still
> before her eyes, what Jason was like, what sort of clothes he wore, the
> way he spoke, how he sat on his chair, his walk as he went to the
> door.[9]

No one who has not heard the Oghuz version at this point is likely to be able to
guess it:

> Now Kan Turali stripped off his veil. The girl was watching from the
> palace and she went weak at the knees, her cat miaowed, she slavered
> like a sick calf. To the maidens by her side she said, 'If only God Most
> High would put mercy into my father's heart, if only he would fix a
> bride-price and give me to this man! Alas that such a man should
> perish at the hands of monsters.'[10]

One notes, too, throughout the Oghuz version the vivid directness and sense of
participation which an oral style can engender:

> They went and brought out the lion and let him into the square. The
> lion roared, and every single horse in the square pissed blood. Kan
> Turali's young men said 'He has escaped the bull; how will he escape
> the lion?' And they wept together. He saw his warriors weeping and
> said: 'Take my arm-long lute and sing my praises. Shall I turn away
> from a lion, when the love of the girl in yellow is at stake?'[11]
> Thereupon his companions declaimed; let us see, my Khan, what they
> declaimed.

The Oghuz tale continues as does the *Argonautica* with the heroine's father
repenting his bargain and deciding to take warriors in pursuit of the couple. As
in Apollonius there is ill feeling between the pair, though in this case for a thoroughly 'heroic' reason: Princess Saljan has done better in the battle than he has,
and out of shame for the likely verdict of public opinion, he resolves to kill her.
She has the same ready answers as Medea herself for this sort of treatment:

I have not embraced you under the many-coloured quilt, I have not held your sweet mouth and kissed you, I have not whispered to you through my red bridal veil. Quickly did you fall in love and quickly did you weary. You are nothing but a pimp and the son of a pimp.[12]

They quickly make up, but not before Princess Saljan has shot a deliberately blunted arrow 'that sent the lice in his hair scuttling down to his feet'.

The final scene does as much as any to establish the overall environment of primary epic:

> With his son and his daughter-in-law, Kanli Koja went into the Oghuz land. He pitched tents on the lovely grass of varied green. When he had slaughtered of horses the stallions, of camels the males, of sheep the rams, he made a wedding banquet and feasted the chieftains of the mighty Oghuz. A gold-decked pavilion was set up and Kan Turali entered his bridal bower, and attained his heart's desire.[13]

Here, then, we see what a more basic and unvarnished epic treatment of the *Argonautica* could be like. Not for the reciter the image of a librarian-poet: the Oghuz are a nomadic people with no Alexandria as the centre of their world. The hard grind of warriors proving themselves and being seen to do so is all that matters.

Jason and Medea: the fairytale

Dede Korkut offers us, then, an unbroken presentation of the whole story as a rough-and-ready warrior culture would have wished to hear it. But it is only when we come to Basile and his successors in the seventeenth century and beyond that we can really see what the story looks like when presented as what we now understand by a fairytale rather than a myth or an epic. Here are two variants from Basile and a modern Italian one:

Pentamerone 2.7	Crane no.15 (and notes)	*Pentamerone* 3.9
Prince is cursed by the ghost of an old woman whose pot he broke	Prince is cursed by the ghost of ghoul whose pot he broke	
He falls in love with ghoul's daughter Filadoro	He falls in love with ogress's daughter Snow-white-fire-red	He falls in love with blood-sucking sultan's daughter Rosella
She helps him by magic with tasks: digging an orchard, and cutting wood	Daughter makes ogress drunk	Daughter makes mother fall asleep
They flee	They flee	They flee with valuables
	She has to throw seven balls of yarn behind	He cuts off hands of mother pursuing in a tree leaf turned felucca

	Obstacles: mountain; razors and knives; river	
He forgets her once they are home, the moment he kisses his mother	He forgets her once they are home, the moment he kisses his mother	He forgets her name once they are home
		Neglected, she arranges a night with three suitors
A dove reminds him just as he is about to marry again	A dove is made by neglected girl to remind him of her	Recognition by ring-token

The tales are obviously one and the same: one chooses to omit the initial tasks, while only one of the three offers the extended range of obstacles. But we are obviously enough on Medea's tracks. What is odd is a motif found only in the last of the three. The retaliation motif in which the neglected wife also 'plays away' but deliberately keeps the suitors from consummating does not occur in quite those terms in Euripides' version of the Medea story: instead Medea seeks refuge with King Aegeus of Athens, promising to cure the latter's impotence. We do not know that she intends to sleep with him to do so; we assume a medicinal cure, and the motifs would not be close enough to be obviously parallel on their own. But the context makes it very clear that they are: the heroine's interlude with a somehow securely impotent suitor is an early part of the story. We should also note another surprise – the presence of a 'snow white' lady in both the last two, to say nothing of a 'bluebeard' theme in the last. We should constantly bear in mind that the romantic repertoire of folktale may often conceal a larger complex than we at first realise, sometimes glimpsed in compound tales and mythological versions.[14] The tale is very fully represented in Europe and beyond.[15] As a full and challenging example of our theme in a large tale-complex we might note the Scottish tinker version, *The Green Man o' Knowledge* recorded as late as 1954:[16]

> Jack is a good-for-nothing who goes to seek his fortune and passes into the Land of Enchantment. He takes on 'The Green Man of Knowledge' who lives 'east of the moon and west of the stars' and beats him at cards; he decides to follow the Green Man; progressively older figures guide and advise him and provide fantastic transport. The Green Man's daughter is put into Jack's power when he steals her clothes as she is bathing. The Green Man sets him tasks – of retrieving his wife's ring, building a castle in sixty minutes, and clearing a wood of ants in half that time. The girl accomplishes the tasks for Jack, and tells him to take the ogre's mule rather than his horse on the return trip; the mule – which is the daughter herself – tells him to take water from her ear and ask for lakes, seas and rivers behind and a clear path in front; this is repeated with hills, mountains and dales from a spark of stone, then by fire, hell and pits from a spark of fire. He is not to kiss anyone else for a year or he will lose her; he kisses his dog, forgets her,

and promises to marry the miller's daughter, having forgotten all about his benefactress. She comes as a ragged girl and entertains the guests with a cock and hen, which prompt Jack to remember her, and they marry after all.

Such a version is about as vernacular as the tale can be, with a constant atmosphere of farmyard or fireside rather than a world of heroic epic. Its opening hints at the 'normal' folktale opening, where the hero is cheated into his adventure, but in this telling the motif has been carelessly abbreviated: the ogre should beat the hero in a second card game and so compel him to come into the enchanted kingdom where the tasks have to be performed. This is represented in the classical tale as told by Apollodorus 1.9.16 (not in Apollonius) by Pelias' cheating Jason by asking him how he would deal with an enemy fated to kill him: Jason's reply ('send him for the golden fleece') is then assigned to the unfortunate hero as a fatal task. This kind of opening can be an alternative to, or may be combined with, a narrative of how the hero finds the kingdom where he must perform the tasks, a sequence we shall now look at as a tale in its own right.

The outward voyage: *Six Go Through the World* (*AT* Type 513A) and *Land and Water Boat* (*AT* Type 513B)

The characteristic of the prelude to the obstacle flight in the fairytale is usually supplied by variations on a story of recruiting experts, all of whom have a specialist skill: running very fast, hearing the language of birds, or the like. Usually in modern oral versions there are up to six of these so that the hero himself makes a seventh. These specialisms are duly reflected among the Argonauts (the strength of Heracles, the sharp sight of Lynceus, the musical power of Orpheus, and the rest), but, whereas in the fairytale the exercise of the six specialisms constitutes the bulk of the tale, not all fifty of Jason's crew can be singled out in this way, nor can each be made to help out the expedition in a single adventure. The fairytale subtype with 'the land and water boat' has a king's daughter as the prize for the man who can produce the boat: he may be a third son where the other two have failed; and he may in the end have the boat made ready by a mysterious stranger, corresponding to the divine help of Athena in the classical tale. The plot can cover the king's resistance to parting with his daughter, setting tasks for the champions rather than the hero and the king's daughter; there will be looting of his kingdom or its treasure and all connected with the bride, and the king has to be eluded before the bride can be brought back.

That this covers almost the whole plot of the *Argonautica* is immediately clear. More interesting is the idea in the classical tale that the Argo is generally regarded as a water-ship which goes over land only incidentally, where its counterpart in the fairytale tends to be more generally amphibious. In this instance, we are left wondering whether an original *Urform* of the tale actually had more prominence for the amphibious nature of the craft. It is plainly impossible for Apollonius to produce a romance with any semblance of realism if the Argo simply slices through woods as the ship in Calvino's modern Italian version of *A Boat for Land and Water* is able to do.[17] Another interesting difference is that in folktale versions the champions are often recruited en route, rather than at the beginning as in the *Argonautica* – an obvious difference between shipboard and land-based versions of the tale. One of Calvino's champions is so strong that he lets a mountain fall after the land-and-water ship is past.[18] This looks like a version of the clashing rocks episode, the Symplegades, in the Jason story. There are a number of further correspondences between episodes in the outward voyage in the Jason story and episodes in the modern tale. Indeed, the voyage element is often omitted, but one or more of the episodes contained in the classical forms of it are stretched to provide the whole preliminary part of the tale. Sometimes the hero has a preliminary competition with the ogre whose daughter is to help him, quite aside from the three tasks themselves – such as beating him at cards or some other game, as noted above;[19] this episode may be covered by the extended episode of Amycus the boxer in the classical tale. Sometimes the modern hero is tricked into the ogre's power at the very outset, as we have noted – a handling which may represent a conflation of the roles of Pelias and Aeetes, the person who imposes the search for the fleece and the king who imposes the tasks related to gaining it. This is the case in the English version *Nicht Nought Nothing* (Briggs 1.424). Sometimes the ogre's house or kingdom can only be detected by a quest in which the hero consults three enormously old and progressively older figures;[20] this corresponds to the consultation of the blind prophet Phineus, sometimes presented as having exchanged his sight for long life. Gantz doubts whether this can be identical with Phineus, the son of Lycaon, who ought to have perished in the flood;[21] but this would actually make good sense, since it is precisely an antediluvian character that we need, and as early as Hesiod this seer had chosen long life in preference to sight.[22] Sometimes a prominent feature of the outward journey is a 'battle of the birds' episode:[23] one thinks of the heroes' battle against the harpies or the iron-winged birds in the classical tale,[24] especially the former, where the Boreadae Zetes and Calais themselves can take an aerial form and can thus be felt as aerial forces on the side of the heroes.

The tasks themselves are interesting in the fairytale tradition: they might include the draining of a loch or the building of a castle or the cleaning of a stable.[25] The obvious connection of the last with Heracles' cleansing of the Augean stables is to be noted, and might be seen as a pointer in the direction of a more important part for this ultimate hero in the voyage of the Argonauts than is reflected in Apollonius.[26]

A modern Arab version is of special interest as a present-day Middle Eastern presentation.[27] The girl is not the real daughter of the ghoul, but a victim he has kidnapped; the hero is the girl's fiancé come to claim his bride. There are no tasks, but she has to protect him from the ghoul who addresses her as a daughter and identifies three magic objects; the couple then elope from his castle and use the objects one by one. The ghoul finally curses her so that she acquires donkey-like features; this time the hero refuses to forget her or put her away and take a rival bride. The ghoul sends a magic mirror and comb to restore her form and the couple marry.

The fate of Pelias: 'The Blacksmith and the Devil' (*AT* Type 735)

The Jason tradition also encompasses an incident after the arrival back home in Iolcus, in which Medea kills Pelias. The modern folktale versions tend to run along the following lines:

> A saint or a devil arrives at a smithy: he amazes the smith by taking off the leg of a horse and effecting repairs, before replacing it as new. He then resuscitates an old man by the same supernatural process, usually in a furnace. The smith now tries his hand on his own father, with disastrous results.

This story is obviously as old as the story of Jason, Medea and Pelias. First Medea rejuvenates Jason's aged father Aison (or Jason himself, less probably, in some versions) by immersion in a boiling cauldron; she then demonstrates with the animal, in this case a ram in a cauldron, to Pelias' daughters; they then apply the remedy to their father, with the usual catastrophe.

The modern folktale variations are conditioned by the need to employ figures with 'normal' supernatural powers: Jesus Christ or the devil are the obvious candidates. The means of regeneration requires a high temperature; hence the blacksmith and the forge are natural choices for agent and setting in any 'normal' context (as opposed to magical encounters in another world with a cauldron of renewal or the like, as in medieval romance). When told as a tale on its own, the story usually has a distinctly moral nuance about it: the amateur tries the regeneration out of some sense of pride or conceit, as when the disciple Peter attempts a miracle which only Jesus Christ can perform; sometimes there is a tailpiece in which the more powerful saint or miracle worker comes back and puts things right. One can see the tale overlapping naturally or even converging with that of the sorcerer's apprentice (cf. *AT* Type 1525, Christiansen *ML* 3020).[28]

We are in a position, then, to see that the popular traditions surrounding the three-task hero and his lady accomplice go back to antiquity, in some respects considerably further than Jason. We can notice, too, that the config-uration of the outward journey is often rather different from what Apollonius' *Argonautica* might lead us to expect: it is sometimes as if the narrator cuts from Pelias to Phineus and/or Amycus and ignores the ship and the experts. From such divergences, we may be right to have the feeling that this is a story on the evolution of which the last word has yet to be said.

At this point, however, we should draw attention to a classical text which sets out to paraphrase an episode of 'Jason and the Argonauts' for the attention of a child. The fifteenth of the Elder Philostratus' *Eikones* offers us partial telling of the story of the fleece, featuring a specific episode described in a painted version to which the child is being introduced.

The Argo has already sailed through the Bosporus and the Clashing Rocks, and already it is cutting through the surge of the [Black] Sea; Orpheus is charming the sea with his singing, and the sea is listening, and the water is lying still under the spell of the song. Now the ship's cargo is the Dioscuri and Heracles, and the Sons of Aeacus and the Sons of the North Wind, and all the offspring from the demigods who flourished then. The keel fitted underneath the ship is [from] an ancient tree, the one Zeus used to deliver his prophetic answers at Dodona. Now this was the reason for the voyage: in Colchis there lies a golden fleece from the ram in olden times that is said to have ferried Helle and Phrixus through the sky. To capture this fleece is the contest Jason is taking on, my boy: and it is certainly a contest, for some dragon is wrapped round it to guard it, with a fearsome look and not a thought for sleep – that is why Jason is in charge of the ship, since he is the reason for the voyage. And Tiphys, my boy, is at the helm; they say this man was the first to be bold enough to pilot a ship, which no one had the courage to do before; and Lynceus the son of Aphareus has been assigned his post on the prow, for he is skilled at seeing things from a long way off and in looking far down into the sea: he is the first to see submerged rocks, and the first to welcome the faintest hint of land.

But now I think even Lynceus' eye is terror-struck at the onset of a phantom, which had made the fifty oarsmen break off their rowing as well. Of course Heracles is not put out at the sight, since he has met many like it, but the rest are calling it some sort of miracle. For they are looking at Glaucus, the sea-god. They say that once he was a man living in ancient Anthedon and that he tasted some kind of grass on the seashore, and that when a wave crept up on him he was swept away into the haunts of fish. But at this moment I expect he is delivering some oracle – for he has great skill at this. But in appearance – the curls of his beard are drenched, and they are foaming like springs, while his locks are waterlogged and drain onto his shoulders all the sea water they have picked up; his eyebrows are shaggy and join together as if into one. And what a big arm he has (*pheu tou brachionos*), with all its exercise against the sea, always taking on the waves and smoothing them for his swimming! What a breast (*pheu ton sternon*), spread over

81

with a hairy covering of tangle and seaweed, while his belly below is changing and is already beginning to tail off: it is clear that the rest of Glaucus is a fish, from the tail raised and curling towards his waist; and its crescent has the colour of sea-purple. And kingfishers too fly round him, singing about human deeds (for they, like Glaucus, have changed from men), and showing Orpheus that they too can sing, so that not even the sea is without music.

Philostratus has selected a children's subject – a heroes' quest encountering their first sea monster; and the narrator has fixed the child's attention on the moment when the magic lookout and the crew alike take in this portentous creature. He has packed in the basic details about Jason and the fleece, and alluded to a whole cavalcade of wonders: the magic wood of the Argo, the magic sight of Lynceus, the magical transformation of Glaucus and his merman-like form, and that of the kingfishers. The decorative detail adds a touch of 'Disney-dust' to the whole ensemble, with Orpheus' contribution calming the sea, and the kingfishers' cries vying with it; two direct addresses to the child remind the adult reader of the supposed audience, as do the redoubled exclamations at Glaucus' arms and chest. In spite of Philostratus' rather self-consciously naive or pseudo-naive artistry, we have at least a trace of children's storytelling as it must have been.

6

THE 'INNOCENT SLANDERED MAID'

In the majority of tales reviewed so far we have noticed the emphasis on the misfortunes of an innocent heroine, though often in contexts where these are secondary to some other emphasis in the story. But we can also point to a group of overlapping tale-types where the heroine is presented as a victim of some kind of major set-up or slander, and where this misfortune in turn triggers off a whole complex of misadventures which it will take the rest of the tale to resolve. It will be helpful and indeed clearer if we offer a composite or general version that broadly covers *AT* Types 882/883, 'the wager on the wife's chastity' and 'the innocent slandered maid':

(a) A heroine is either raped or seduced or supposedly seduced by a conspirator or conspirators; at some stage she may be framed for child murder as well as unchastity;

(b) she is the victim of a murder attempt and is captured by pirates or robbers or put to sea in a boat or abandoned in a wood or otherwise exiled abroad at the behest of her father or husband;

(c) she arrives at some position of trust or authority (often necessarily by disguising herself as a man), and may contract a second liaison in her new life;

(d) she is able to participate in or contrive the exposure of those who have wronged her and take revenge on the person responsible for her misfortune;

(e) she has her searching lover/husband/kinsmen in her power;

(f) she escapes and reverts to her first relationship, sometimes also rescuing her child/children in the process.

The number of permutations emphasise the flexibility of the scheme, but the overall mechanism is clear enough. It will immediately be seen that certain configurations of the plot must be predetermined by a narrator's individual choices: the heroine cannot convincingly pose as a man in versions where she is or becomes pregnant, and it tends to be the former motif which is most consistently prominent. Here are several examples of the variation to which the modern tale lends itself:

Italian\ (Calvino 1982: n. 157)	Spanish\ (Taggart 1990: 49)	Italian\ (Calvino 1982: n. 176)
A king of Palermo boasts about his wife's chastity; a jealous knight pretends to have slept with the girl	A priest tries to seduce a young girl, and she throws him down a well; he accuses her	A king marries a girl, but in his absence a jealous courtier who has tried to seduce her slanders her to her husband
The angry husband assaults her and leaves her in the wilds for her presumed unchastity	Her father arranges to have her murdered for trying to kill the priest	The angry husband agrees to an unspecified punishment
	Shepherds give her men's clothes	A goatherd gives her men's clothes
	She is disguised as secretary of mayor, whose son she marries	She is disguised as master-thief
She is looked after by doctor and wife; she cares for their child, but is framed by a slave who kills the child	The son goes to war; parents abandon her; thieves steal the child	
	She dresses as a man in the next town and is steward to her husband's mess	She captures her husband
All parties who claim her – father, doctor, husband – hear magic objects reveal her story	At a wedding meal she reveals all who have wronged her, and they are hanged	She summons husband and minister to a meal; thieves pardoned and minister executed
She is reconciled to husband; slave is punished	She lives happily with her husband	She lives happily with her husband

The modern oral tradition of these and very similar story patterns is widespread in Europe and the Near East, and there are several quite distinctive forms: the girl is sometimes entrusted to a priest who assaults her, tries to frame her, and is entrusted with the task of killing her; there may be a single marriage abroad, or again an intrigue with a jealous rival, sexual threats, and sometimes even the murder of the child(ren); but most conspicuously the plot tends to culminate in a final showdown scene in which the girl collects all those who have wronged her in the one room, and forbids anyone to leave even under pressure of urgent calls of nature; she then exposes all her malefactors in turn and appropriate punishments are meted out, before she identifies herself to her (generally only one true) husband.[1]

The modern tale has been recognised as early as Boccaccio's Tale of Sir Bernabo in the *Decameron*:[2]

One of a group of Italian merchants hears the hero boasting of the chastity of his wife. He puts a wager on it and frames her as an unfaithful wife by bribing a serving-maid to give him access to her room, thus enabling him to observe a birthmark and steal tokens. The outraged husband is convinced that his wife is having an affair, and arranges to have her murdered. A *Scheintod* takes place and she is shipped to Acre instead, disguised as a man; she becomes an inspector of merchandise; eventually she meets her traducer, who actually explains the frame-up to her. She also arranges for her husband, now impoverished, to come to a rendezvous before the sultan; before the court she reveals herself as a woman, and is reconciled with her husband. The betrayer is executed.

Variations on the story were in fact widely current in late medieval and Renaissance traditions, and it eventually found its way into the plot of Shakespeare's *Cymbeline*. Boccaccio's version begins almost identically with the mainspring of Calvino's n. 157, but we note an entirely natural showdown trial rather than the magic talking objects of fairytale which surface in the modern Italian tale. There is no child and no child murder because, as noted, disguise as a man replaces and effectively precludes the heroine from acting as doctor's maid. The other essential difference is that the task of framing the girl and stealing the tokens is done differently, but only slightly so.

The plot of 'the wager on the wife's chastity' merges very easily into the extended modern type *AT* Type 883B, *The Innocent Slandered Maiden*. The earliest western European example known to me is the so-called *Tale of the Count of Ponthieu*, a brief thirteenth-century French romantic prose tale:[3]

The heroine is raped by a gang of robbers; she strikes her husband to spare him the shame of taking her back. She is cast adrift by her outraged father who disowns her; she is picked up by a merchant and sold to the sultan of Al-Mairie. A marriage of necessity gives her two children by the sultan. When her husband Sir Thibault comes in search of her she saves him and her father, his companion, from death, without revealing their identity. Sir Thibault goes on to acquit himself well on a military campaign in the sultan's service. Thibault's wife is now sent back to France for a health cure, with both Thibault and son; a daughter is left with the sultan.

Here we have no showdown scene, and a very different way of setting up the wronged innocence of the heroine. One further version, considerably divergent again, uses what appears to be an equivalent of the name Thibault, Boccaccio's tale of Tedaldo:[4]

Tedaldo's true love is a mistress, not a wife, and her husband is still alive. He feels that she has cooled her affections and goes off; meanwhile her husband is put on trial for the suspected murder of Tedaldo. The latter comes to her in disguise as a pilgrim and confessor, and sleeps with her (having found out that their impasse was not her fault). He then turns up at the husband's trial to save him from execution; after the trial the old triangle resumes.

Here we have no pregnancy, *Scheintod*, or romantic adventures, but we do have the lover's dramatic intervention in the trial scene as the natural climax.

How old, then, is the tale-complex altogether? We can point to a very detailed and sophisticated version as early as Chariton's novel *Chaereas and Callirhoe*, of perhaps as early as the first century BC or AD. This work is usually taken not only as our first complete Greek novel, but as a demonstration of the type's essential Hellenism on the one hand and its simplicity on the other.[5] It has also generally been assumed that the plot is an invented one,[6] that such invention reflects somehow or other the *Zeitgeist* of the Hellenistic world,[7] and that in the use of such a plot Chariton had no successors to speak of. All such impressions call for at least another look. It is possible to show that Chariton's work is in fact one of the most sophisticated treatments of this specific folktale-complex, which certainly occurs in some form elsewhere in antiquity; and we may also at least suspect that Chariton's handling can scarcely be seen as the first of its type, and that more obviously popular handlings can in turn tell us a great deal more about Chariton's own shaping of his material. Here, then, is an outline of *Chaereas and Callirhoe*:

> The hero and heroine are two young aristocrats of Syracuse, married by popular acclaim the moment their love becomes known. Malicious rivals contrive to split the pair by making Chaereas jealous of a bogus love affair which they pretend Callirhoe is having. He kicks her and she swoons, apparently dead; she is buried, the body is removed by pirates, and she is sold in Miletus to the seigneur of the town, Dionysus. To protect the unborn child she is expecting to Chaereas she marries Dionysus; Chaereas comes looking for her and is captured by a Persian satrap; court intrigues follow, resulting in a court case in Babylon at which Chaereas is produced alive, just as the King of Persia is himself becoming interested in Callirhoe. A war breaks out, and Chaereas wins Callirhoe in a naval campaign against the king, while someone tries to persuade him to regard his own wife as spoils of war; she leaves her child with her second husband Dionysus and returns to Syracuse with Chaereas.

The nearest point of comparison is once more Calvino's n. 157, a Sicilian variant actually set in Palermo, as Chariton's version in turn is set in Syracuse. In Callirhoe's case, instead of looking after a rescuer's baby and being framed for its murder, as in the modern Sicilian tale, the heroine actually marries a rescuer and has his child, a very considerable complication in the story as a whole. The punishment element is different as well: one notes that the person who should really be exposed is the Syracusan aristocrat who engineered the deception over Callirhoe's chastity; instead the only person brought to justice is Theron the pirate, a minor cog in the machinery of the plot. This may well be no more than a matter of political realism: Dionysius of Miletus has only very limited influence under Persian sovereignty, and Callirhoe is never sufficiently close to the King of Persia to persuade him to bring the tyrant of a western Greek city-state to execution.

It is noteworthy that two of Calvino's other examples from Palermo also fit the two halves of the tale of Callirhoe:

Calvino (1982: 158)	*Chaereas and Callirhoe*
King marries foreign princess	Grandee marries daughter of enemy politician Hermocrates
Rival sends her love-tokens, which elderly go-between passes off as bribes	Rivals plant love-tokens; then arrange further trick, of apparent entry of false lover to husband's home
He complains to king that princess is wearing his tokens but not granting favours	Chaereas thinks wife is seeing lover
King orders princess to be drowned at sea	He kicks princess; she is taken by sea
Captain puts her ashore and she is picked up by second ship and shipped to king's brother, Emperor of Brazil	She is put ashore and sold to household of fellow-grandee Dionysius of Miletus
She disguises herself as man and begins as clerk, ends up as viceroy and is sent to administer her husband's kingdom, since he is now mad with remorse	
The truth comes out: suitor is guillotined, old lady is burned	The truth comes out; pirate tomb-robber is crucified
Calvino (1982: 160)	
Jealous right-hand steward envies wife of left-hand steward and alerts king to her beauty	Jealous governor Mithridates envies wife of Dionysius and alerts King of Persia to her beauty
King visits her and leaves love-token	King visits her and endeavours to seduce her
but is prevailed upon to back down	but is prevailed upon to back down
Wife's innocence in the face of the king's attentions is made clear	Wife's innocence in the face of the king's attentions is made clear

It should be clear, then, that Chariton's account offers us the fullest known version of the popular tale: a luxury literary production of even larger scale (though less linguistic ambition) than Apuleius' *Cupid and Psyche*. But we should be tempted to look back still further, just as we have done for *Cinderella* and *Snow White*.

Mythical versions: Callirhoe, Helen, Iphigenia, Thetis

We should suspect from its large scale and unusual variant that Chariton's version is not the original of this simple and very basic love-triangle tale. When we look in the first instance for actual mythical realisations of a girl by the name of Callirhoe the results at first may seem disappointing: the name itself occurs in Hesiod as the name of a nymph;[8] but there are also two complete stories, at least one of which seems to have the flavour of myth as such, though the other might be more readily regarded as racy novella. Pausanias preserves a story in which a girl called Callirhoe is wooed by a man named Coresus, and undergoes a fortune similar to that of Iphigenia. She must be sacrificed, in this case to avert a plague, but at the altar Coresus relents and kills himself instead.[9] In the other tale, Callirhoe is raped at the waterside by one Cimon, who has spied on the nymphs calling on the river-god Scamander to take their virginity; by impersonating the god he does just that, and she only finds out by spotting him in a procession; the truth comes out, and angry citizens drive him out.[10] The tales have little in common with one another, though the second might well deserve the rubric 'innocent slandered maiden'. But if there is a closer connection with 'our' tale of Callirhoe, it must continue to elude us. There is, however, a considerable degree of overlap between Chariton's story of Callirhoe and some of the post-Homeric traditions about Helen in Herodotus and elsewhere, but it should be stressed at the outset, as it has not been in the past, that the relationship here is between *Chaereas and Callirhoe* and the Helen story, not with Euripides' *Helen* as such.[11]

Helen married to Menelaus	Callirhoe married to Chaereas
Kidnapped by Paris	Framed by Tyrant; kidnapped by Theron
Arrives in Egypt	Arrives in Asia
Reported by local governor	Reported by local governor
Menelaus searches in Asia Minor	Chaereas searches in Asia Minor
Image of Helen in temple as 'stranger Aphrodite'	Image of Callirhoe in temple as 'stranger Aphrodite'
Thon sends report to King Proteus	Dionysus sends report to King of Persia
Who keeps custody of Helen till Menelaus arrives in Egypt	Who keeps custody of Callirhoe; Chaereas arrives in Egypt

One constant throughout most versions of the story is the close connection between the Callirhoe figure and the sea: in mythical terms she would obviously be appropriately cast as a water nymph.[12] If we look at the history of probably the best connected of all water nymphs, we find ourselves with yet another version of Callirhoe:

Thetis is wooed by and married to Peleus. But Poseidon the God of the Sea and Zeus the King of the Gods are both interested suitors. Only under extreme pressure of an ominous future does Zeus finally back down, and Thetis remains with Peleus, to whom she bears a pre-eminent son.

The story, when presented in this way, shows its essentially threefold structure, with some sense of escalation from the human husband to the sea lord to the sovereign.

On the evidence so far, then, we can suggest that Chariton probably did not invent the plot of *Chaereas and Callirhoe*, but used a relatively unusual and particularly elaborate form of the 'innocent slandered maid' complex, which recurs as no fewer than three separate novellas in Boccaccio. We are particularly in the dark in this case as to the history of the tale's development or elaboration. It is in this particular that Chariton's version is of special interest. What he might have lacked in originality he certainly did possess in artistry. What is elsewhere a very slim story or a relatively bald narrative is here given neat and smartly succinct literary touches, as well as a human sensibility rarely encountered in standard folk and fairytale.

Callirhoe goes for a better offer after all? (*AT* Type 612)

So far we have noted the usual option in the 'innocent slandered maid' tale, that the heroine's main concern is with virtue, and that she returns to her first love or first husband. But suppose Callirhoe had not been that sort of girl and had gone instead for the better offer? What of varieties where the girl deserts the original hero and goes off as a matter of choice rather than necessity with the more powerful suitor? This gives rise to an overlapping type *AT* 612. The modern tale (as in the Grimms' 'The Three Snake-Leaves') can be presented as follows:

A young boy and girl decide to get married. They have a pact that each will be faithful unto death to the other to the extent of swearing an oath to attend the other in the tomb. When the girl is left for dead in the tomb the man mourns faithfully for her. In the tomb he finds a way of reviving her by watching an animal (a snake, a lion) revive its partner (the story of Polyidus). She is desired by a rival who sets her up and kidnaps her, or she is not to go near water, to avoid being kidnapped. She disobeys and is kidnapped by a foreign king or by pirates who take her to one, or the kidnapper is concealed in her house and forces her away. When the first partner goes in search of her, the second partner tries to have him killed, sometimes by the 'Joseph' set up of planting valuables on him; he is to be executed, but is rescued at the eleventh hour through the good offices of a faithful companion;

eventually he becomes a general and is able to see to the punishment of the unfaithful wife who has supported or connived at his murder.[13]

We can now compare this model (as at Grimm no. 16) with *Callirhoe*:

Three Snake-Leaves	Callirhoe
Princess insists that suitor accompany her to tomb	General's daughter
When she dies he stays with her in the tomb, but revives her by magical means	When she dies he mourns her at the tomb; a robber revives her
Later a rival suitor has her kidnapped	She is kidnapped
She is taken by him aboard ship	She is taken by pirate aboard ship
She connives at the killing of her husband; he is saved by his faithful friend	She is the (ultimate) cause of her husband's impending execution; he is saved by a faithful friend
She and the guilty captain are brought before the first husband as general	The guilty pirate is brought before the first husband
They are put to sea and drowned	He is crucified by the seashore

The story relies on a number of elements which are present in several different antique traditions. Much of it is closely related to the story of *Chaereas and Callirhoe*, with the distinction that the wife remains faithful through all the complications of a second husband. But the 'unfaithful wife' version is actually encountered very early, in the Egyptian *Tale of Two Brothers* from around 1200 BC; both the ancient and the modern tradition of this tale share key motifs with the traditions of Joseph. But traces of traits resembling Chariton's version also turn up in the mythology surrounding the family of Minos of Crete. This is the first mention known to me of the Polyidus story, but it is Minos' son Glaucus, not a daughter, who is healed by the animal magic, and by a physician, not a husband.[14] Two of the daughters of Minos' son Catreus have similar adventures to those of Callirhoe, Aerope being the innocent party in a seduction by a servant, to be handed over to one Nauplius to be drowned, or to be taken with her sister to be sold to a husband Pleisthenes ('full-strength'); while Apemosyne is kicked by her brother when she protests she was violated by Hermes. Moreover Catreus' much more celebrated sister Ariadne has two partners, the second, Dionysus (Callirhoe's second husband has this name); there is considerable ambiguity over the relationships between Ariadne and the male pair.[15] Secondary traces of Chariton's version surface in the modern tale, such as the social imbalance between husband and wife and the fact that the marriage is engineered by outside pressure (without the knowledge of the couple, Chariton;[16] without the knowledge of the parents, Calvino 194). The two Italian variants produced by Calvino are from Sicily (the base of Chariton's tale) and from Sardinia. In the Cretan examples, as in Chariton, the dominant figure is a king or commander inimical to Athens.

The relationships can be presented as follows:

Folktale	Chaereas and Callirhoe	Two Brothers
Boy saves girl at tomb	Youth buries his dead wife at tomb	Brothers make pact to be faithful to death
Girl is not to go near the sea	She is rescued by pirate	
She is kidnapped by foreign ruler, and becomes his wife	She is kidnapped by pirate to the foreign ruler and becomes his wife	Wife is kidnapped to foreign ruler and becomes his wife
The husband follows her, but an attempt is made to kill him	The husband follows her, but an attempt is made to kill him	The husband follows her, but three attempts are made to kill him
He eventually gets the couple into his power	He eventually gets the couple into his power	Pharaoh dies and son succeeds; he punishes guilty wife
He punishes the guilty wife and second husband	The wife is innocent	
and returns as general	and he returns as general	and succeeds to the kingdom

All in all, then, we should strongly weigh the evidence for continuity in the transmission of both of the major forms of this tale over several millennia. While the traces of Callirhoe's story in classical myth are fugitive, it is equally clear that the many modern variants are unlikely to come directly from Chariton (and certainly could not have entered oral tradition over a wide area from a text only available to scholars from an *editio princeps* as late as 1750). And it is clear that there was a medieval popular tradition of the story. The persistence of Sicilian variants in the nineteenth century do suggest that Chariton himself may well have used a local or locally coloured version of the story, rather than tried to construct it from scratch as some kind of quasi-historiography. It is a comment on how far the study of oral storytelling has parted company from that of formal literature that it should have taken till now to trace this common popular tale-complex back to antiquity at all.

7

BUTCHERING GIRLS

Red Riding Hood and Bluebeard

For heroines of the 'innocent slandered maiden' type we can expect a murder attempt, but the tale does not really centre on the murder episode as such, and the heroine for her part does not do a great deal to avert her fate, although she may show considerable initiative in variants where she is disguised as a man. Other tale-plots are, however, considerably more inclined to indulge an appetite for ghoulish horror, at times apparently for its own sake, and the 'compassionate executioner' is not likely to be on standby either. Tales of plucky young girls who elude being devoured or murdered by an animal or human predator are well entrenched in the modern repertoire. The best known are *Little Red Riding Hood* (*Little Redcap*) and *Bluebeard*; both are often felt to be tales of relatively limited distribution and obscure early history. Once more there is a great deal of further exploration still to be done.

Red Riding Hood (*AT* Type 333)[1]

The Perrault version of *Little Red Riding Hood* is the first available example of the modern tale, and also the best known:

> The girl in the red cape has to cross the wood on an errand to her grandmother. In conversation the wolf elicits details of her errand, comes to the grandmother's house by a different route, and swallows both.

Not until the Grimms does there appear to be a happy ending, in which the wolf is forced to disgorge the victims still alive and is then himself killed by having his belly weighted with stones; a second wolf in a clumsy doublet attack is then drowned in a water butt. There is also an all-animal version, in which a wolf swallows all but one of seven goat's kids, and once more is drowned (*AT* Type 123).

In the most extensive modern discussion, Jack Zipes accepts the theory that the tale itself is of little more than local distribution in western Europe in the first instance, with an evident epicentre in lycanthropy trials as late as the seventeenth century in provincial France.[2] But the picture is always changing. We should note an earlier and different looking tale at least in neighbouring north Italy. In Boccaccio's *Decameron* (9.7) there is a rather more ordinary wolf-meets-girl story:

> Talano d'Immolese dreams that his wife Margarita is caught by a wolf, and warns her not to go to the wood the next day. She is at the best of times a quarrelsome wife and goes into the wood, suspecting that her husband has a lover's assignation there. She is indeed caught by the neck by a wolf, and is only rescued by chance by some shepherds; she bears the marks on her neck and is more respectful of her husband in future.

This is obviously, like Red Riding Hood itself, capable of being 'read' as a cautionary tale, but this time a more obviously adult one: the woman is married and there is the suspicion of the husband's affair. The wolf does catch the woman, and is forced to let her go; but there is no gross violation of probability as there is in the wolf's disgorging a child alive – let alone talking to her in the first place. The anticipatory dream of capture in an animal's mouth and dispute between husband and wife over the value of the dream gives the story affinities with Chaucer's *Nun's Priest's Tale*; but it does deserve at least a mention in the context of Red Riding Hoods.

Equally unmentioned in discussion of any Red Riding Hood canon are examples where the victim is not a girl but a boy – a possibility which might serve to qualify some of the more extreme feminist readings of the tale. A modern Persian example runs as follows:[3]

> A little boy is sent through a wood by his mother to take food to his father who is working in the fields at the other side. He meets the wolf and the usual conversation takes place; the wolf gets to the house where the father is staying, but he is not at home. When the boy comes home the wolf invites him to rest in bed. The boy takes his clothes off and comes to bed beside the wolf, and once more the usual conversation takes place; the boy is under the impression till the last moment that the wolf is his father – who returns in time to kill the wolf with a single stroke.

It is not clear whether this is a radical remodelling of the Perrault version: it certainly owes nothing to the oral strain of the tale that survives in France in Delarue's now well-known nineteenth-century peasant version from Nièvre,[4] with the girl forced to drink the grandmother's blood, but pleading a call of nature to escape. It seems odd that the wood is there and the dialogue so closely identical, even though oral recital tends to maintain the 'jingle' element as the most stable. ('All the better to "x" you with...'). It seems suspicious that the two paths through the wood are kept as they occur in Perrault, and oddly inconsistent to have it necessary for the father to be staying far enough away to require lodgings if a child is to be sent on an ordinary errand. It may simply be the case that this is a 'remake' for a more male-oriented society, or that it is a man's version in a society where women may have their own tales.[5] But even if that is so, it establishes that there may be reason for a male version in the Near East. There are other such versions: Tom Thumb may be swallowed first by a cow, then by a wolf, and is able to entice the wolf home and encourage it to eat too much to escape before calling on his father, who kills the wolf and rescues him.[6] Andrew Lang published a French literary version in which the girl is called Little Golden-hood ('the colour of fire') in which the magic golden cap was made by the witch-grandmother and is eaten by the wolf, burning his throat and bringing about his capture.[7]

Little attempt has been made to ask whether this much-loved fairytale is as old as the Ancient World. Perhaps the most completely satisfactory all-round analogue from antiquity is to be derived from a notice in Pausanias (6.6.7–11) about the famous boxer Euthymus of Locri in southern Italy. He was visiting nearby Temesa when he heard about a custom currently taking place there. Every year they had to offer a virgin 'bride' to a local spirit – of one of Odysseus' crew, long ago stoned to death as a rapist. The spirit – known by the neutral term of *Heros* – had a temple precinct in which the virgin had to be left (in Callimachus the spirit simply calls for a bed, and for those who brought her not to look back).[8] Euthymus entered the shrine, took pity on the girl, accepted her offer of marriage in return for saving her, fought and defeated the spirit, and drove it into the sea. Pausanias had also seen a picture of Euthymus' feat – in which the spirit was depicted as dark and terrifying *and wearing a wolfskin*. We have no actual swallowing of the girl and no red in her clothing, but the evidence relating to Callimachus' version indicates that in the rite defloration normally took place. Otherwise we have everything we need: deaths for the wolf-man involving first stoning, then (presumably) drowning; Euthymus as the huntsman; an enclosure with a bed, as in the fairytale's cottage scene; and a sexual motif. We have the wolf named in the picture as Lykas ('Mr Wolf'); but the 'girl that got away' remains unnamed.

There are a number of other candidates. If none is so good a match, a number actually involve the element or implication of 'red' in the girl's name or general identity. We can begin by asking whether any ancient hunter associated with a girl named 'Miss Red' *also* killed a wolf-man? No single mythographic source offers us an answer, but when we combine two scraps of evidence, one from Greek tragedy and one from later mythological narrative, we find a candidate. We are told in Euripides' *Heracles* that the hero has an enemy Lycus ('Mr Wolf'), who has killed Heracles' father-in-law Creon and the hero's own wife Megara and her children; Heracles will of course despatch him in due course. And we also know from the *Megara* attributed to Moschus that Megara, the wife of Heracles, had a sister Pyrrha ('flame-red'). We have no details, but we are entitled to infer that the reasons for Heracles' vengeance on Lycus include the desire to protect the surviving members of his wife's family.[9] We might put it briefly like this: 'hunter Heracles kills wife-killer Wolfman; sister Redgirl survives'.

Nor is this obscure Pyrrha the only 'flame-red' candidate available. A scholiast to Lycophron reports that Thetis was able to turn a real wolf to stone with her gaze when the wolf is sent to ravage her husband Peleus' flock.[10] Apollodorus credits her with the ability to change to fire, and so she too can be claimed as a 'flame-girl', though not in name; her activities in galvanising her son Achilles with fire point in the same direction. She doubtless had plenty of time to learn the craft; she and Eurynome held Hephaestus concealed for nine years, and he provided them with ornamental buckles, floral ornaments and necklaces (*Iliad* 18.398–405). We might note that lithifying the wolf by a look is a more supernatural and efficient variation on filling the sleeping wolf's belly with stones, the nearest to 'lithification' we find in the Grimms. We might also notice that the proverbially stormy relationship between Thetis and Peleus interestingly corresponds to the bad relationship between the husband and wife in the Boccaccio tale already noted.[11]

We have however no information that either Pyrrha, Heracles' sister-in-law, nor Thetis was actually *swallowed* by a wolf (a detail not always present in modern variants either).[12] But there is yet another candidate – we do have the story of Lycaon and Nyktinus, in which the father sacrifices his *son* to Zeus: the offering is unacceptable and he is miraculously reconstituted, while Lycaon is transformed into a wolf.[13] In Ovid's flood story Miss Flame-red (Pyrrha) is one of the survivors of the flood (*Met.* 1.348ff.), while the wolf is among the victims who drown. In all these cases, except that of Euthymus and Lykas, we have a sense of looking at the essential ingredients but never being able to assemble them in quite the right way, although the drowned wolf *does* actually occur in Grimm, as we have noted.[14] There is yet another version involving a Pyrrha in a quite different way: a mother, the nymph Thetis, sends her child for safekeeping to the home of King Lycomedes ('wolf-sly'?); the child comes as Pyrrha ('flame-red girl'); she is flame-red because she has been galvanised by her mother in a fire, and is almost entirely indestructible. But she is really a boy in disguise, and it is not long before she has made Lycomedes' daughter Deidameia pregnant.[15] This of course is part of the story of Achilles. The possibility of a cross-dresser's dialogue ('O what an "x" to "y" you with') suggests itself in such a situation, but we have no trace of any such. Yet it is really taxing coincidence very hard to see all this as random. The girl's dangerous enemy in woman's clothes is in the text, but the wrong way round. It is as if this is a counter-Red Riding Hood, like the satirical Thurber version where she slugs the wolf with the revolver she has been carrying in her basket. On the other hand, this particular Pyrrha's mother has herself turned a wolf to stone, as we have seen.[16]

We might also note an anonymous tale casually alluded to by Horace where a male child is brought alive from the belly of the Lamia: *neu pransae Lamiae uiuum puerum extrahat aluo* ('do not [in a poem] drag out the boy alive from the belly of the Lamia').[17] It might be objected that the Lamia is a cannibal ogress, not a wolf, but de Nino knew an Italian version in which the wolf's part in what is otherwise quite clearly a Red Riding Hood tale is indeed played by an ogress (and once more where the resourceful heroine escapes and kills the ogress rather than being swallowed).[18] The Red Riding Hood story may be relatively uncommon in Italy, but on this evidence it ought to be very old indeed.

Modern tellers and students of the story have not been slow to find sexual symbolisms in the close association of the young girl and the wolf, especially in the frequent instances of the wolf's requiring the girl to strip prior to entry into the wolf's bed. These elements, too, are to be found at least hinted at in antiquity. There are two pastoral pieces in Greek, one by Theocritus and one by Longus, in the same general tradition that deal with the adventures of someone with a wolf-related name. In Longus, a lustful girl called 'Little Shewolf' (Lykainion) entices the naive young Daphnis into the depths of the wood and offers to initiate him into lovemaking; there is a pretext that one of her geese has been captured by an eagle and needs to be rescued. He even offers her the produce of his flock as a 'reward'.[19] There is also an earlier episode in the same text in which the oxherd Dorcon puts on a wolfskin in order to rape the heroine Chloe, until he is foiled by dogs, then killed by pirates.[20] In the case from Ps.-Theocritus 27, Daphnis is the son of Lycidas (i.e. 'son of Wolfson'). He entices into the woods a daughter of Menalcas; after laying her down on his sheepskin he forces her to make love, having torn her dress so that she is naked.[21] There is also a standard sexual symbolism in Latin: a brothel was a *lupanar*, and prostitutes were required to wear purple-bordered togas. It does not take much adjustment of vision to see the modern tale as 'scarlet woman en route to the wolf-lair...'. The sexual symbolism was realised early enough in the modern history of the tale, as underlined by Perrault and his first English translator Robert Samber.[22]

What conclusion, then, can we suggest overall? It seems clear enough that, despite the absence of a name for the heroine in Pausanias' story of Euthymus and Lykas, we do have one good clear 'take' of the traditional Red Riding Hood in antiquity; and a whole dossier of other partly converging hints surrounding a girl with a 'flame-red' name and associations;[23] the circumstantial evidence of a 'Heracles and Pyrrha' version is likewise strong. The available materials offer us two things: the skeleton of a story in which a child, male or female, is threatened, raped or eaten by a figure with wolf or ogre associations, then disgorged or otherwise reconstituted with or without the substitution of a stone, while the wolf-figure is drowned or killed, and a 'flame-girl' (in whatever sense) survives the drowning to see new life brought from stones. The tally of Red Riding Hood candidates is quite impressive: Pyrrha, sister of Megara, on the sidelines of a story in which Heracles disposes of the murderous Lycus; Pyrrha, wife of Deucalion, surviving the flood in which the wolf-king Lycaon is drowned after murdering a victim reconstituted by Zeus, and herself drawing life from stones; two Rheas – one married to a cannibal ogre from whom she saves both male and female children, including a flame-girl Hestia, by placing a stone in the ogre's belly, and another associated with a wood, worshipper of Vesta, frightened by a wolf; Thetis, a fire-goddess in several senses, who turns a wolf to stone; her son/daughter Pyrrha who seduces a wolf-king's daughter; the unnamed boy disgorged from the belly of the female ogress; and the unnamed girl rescued by Euthymus from the wolf ghost earlier stoned and later drowned. But there is also just a hint of some kind of 'allegories of adolescence' in which the form of a wolf is associated with the role of a predator, often and obviously enough with sexual overtones.[24] I do not doubt that wolf stories can emerge wherever there are wolves; but it is difficult to dislodge local tradition from the tale-type both in Italy and elsewhere in antiquity.

Bluebeard (*AT* Types 311/312)[25]

Hitherto it has not been possible to produce a clear connection between the celebrated Bluebeard tale and ancient mythography: the story of a serial killer whose victims know too much might so readily be rooted in recurrent reality as to make an ancient prototype unnecessary. Nonetheless, there are at least some stylised features of the story that will indeed point to one or more versions from the classical world. The modern tale can be described as follows:

> A single sinister aristocratic figure, Bluebeard, engages a series of (usually) three servants or wives from the same set of sisters. Each is subjected to a test taboo: they have the free run of the house except for a forbidden door. Bluebeard absents himself and tests each wife: the first two open the door but betray their deceit by letting an egg fall into the blood of the forbidden chamber, a flower wither, a key become bloody,[26] or the like. The third takes a precaution so as to remain undetected, and is able to revive her sisters, smuggle them out, and send for the help of a brother or similar agent in the nick of time; Bluebeard himself is usually killed.

That represents the tale as familiar from Perrault. The resourceful surviving wife in the Grimm's version, 'Fitcher's Bird', makes her escape in a peculiar disguise of bird feathers stuck to her body with a coating of honey. There are also two closely related tale-types that tend to merge with *Bluebeard*: a *Robber Bridegroom* tale (*AT* Type 955) tends to have only the one girl; there is also a version where the Bluebeard figure is quite clearly detected to be the devil, and his house as hell (*AT* Type 312B). The oral tale enjoys wide circulation in northern European traditions, being particularly strong in Scandinavia; samples elsewhere tend to be sporadic, but a full modern investigation has not been done. Particularly suggestive is the fact that some versions, notably Italian examples, have the devil as the bridegroom and hell as the forbidden chamber; or they feature a dragon as the horrid bridegroom or employer, and his efforts to make the reluctant wife or servant eat human remains; similar motifs occur in 'primitive' renderings of Red Riding Hood, and some filiation between the two is not to be ruled out entirely.

The Opies produce a respectable trickle of literary versions going back as far as a hagiographic tale of St Tryphine set as early as the fifth century AD, and thus already edging back, at least in their dramatic date, to the very threshold of antiquity.[27] But it can be pushed back a good deal further. The story has a number of connections with the lore attached to Minos of Crete. The principal theme would be the fact that he is cursed with being unable to sleep with women without fatal results to the women themselves. This in itself would produce a string of fatalities, until he is apparently cured by the ministrations of Procris, who is herself, as we shall see, already involved in *another* Bluebeard-type adventure as a daughter of Erechtheus.[28] But Minos also possesses the palace at Cnossus whose abundance of rooms and labyrinthine character is archaeologically attested; the right kind of site for the motif of the 'forbidden door'. Bluebeard put each disobedient wife into the bloody chamber with the corpses of her predecessors. We know that Minos is not above shutting a living person in with a corpse, as he does in the separate adventure of Glaucus and Polyeidos;[29] that he demanded the tribute from the Athenians including seven young women at a time; and that he was sexually attracted to at least one of the victims who travelled over with Theseus.[30] We do not know the circumstances under which he would have introduced them to the Minotaur, but there would certainly have been a suitable context for a 'room taboo' test here. Minos could have tested the women by courting each of the victims until she opened the forbidden door, after which, as a result of her disobedience, she might conceivably have been killed by being shut in with the Minotaur behind it.

More certainly, however, Minos *did* possess a peculiarity close to the Bluebeard of the fairytale: he bribed Nisus' daughter Scylla to let him have her father's purple lock on which the safety of the city of Megara depended.[31] One notes that in Ovid's retelling of this adventure Minos rides a white horse and wears a purple covering: Charles Dickens' nurse's version of the story, *Captain Murderer*, by far the ghastliest known to me, has the villain ride a white horse with a red stain on its back covered by harness.[32] Minos himself also has subterranean associations, since he becomes a reputable judge of the dead, following a Homeric tradition friendly to his reputation. But this could easily help to account for the conflation of his story with that of devils. The end of Minos in his human form, killed by Coccalus' daughters with boiling water or pitch while he vindictively pursues Daedalus, would not be inconsistent with the usual end of Bluebeard tales where he is murdered by the last of his intended victims.[33] Minos, then, has more than enough qualifications to take the Bluebeard accolade in his own right, and the purple lock is likewise hard to argue away when associated with someone sexually destructive to women; though there is no single simple narrative thread, and no single source that preserves the tale intact. Procris cures his trait of being fatal to women, but has her Bluebeard-style come-uppance with someone else, her own absent husband Cephalus, and that is treated as a romantic fatal accident in Ovid's classic version in *Metamorphoses 7*.

It might be emphasised that traditions concerning Minos are as fluid as those concerning Bluebeard himself. What has hampered identification is the stability of details like the Minotaur and the Bull of Pasiphae, which tend to obscure the more incidental and no less sinister other tales of this elusive and tantalising figure. One factor in favour of Minos is that once more his story has a legendary character to it: someone something like this existed in some sense, and so he joins the murderer of St Tryphine among the rogue's gallery of fore-bears for *Captain Murderer*. We may be tempted to strengthen our suspicions by looking at the story through the perspective of Procris herself:

Bluebeard's wife	*Procris*
Sisters are killed by murderous husband with blue beard	Sisters are sacrificed during threats from enemy king Eumolpus, son of sea-god Poseidon, a deity described as caeruleus (sea-blue) [34]
Husband has forbidden chamber	Eumolpus is a priest of Demeter and the underworld queen Persephone, and institutes mystery rites at Eleusis
Husband tests wives by going absent	Procris' husband Cephalus, son of Deion ('Murderous') or of Hermes, [35] goes off to see whether his wife will remain faithful; she fails the test, by sleeping with a stranger, or husband in disguise, for gold
Bluebeard locks women in with corpses	Minos locks a living man in with a dead one
Brides of Bluebeard do not survive to tell the tale	Procris goes to Minos, the man with the purple lock, whose lovers do not survive sleeping with him
She takes precautions against the bride-test	She takes precautions against his fatal embrace and survives
She leaves Bluebeard disguised as 'Fitcher's Bird'	She disguises herself as a man and rejoins Cephalus under the name *Pterelas* ('winged')

These matches work well on the whole once we grasp that it is Procris who seems to move from one Bluebeard scenario to another. But we must stress the sense that we almost always seem to be dealing in this context with halves of stories.

There are also other candidates in antiquity for Bluebeard's victims. Curiosity in opening a forbidden object is central to the tale, and the Opies noted in passing the story of Pandora and the forbidden jar, though only to make the point that 'the effect of female curiosity' offers a theme of great antiquity.[36] But the Pandora theme deserves to be pursued further.[37] It has to be noted that another, or an apparently other, girl by the name of Pandora is, like Procris, one of the daughters of the ancient King of Athens, Erechtheus, and in their tale we may have something of what is missing in Hesiod. One of the daughters has to be sacrificed at the behest of Delphi to ensure Athenian survival in the war against Eumolpus of Eleusis,[38] and two other daughters give their lives in sympathy. A fourth daughter, Procris, fails a fidelity test set by an absent husband with an ominous pedigree: Cephalus, son of Deion ('murderous').[39] Any conflation of the two Pandoras, and any attempt to conflate the fortunes of the daughters of Erechtheus, will produce a further Bluebeard tale automatically – and a conveniently expurgated example at that, with simply a forbidden box of evils rather than a forbidden bloody chamber.[40]

The motif of 'the devil's bride' can also be pursued through a further mythological route: the story of Persephone has the girl taken from a flower meadow by force by Hades into the underworld;[41] there she violates a food taboo and the breaking of the taboo puts her into Hades' power for at least part of the year. Our mythographic sources do not explicitly represent the eating of the pomegranate seeds as a food taboo as such,[42] but it might be inferred nonetheless: if one touches the egg in Bluebeard's forbidden chamber, one must join the rest of the dead; if one eats the pomegranate seeds in Hades' kingdom, one must stay in the realm of the dead.[43] Underworld taboos can be shown to operate inexorably much earlier in a similar context (the confinement of the Sumerian Enkidu in the Nether World).[44] And indeed the Sumerian story of *Inanna's Descent to the Nether World* already has the goddess stripping off her seven garments to enter the Nether World, only to remain as a corpse on a hook until her extradition can be arranged.[45] Her death has occurred after her admission beyond the Seventh Door.

There is also a related girl in the underworld story reflected in a modern German version (Ranke 1966: 26), where an innocent girl goes in search of her godmother, who turns out to be the devil's wife; one of the sights seen in hell is the burning of infants in the chimney piece; another is the godmother wearing a horsehead. Both features can be compared to adventures of Demeter, mistress of Poseidon (once more a 'sea-blue' god).[46]

The Robber Bridegroom (*AT* Type 955)

The Bluebeard type-tale is closely associated with another, that of the Robber Bridegroom. A clutch of modern Spanish examples serves to convey the nature of the type:

> A group of thieves prepare to rob a house, with one of their number as the 'inside man'. The youngest of three sisters in the household notices his suspicious behaviour. As he is calling his fellow thieves she pushes him out the window. He recovers and comes back for his knives: she

opens the door just wide enough to allow her to mutilate his hand. Eventually the thief with the distinguishing mutilation becomes rich, and parental pressure forces the canny daughter to marry him; he prepares to kill her with the knife that caused the mutilation; but she manages to drown him in a well.[47]

In an extended version of the same tale we have the thief taking the girl to the robbers' den;[48] she kills the gangsters' moll who has been commissioned to cook her, and escapes. In a further version each of three sisters has to handle the corpses: the first two refuse and are killed; a third rescues a sick prisoner and they escape; one of the robbers is disguised in a dogskin and finds her,[49] but she gives the alarm; she marries her co-escapee.

This sequence of distinctively bloodcurdling robbers' episodes in which a humble, weak creature eludes the artful organisation of a robber band is already to be found in only slightly rearranged form in the robbers' tales in Apuleius. There are three tales – of a robber who loses a hand nailed to the door by the owner, a second thrown out of a window by an old woman, and a third trapped in a bearskin and betrayed by a slave (*Met.* 4.9–21). In the Spanish group these are all perpetrated by the same quick-thinking youngest daughter. But Apuleius does offer the girl at the robber's house in the person of Charite, and she too finally mutilates a robber, her husband's murderer (in this case, by blinding, *Met.* 8.13); he certainly has a robber's name, Thrasyllus, and indeed is said to have associations with robbers (*Met.* 8.1), though not specifically with the band already mentioned. The correspondence works like this:

Robber Bridegroom	Tale of Charite
Youngest sister	Young girl
is detained at robber's den, but escapes	is detained at robber's den
She detects and wounds robber by cutting off his fingers in a door;	She hears tale of robber wounded by having hand cut off in door;
by pushing him through a window;	of a second robber pushed through window;
by killing him in an animal skin	of a third robber killed in animal skin
She marries the man she has mutilated, and has great difficulty in being rescued at the last minute	She is prepared to sleep with murderous robber, but mutilates him before bringing about both their deaths

Apuleius' complex web of robber stories is considerably more romanticised than the folktale versions by the complication that Charite marries a fiancé who merely *poses* as one of the robbers, Haemus, ('Captain Blood') before being killed; but the basic framework is in place and must reinforce the view that Apuleius' novel has close affinities to folktale in general.

We are in a position to see, then, that the tales of extreme cruelty to resourceful women exhibited in *Red Riding Hood*, *Bluebeard* and *The Robber Bridegroom* are indeed to be found in antiquity, though seldom in an obviously coherent form. We should stress the importance of looking at the whole of the mythological tradition of any given story: a well-known version in Ovid or elsewhere is unlikely to present all the details necessary to relate any given ancient version to the modern tale-type, and it often requires the assembly of a good many hybrid outlines before we are in a position to see that most of the features now known in a tale already exist in antiquity in some sort of stable relationship to one another. Seldom, too, are we able to make any progress towards constructing an archetype of any given tale. The variants encountered in surviving literature are at least as varied and confused as their modern counterparts, suggesting that the tales themselves are already old.

8

MAGICIANS AND THEIR ALLIES

In addition to *Maerchen*-type romantic fairytales, the repertoire of oral folktale includes a considerable variety of picaresque or horrific stories, which on the whole tend to be more stable in their transmission than the tale-types we have considered so far. This makes it possible to discuss them in a more compressed form, and examine a number of often closely related types together.

The Sorcerer's Apprentice (*AT* Type 1174; Christiansen 3020)

One devil's disciple-type story does indeed have ancient roots and offers us a clear single 'take' of the tale in the classical period: this is none other than the celebrated (and now doubly Disnified) *Sorcerer's Apprentice* itself. As a result of the general and local witch-hunting manias of the Middle Ages and the seventeenth century, there has been obvious scope for local colouring in more recent forms of the tale. Often, in modern versions, the story relates to the wrongful possession of a forbidden Magic Book of which a named and prestigious magician is the rightful controller: in not a few of the Norwegian cases known to Christiansen this sinister figure is a Christian clergyman, while in a Scottish version Donald Duibheal Mackay studies with Satan in Italy.[1] Often the story relates in particular to an inability to handle the demonic servants which the Magic Book controls. The inexperienced operator may have to employ a whole range of impossible tasks for the demon(s) to perform (twist a rope of sand, pick up grains of sand, untie the knots in a fishing net, or suchlike); often such tasks have some connection with water, such as emptying a lake, carrying water in a sieve, or similar absurd operations. The rightful owner should then return, by instinct or in response to summons, and exorcise the devil, sometimes leaving traces of the incident behind that can be connected with a specific locality (hence the classification of the tale as legend). In a Scottish version the master leaves his book unsecured and the apprentice finds little men marching out of it.[2] In an Irish example the book is none other than Oliver Cromwell's Bible: in common with local Irish tradition, the tale regards him as the devil incarnate.[3]

The most celebrated version in antiquity is Lucian's 'Sorcerer's Apprentice' tale, which forms the final story in the *Philopseudes*: this is a particularly well-crafted example of a *Kunstmaerchen*, an artistically worked literary fairytale, and it does not require commitment or belief on the part of the sceptical Lucian to produce a 'correct' version of the story:[4]

> A young Greek called Eucrates is touring Egypt and in the course of a trip on the Nile encounters Pancrates, an amazing magician, to whom he is apprenticed; the latter does not require any domestic servant, but instead enchants household objects, a broom and a pestle, to undertake domestic tasks on their own. Eucrates overhears the spell and in the sorcerer's absence is able to activate the magical servant. Unfortunately he is also unable to stop its activities once started, having only overheard the first half of the spell; splitting the animated pestle with an axe only divides it into two servants instead of one. Only the returned sorcerer can put a stop to the now three magical servants, and having done so he disappears. Eucrates still knows his half of the spell, but dare not use it for fear of the consequences. Thereafter, he travels on to Memphis, and the great stone colossi of Memnon deliver him an oracle.

One notes that several such traditions are preceded by a trip on water, or arise out of one; this is true not only of Egyptian examples mentioned below, but also of the Scottish disciple of Satan, Donald Duibheal Mackay, whose activities are localised in Caithness and Sutherland.[5] He takes a boat into a cave and is given a casket with a book by a fairy, but is forbidden to return to the cave. When he wrongfully opens the book he is confronted with a swarm of fairies clamouring for tasks. On one occasion a third party causes the task to be aborted by an unwelcome interruption. This corresponds to the motif of the returning magician, but in the instance of Mackay the spell is broken for good when he sets a task beyond the fairies – to twist a rope of sand for building a bridge from Caithness to Orkney. One notes that Lucian's version has the seemingly irrelevant information that Eucrates received an oracle from the famous Colossi of Memnon.[6] We should dismiss this as a purely decorative detail thrown in to emphasise Eucrates' credulous outlook, but the Scottish example raises the possibility, as do several of its Norwegian counterparts, that it hints instead at knowledge of a slightly different version of the story. When the magician puts an end to the spell, he may himself turn to stone, which can be seen to this day.[7] Lucian would not wish any such monument to Pancrates to 'prove' the story: he is trying to manoeuvre the teller into a position where only the use of the half-learnt spell can prove that such magical servants could ever have existed. We should note, too, that the apprentice likewise splits the head of the intruder in the Scottish case, as Eucrates breaks the pestle into two.

Once more, however, there is at least a genuine native Egyptian predecessor. Lucian's spell is an oral one, but the native Egyptian approach tends to be bookish – the novice Naneferkeptah who went down to obtain a magic book from a tomb without its rightful owner's permission finds not only that he starts a flood by operating its spell, but that everyone in his family is drowned, eventually including himself.[8] One notes, too, that Egyptian magic in the narrative tradition does a good deal of water engineering: not only does the rod of Moses drain the Red Sea, but the magicians Djadja-em-ankh and Djedi in the Westcar papyrus can pile up the sea to find a lost gem on its bottom, or can let the river level fall for a Pharaoh to travel over it.[9]

Allied to the *Sorcerer's Apprentice* is tale-type 753, in which an expert magician or miracle worker resuscitates a corpse, but when an amateur tries to do the same disaster ensues; the expert may or may not put matters right. This is illustrated in classical literature, as we have seen, by the case of Medea's resuscitation of Aeson and the lamb, while the daughters of Pelias fail to apply the same recipe to their father.[10]

Trickster avoids Death (*AT* Type 332)

This whole group of tales admits of considerable variation: it is related to the group that includes 'Godfather Death', where a man is given a sack to imprison Death;[11] or where Death makes a compact with a man to act as a physician, who saves all patients unless Death stands at the head of the bed. When he saves even one of these, a princess, by a trick, Death is out to get him in turn. But he can still hold out; by refusing to recite the obligatory prayer before Death can take him, he stays alive.[12]

These types of tale are represented in antiquity by the story of Sisyphus. So far as I know there is no version where the means of imprisoning Death is a magic sack – so common in the modern versions – but according to Pherecydes he does bind Death till Ares releases him. The continuation in Pherecydes that Sisyphus cannot be killed till he has received his wife's burial rites has its equivalent in El-Shamy's modern Egyptian version where the death-defying trickster flatly refuses to say the Koranic prayers without which Death cannot take him.[13] The ultimate fate of Sisyphus is divergent from the modern folktale conclusion. Sisyphus never succeeds in rolling the stone right up the hill in the underworld,[14] whereas in the popular tale his counterpart does succeed in getting into heaven by a stratagem. There is, so far as I know, no equivalent of this version, at least for Sisyphus, but it may be that his role has been allowed to overlap with that of Asclepius, who does of course get into heaven by being deified, but whose exploits also seem to figure in folktales of the 'Godfather Death' type, where he goes against orders in rescuing souls so that the doomed do not die.[15]

Aladdin (*AT* Types 560–562; 566–567)

The tale of *Aladdin and the Lamp* is the most obvious example of a tale of oriental origin and colouring that is now at home in the repertoire of Western fairytale,[16] thanks in large measure to Galland's translation of the *Arabian Nights* into French at the beginning of the eighteenth century (though in fact Galland did not translate his tale from a manuscript of the *Nights* themselves).[17] But we are entitled to suspect that some Western versions of the story reflect a different tradition to Galland's transmission of the tale, which is in any case part of a larger complex – *AT* Types 560, 561 and 562 are really handling the same basic framework with major differences of detail: the magic object in 560 is usually a ring rather than the characteristic magic lamp of Aladdin; and Jewish-oriental tradition can produce a whole repertoire of objects which the hero can use to win the princess and foil a rival suitor.[18] Type 560 features animal helpers in the first instance – most characteristically, a snake. When the hero helps it, the snake's father, the king of the snakes, gives him the magic object that will provide the foundation of his good fortune. Ranke was unable to extend the known elements of the tale any further back than a couple of centuries before Galland, and that only for the common motif of the elopement of the princess. Some idea of the diversity that is possible in a tale so generally familiar can be seen from a German oral example recorded in 1937 (Ranke no. 40):

> A poor tailor accidentally summons a supernatural creature – a green man who is a mountain ghost with a club foot and a hoof, and who takes his son Johann in response to an unguarded 'invitation'. The young Johann is to obtain a book and a lamp from inside a mountain. After going through nine gates he finds the objects, but overstays in the seductive garden he finds there and sleeps for an extraordinary number of years inside the mountain. When he returns the creature has gone and, except for his mother, his family has died off. The supernatural servants in the book provide both food and wealth on request and he has them build a palace so that he can woo the prince's daughter, whom he marries. The creature reappears in disguise, exchanges book and lamp for new replacements with the gullible wife; he then transports wife, palace and objects, leaving Johann to languish in the prince's prison. The hero recovers the crucial objects when he encounters a dead horse on the road, and a dung beetle and an ant persuade him to open up the horse's brain and belly; in return they give him the powers to change into their shape (and so obtain mobility and near invisibility). He uses the invisibility to snatch the queen back on the night of her wedding to the creature, recovers palace and objects, and kills his rival. He and the princess live happily ever after.

There is no doubt that this is *an* Aladdin, but it is hardly 'our' Aladdin. It has an extended beginning, differently and more supernaturally coloured, explaining the 'devil's bargain' nature of the lad's apprenticeship; and the second movement of the action, the recovery and thwarting of the green mountain spirit, is obtained by an entirely different set of magical operations motivated by helpful animals more reminiscent of materials in *AT* 560, the 'magic ring' variant.

We can add at least fifteen centuries to the certain antiquity of the tale by noting two versions told of Gyges of Lydia, an historical figure of the seventh century BC.

> Gyges (or an ancestor of the same name) is a shepherd serving a royal master; he descends underground after a landslip and recovers a ring from the body of a dead giant inside the doors of the belly of a bronze horse. The ring confers powers of invisibility. He sleeps with the queen and kills the king, whom he supplants.[19]
>
> Gyges, the favourite of his royal master, intercepts the queen about to marry the king he serves. He kills the rival suitor on the wedding night and marries her himself.[20]

These two pieces alone, from Plato and Nicolaus of Damascus respectively, represent a combination of the first and second of the hero's magical adventures: here the horse with the belly to be opened is actually found *inside* the underground chamber, instead of in a separate adventure as in Ranke's folktale version.[21] Plato has minimised the magic element and Nicolaus has cut it out altogether, but it is impossible to argue away the fact that a combined version of AT 560 and 561 was available by Nicolaus' time, the first century BC, at the very latest.

Half-Cockerel (*AT* Type 715)

Consideration of magical tales of an Aladdin type lead naturally into stories where a humble master is helped beyond locked doors by a different kind of magic helper, a humble but invincible animal rather than an evil magician. A relatively unfamiliar fairytale in England, but widespread throughout Europe, is the tale of *Demicoq*. Delarue gives a modern French version as follows:

> Two women had a rooster. They split it in two, and one ate her half, the other kept hers. While scratching about, Half-Chick uncovered a bushel of money, but a miller, who happened to pass by, took the money, leaving only three heads of wheat in exchange. To right the wrong, Half-Chick, followed by a fox, a wolf, a colony of ants, and a river, went to the miller's house. They did so much destruction that the miller had to return the money. Half-Chick carried it back to the good woman, and they lived happily together.[22]

This is not only one of the world's oldest tales, but one of the most versatile: we have an ancient Akkadian form (with its modern Near Eastern analogues), as well as the modern European versions, and an almost unnoticed ancient Greek literary working.

The basic structure is as follows. A poor person has an animal or supernatural companion. Cheated by some more powerful agent, the poor person needs the amazing odd companion to bring about revenge, which involves a number of different identities. In the case of the coarse German version printed by Ranke,[23] the cockerel goes round actually absorbing larger animals into its (magically infinite) backside, then disgorging them at critical moments. It is that variation that gives us our main clue for linking the tale to antiquity.

In the second century AD the Near Eastern satirist Lucian writing in Greek produced the following tale in his Dialogue *The Cock*:

> A poor man Micyllus has a cockerel, and little else. The bird informs him that his neighbour Simon has stolen their only earthenware bowl, and now insults him with his nouveaux-riche airs and graces; while a certain Eucrates, a rich grandee, has invited Micyllus to his house, but merely as a substitute guest. The cock reveals that he himself has had a number of identities in his travels through time: he has been a number of people, including Pythagoras, but also a number of different animals, including a horse, a jackdaw and a frog. By pulling a magic feather from his crop, Micyllus can open doors and thus can gain entry to the offenders' houses. He gets his revenge by beating the now miserly Simon invisibly, and by watching the sexual humiliation of Eucrates and his wife by servants, before returning home with his companion the cock.

This story is obviously 'our' tale.[24] The main difference is that fairytales, while acknowledging multiple metamorphosis, do not embody transmigration as a philosophical doctrine, a natural cultural feature in Graeco-Roman educated literature. But the idea of the cock having been many people corresponds very neatly to the literal notion of the cock having various animals he has picked up along the way somehow absorbed 'inside' him. (In a modern Near Eastern version we have the cock being killed more than once, thus coming just as close by another route to transmigration.)[25] The magical power of the hindquarters is hinted at with the magical powers of Micyllus' companion's tail feathers.

In this working the debacle at the rich man's house is curtailed to a single blow, but the motif is there nonetheless. The sexual humiliation of the villain is not in the European versions. It seems to be present in Dawkins' version from Asia Minor,[26] but the text is corrupt and Dawkins declined to declare what he suspects is really happening: what should follow is that the cock escapes through the backside of his enemy. Such a motif would ally the tale to chap-book versions of *Tom Thumb*, where Tom goes right through a cow to be evacuated in the natural way – again a detail which presents difficulties for some modern retellings of the story.[27] This makes good sense: the whole idea of Half-Chick is that he is a weak and insignificant creature who makes up for his lack of physical strength with amazing resourcefulness and resilience.

A form of the tale before Lucian's is indicated by the Akkadian folktale first published in 1956 as *The Poor Man of Nippur*.[28] This is so close to modern Israeli versions already published before its discovery that they can be summarised together:

> A poor boy acquires an animal companion (goat, hen, cock, cow). He gives a present to the mayor, but is humiliated, given an insulting meal and cheated of his animal. He sets up the mayor by a trick, and beats the mayor in a temple after falsely accusing him of theft, before dressing as a healer and attacking him twice more.[29]

We should note that the animal the boy is cheated out of is often a cock or a hen, and in a modern Turkish version the boy himself is actually nicknamed 'Brother Cock'. A distinctive episode in the modern tale has the rascal bent on revenge disguising as a woman, then murdering the robber, or raping daughters and injuring their father in bed, presumably by buggery. Lucian delicately leaves this to servants. One notes that in Lucian there are really two adversaries – Eucrates and the nouveau-riche Simon. In *The Poor Man of Nippur* this is rearranged: the hero borrows a chariot from the king to get even with the local official, whereas in Lucian Micyllus only dreams of kingship.

It seems proper to assume that the tale has a continuous history. The eccentricities of Lucian's version, in particular, are still well encoded in the modern popular west European versions. There are also affinities to *The Wonder-working Doll* and *The Goose* in Straparola and Basile. The doll and goose attach themselves to the hindquarters of the prince; one thinks of Eucrates as a target for homosexual rape by a servant in Lucian's version.

If we attempt a scheme for all the versions it might run like this:

> A poor person; humiliation, theft; strange companion with magic posterior; prince, dignitary humiliated; wealth restored.

Note that Lucian's version does not have this last and logical motif of 'wealth restored', for the good reason that he emphasises Cynic colouring with its emphasis on *autarkeia*, self-sufficiency – the poor should be content with their lot and not envy the rich victims of debauchery and corruption.

As far as the early history of such tales is concerned, Heda Jason (1980) sounds a cautionary warning: it is a hopeless task to try to reconstruct or date vanished archetypes because our earliest versions of the stories are so very ordinary. This is certainly true of *The Poor Man of Nippur*. But we can see clearly enough that the story is one of the basic plots of both fairytale and rogue tale: it balances on the borderline between realistic novella and magical morality tale. It also invites resourceful expurgation of the sexual theme in some versions, and uninhibited exploitation of it in others.

Master and pupil (*AT* Type 325; cf. Christiansen Type 3000), *Escape from the Black School at Wittenberg*

We end as we began with magician and pupil. The modern form of this widespread magical tale might be seen as an obverse to *The Sorcerer's Apprentice*: this time the magic is made to work invariably to the assistant's advantage. The events can be characterised as follows:[30]

> A man is forced somehow to entrust his son to the devil for a year for his education; the boy learns how to metamorphose into animals, and he can be recovered only if his father can distinguish him; he changes into various animals for sale to make money, but the devil claims him back, usually in the guise of a horse, and there is a final sequence of quick-fire metamorphoses into animals or objects out of which the young man finally gets the upper hand over his evil master.

An ancient example outside the Graeco-Roman world of the contest of magicians has been noted by El-Shamy in the course of discussing modern Egyptian versions. The Satni-Texts in Demotic of the Graeco-Roman period show a young boy successfully competing against an Ethiopian magician and driving him and his mother back to Ethiopia by a series of feats of counter-magic: the Ethiopian produces fire, and the Egyptian boy produces rain to quench it; or the Ethiopian turns into a gander, and the Egyptian produces a fowler with a knife.[31] Were there any equivalents in the classical world? The capacity for multiple metamorphoses is given by Poseidon to Periclymenos, son of Neleus, as early as the Hesiodic *E Hoiai*:[32] his shapes include eagle, ant, bee or snake. The idea of metamorphosis or even a sequence of metamorphoses for sale is found in the story of Erysichthon, where his daughter (Hypermestra) is able to satisfy her father's craving for food by continually selling herself in animal form and then returning;[33] the capacity had been given once more by Poseidon, in this case in exchange for her virginity. We sometimes find female victims of the magician, though the modern folktale may expurgate their 'use' by the evil master (in El-Shamy's example a young female victim is simply hung up by her hair, as so often in *Jack the Giant Killer* stories).[34] But what Ovid's story underlines is that a subsidiary motif of the tale is some parental need to earn money to survive, and so provide the motivation for a whole sequence of metamorphoses.

The most obvious classical example of the story, however, is perhaps suggested by the general outline of Aristophanes' *Clouds*, the original version of which dates from 423 BC: the old Athenian farmer Strepsiades ('twister') is saddled with debt because his son Pheidippides is mad about horses; the son is sent to a school run by Socrates where he will learn unjust argument, and so enable his father to escape his debts, doubtless to enable him to continue maintaining horses. For a while it looks as if the unjust argument will prevail and totally take over the boy. The debate between two *logoi* ('arguments') is portrayed in our extant revised version of the *Clouds* as just that; but in the original version of the play we know that the arguments were represented by fighting cocks.[35] This may have been an ingenious adaptation of the usual sequence in the tale, where the essence of trials between boy and magician is that the combatants must change into different creatures so that a fox, for example, can eat up the cock, or a fire burn up a hair, or the like. The last of these is hinted at in the text, but not in animal form: one of Strepsiades' own bright ideas, inspired by Socrates, is to use a glass to burn the record of his debts.[36] The initial scene at the *phrontisterion* has Strepsidaes met by a pupil, then referred to the master who appears aloft in a basket: folktale variants have the master appear on top of a mountain (Georgian), or flying through the air (Egyptian).[37] And one of the tests for Strepsiades is to be able to distinguish genders: he is taught that a female cock is an *alektruaina* (a 'cockess'). Aristophanes uses the joke as a skit on pedantic sophistic classification of language, but a version of it occurs in the popular tale. In a Rumanian Yiddish version we have the test that the father will only get his son back if he can tell his son from the magician's daughter when both are changed into doves (i.e. to distinguish the gender of doves).[38]

The fashionable satire on sophists in the *Clouds* should not blind us to the essentials of the popular outline. Whatever our ideas about Socrates, there is little doubt that he is perceived in the play as a presiding evil genius whose job is to transform people and alienate them from their traditional roots. His traditional and much-vaunted communication with a personal *daimon* would have offered corroboration enough in the popular mind.[39] Even on the Old Comic stage it might have been difficult to swallow the literal transformation of Pheidippides *into* a horse; the mania for horses in an expensive lifestyle may have been a clever compromise between fairytale and reality. As the story, or at least some version of it, is substantially older than Aristophanes, it seems obvious that the Old Comic dramatist has drawn on popular storytelling, differently reflected in the string of metamorphoses in the Hypermestra story, and that knowledge of the folktale would help to enhance the sinister portrait of Socrates. As well as a proto-scientist, he is being presented with hints of an evil magician.[40]

We can see, then, that the alliance with a demonic figure or the access to powers with demonic associations offers a rich choice of formulae for fairytale (and novella). It should come as no surprise that so many such tales should have a demonstrable resilience over so long a time-span.

9

BETWEEN LIVING AND DEAD

The folktale repertoire contains a number of variations on the possibilities of *revenants*, of mortals who have some reason or another to re-cross the normally inexorable boundaries between the living and the dead. A few have been sporadically recognised or discussed in relation to their ancient occurrences, but this has remained the exception rather than the rule. It is useful to gather some of the most obviously recurrent types together under a single heading.

Laying the ghost (*AT* Type 326A)

The most obvious starting-point is the routine ghost story where the hero is able to lay an unburied ghost in a haunted house. There is a clear and relatively uncomplicated modern version in Briggs (1970: 1.1.308):

> A fearless but reprobate young soldier is sent to his colonel for punishment; he is to find his own food on the way. The only place that has a free meal on offer is a haunted castle. The serving girl prepares a meal, then departs. He addresses the ghost, a lady, who declares that she was murdered by her prospective husband, and shows him the spot where her unburied corpse still lies. He has the corpse properly buried.
>
> The serving-girl offers to marry him, but he reports instead to the colonel, whose daughter she is; he is rewarded with her after all.

Here there is something of a frame story, of the romantic reward for the hero. Often this aspect is far more developed – for example, with the intervention of magical cats in a complex murder plot in which the ghost was again a murder victim and reveals his own story; and again there is a great reward for the courage of the nothing-to-lose soldier.[1] The normal pattern is that of a down-on-his-luck hero (occasionally a heroine), but sometimes we meet a mixture of clergyman and dashing huntsman;[2] recurrent features of the story are the meal and a book to read to while away the time prior to the ghost's entrance.

In the two classical literary versions of the story we have the ghost-story core and little else. The Younger Pliny (*Ep.* 7.27.5–11) tells the tale as a matter-of-fact report on which he is seeking a second opinion, whereas Lucian tells it tongue-in-cheek as a satire of its boastful and superstitious narrator Arignotus (*Philopseudes* 30f.). In both cases it is a person of much more established status who acts as the ghost-layer, Athenodorus of Tarsus in Athens, Arignotus the Pythagorean in Corinth. In each case this is simply a natural extension of his professional calling: the after-life in antiquity is a natural sphere of interest for the philosopher. The variation in specific name and place underlines the status of this story as a migratory legend (Christiansen Type 4020/1). We are told nothing about the ghost's background or manner of death, though his being unburied within a normal house would normally be taken to indicate foul play. The ghost-layer reads in Lucian and writes in Pliny, but neither takes a meal. The only reward is the freeing of the house from haunting and enhancement of the ghost-layer's own personal prestige. Pliny's matter-of-factness preserves a 'correct' version of the story as far as it goes – the ghost attracts attention solely in order to obtain burial:

> (Athenodorus) calls for writing tablets, pen and lamp; he sends all his servants to an inner quarter, and turns his mind, eyes and hand to writing, to prevent a vacant mind from conjuring up imaginary noises and empty fears. First, as everywhere else, the still of night; then the clanking of iron and the moving of chains; he does not raise his eyes, he does not stop writing, but strengthens his resolve and closes his ears. The hubbub becomes more intense and advances, one moment audible at the door, the next in the room itself. He looks behind him, sees the ghost and recognises it from the description. It stands and beckons with its finger as if summoning him. But he gestures it to wait a little and returns to his writing, while the ghost rattles its chains about the writer's head; he looks round and sees it beckoning him as before. Without delay he takes the lamp and follows. It travels slowly as if weighted down with chains. After it turns into the courtyard of the house, it suddenly vanishes. The moment he is alone, Athenodorus gathers some grass and leaves and marks the spot.
>
> (Pliny *Ep.* 7.27.7–10)

Lucian, for his part, has the ghost-layer Arignotus tell the tale in the first person, with emphasis on the boastfulness of the exorcist himself; but an exhausting bout of battling with the ghost does occur in popular versions as well.[3] The nearest to the magic cats of the modern folktale is the repertoire of gratuitous metamorphoses offered by the ghost:

> I took a lamp and went in on my own, and putting down the lamp in the largest room I sat down on the floor and was busy reading; but the spirit confronted me, thinking that he had come up against some layman and expecting to terrify me the way he had terrified the others

– he was filthy and long-haired, and blacker than the darkness itself. And looking over me he tried to get the better of me, attacking from every side to try to overcome me, one moment as a dog, the next as a bull or a lion. But I reached for my most blood-curdling curse, chanted it in Egyptian, and drove him into a corner of a dark room; after noting where he went down, I was able to rest for what remained of the night.

In a very elaborate variant of the modern tale we find the Revd Mr Polkinghorse of St Ives talking for a long time in an unknown language to Wild Harris's Ghost.[4] And metamorphosis of the ghost may occur as well.[5] It is not clear from anything in these two surviving examples whether the tale has undergone expansion after the end of antiquity. (The short form is certainly still found, especially with the decor of local legends of individual exorcists.)[6] All we can say is that the unusual variant of philosopher rather than devil-may-care underdog is less likely in popular tradition and may be the result of remodelling. Pliny, in particular, has taken pains to ensure that his account has nothing fantastic other than the apparition itself, which Athenodorus rigorously tests for 'authenticity' along the way. But on present evidence we cannot attempt to reconstruct an original.

Theft from a corpse (*AT* Type 366)

A ghost may return for other reasons than simply to secure burial; it may also come back to reclaim what is usually stolen property. The revenant may be male or female, and tends to have some part of its anatomy actually *made of* gold (an arm or a leg), which a grave-robber, sometimes a young girl, has contrived to pilfer. Alternatively a husband may pilfer his dead wife's liver (!), or a poor person steal a bone from a corpse to make soup. The corpse visits the thief to reclaim the property (and in so doing may bring about the death of the thief); there may be dialogue culminating in the dead accuser telling the thief that he or she has the article in question.[7] Lucian offers a short classical literary version from the second century AD: in the *Philopseudes* the wife of the host Eucrates comes back from the dead as a ghost to reclaim her golden shoe, in this case merely left by accident behind a couch; having reclaimed it, the ghost of the corpse brings no ill-consequence to her innocent husband.[8] Lucian may well have simply toned down an aspect of the traditional tale to suit his literary context, a set of tales where ghosts tend to act in a benign manner towards those credulous enough to believe in them. We have, however, a native Egyptian example from the Graeco-Roman period where the motif of pilfering is quite clearly established: in the first tale of the Egyptian Demotic Satne-cycle, the buried ghost Naneferkeptah narrates how he and his family met their deaths through the revenge of the gods for his having wrongfully acquired a magic book, which Satne in his turn now proposes to steal from Naneferkeptah's tomb; Satne disobeys both the ghost and the Pharaoh in taking the book, till the ghost contrives a set-up with a courtesan to humiliate him in front of the Pharaoh until the book is returned.[9] Here we have in effect two workings of 'wrongful theft from the tomb' in quick succession, one serving as a cautionary tale to warn against the other. In neither case does the ghost personally come back, but is rather able to work remote magic and contrive misfortune against the thief – in the first case, the death of Naneferkeptah himself and his family; in the second case, simply humiliation on Satne's part – but the type is established in Egyptian Demotic literature as well as Greek.

Godfather Death (*AT* Type 332A)[10]

In a further situation, a mortal is summoned to the underworld in some sort of mistake, and becomes a revenant on being sent back to tell the tale. For example, in the Modern Greek tale *The Shepherd and the Three Diseases* (Megas 23):

> A man is summoned by Plague to deliver a sacrificial lamb to her house for his protection; the souls are represented in Plague's house by lamps; when there the new arrival sees that his soul is not due to die, but his brother's is. He runs off home. When he gets there, his brother dies.

For the presentation of the souls in Plague's house by lamps we can compare the parodic presentation in Lucian's other-world community of Lamptown,[11] where the author-cum-narrator claims to be able to meet his own lamp, and where lamps are executed by being put out (but again, his own is not). For the idea of a House of Plague we might compare the ghoulish *ecphrasis* in Ovid (*Met.* 8.788–808) of the abode of Hunger. The crux of the modern tale is as follows:

> 'There's my house', said Plague to him.
> They went in; the shepherd looked about him, and what should he see, but the whole house full of *kantelas* (oil lamps) hanging from the ceiling and shining as bright as stars. Some were full of oil to the brim, and some only half-full; there were also some just on the flicker, and others on the splutter, ready to go out.
> The shepherd ceased wondering at this to ask Plague: 'Tell me, what are all those *kantelas*?'
> 'Those,' Plague told him, 'are the lives of men. For as long as each man's lamp burns, he will have life. If it goes out, he will die'.
> 'Is my lamp among them?'
> 'Of course it is. Look there!'
> The shepherd looked and saw a lamp full to the brim with oil and shining so bright that it did one's heart good to see it. (He is able to return home to find the death of his brother).

Once more it is Lucian's *Philopseudes* that has an ancient working of the overall theme: a man has been summoned by Hermes as guide of the dead; when he gets to Hades, he finds that it is not himself but his next-door neighbour who has been called. He himself is taken back to the land of the living; then he hears the sound of mourning for the blacksmith next door. Here the vivid motif of the soul-candle in the oral tale is not used. Instead, Pluto in the underworld reads off the names of those who are to die; in Lucian's literary ghost stories those who administer the realm of the dead are literate.[12]

The self-sacrificing wife: Alcestis and her analogues (*AT* Type 899)

In the case of Alcestis it is the classical story rather than its modern analogues that can claim to be better known, and where the story does appear in folk tradition it is treated for obvious reasons as a folktale proper rather than as a childrens' story. Euripides' version is one of only two complete extended treatments from antiquity, though we can trace a considerable tradition in previous allusion or early fragments. The other is the so-called *Alcestis Barcinonensis* (Barcelona Alcestis), a late Latin poetic narrative of considerable sophistication, but clearly looking back to the already classic version of Euripides itself. The latter's handling is as follows:

> Admetus is granted the privilege of being able to offer a substitute for his death, thanks to his previous kindness to Apollo. His parents decline the proposition that they should volunteer to deputise for him, and Death is about to take him when his wife Alcestis volunteers. She is already being lamented on her deathbed when Heracles, a former associate of Admetus, appears and wrestles with Death, who is forced to give up his victim.

There is no difficulty in accepting Trenkner's case that Euripides' version already represents a literary treatment of a popular original.[13] There are a number of modern folktale treatments, and at least one important medieval one, which serves to stress the difference in perspective between a classical literary and a non-classical sub-literary version. The very elaborate, quasi-heroic version in the late medieval Turkish *Book of Dede Korkut* is told in an Islamic context:[14]

> Dumrul sees a dead warrior for the first time and proclaims himself mightier than death himself. Allah is furious, and sends the Archangel Azrael to take his soul. The Archangel comes as a bird, and is dismissed and mocked. He then causes the hero's horse to rear while in the form of an invisible spirit. Dumrul sees his folly and pleads for his life, but Allah will only spare it if a substitute is offered. His parents, too,

116

refuse. Only Dumrul's wife does not resist the onset of death, but encourages him; impressed, Allah orders the death of the refusing parents and transfers their remaining span of years to Dumrul and his wife.

There is no reason to suppose that 'Dede Korkut', the supposedly illiterate Bard of the Oghuz, had any knowledge of Euripides as such; and we can certainly point to the very early insistence in Sumerian mythological tales of producing a substitute for any of the already dead.[15] We should note, too, the warrior aspect of wild Dumrul. This is hardly prominent in Euripides, where Admetus is an out-and-out coward throughout; though he had in the previous part of the story been able to *pose* as an outstanding heroic champion at least, but only with Apollo's help.[16] The Muslim version concurs with an allusion in Plato's *Symposium* in which the gods send Alcestis back out of admiration. But Gantz may be wrong in assuming that this has more the air of an older version than Heracles' literal battle with Death himself (Thanatos) for her life, which certainly has a naively literal quality.[17] The tale is found as a folktale in the Near East still, both in Greece itself,[18] and in the early twentieth-century Armenian variant 'A Tale of Love';[19] and we can point as well to a fourteenth-century Yemeni Jewish text.[20] What is most subject to variation is the nature of the principal character's offence, which, in the case of the Jew, is no more than ousting a stranger from his 'own' place in the synagogue, and any reason is absent altogether in Euripides' version. The parents may also vary in their behaviour; their refusal is outright in Euripides and *Dede Korkut*, but both are prepared to volunteer until they feel death actually take a hold of them in Schwartz's Jewish version.[21]

The essence of the tale is also found in a lower cultural context as an anti-wife sick joke. In a much-compressed modern Egyptian story, a cowardly husband and proverbial fool Goha encourages his wife to dress in a coquettish way so that death will fall for her and take her first.[22]

The curious case of Philinnion (*AT* Types 307/407/425?)

The commonest motivation for coming back from the dead, or not going away in the first place, is the bond with a lover. We have a substantial fragment of a highly realistic ghost story quoted as the first of the miracle stories of Phlegon of Tralles:[23]

A lodger in a household discovers that the girl who comes to make love to him every night is in fact the ghost of the daughter of the household, dead for six months past; when disturbed by the intervention of the parents, the girl disappears for good; the fact that the corpse is found at the house while missing from the tomb serves to confirm the identification.

117

Hansen cites several folktale analogues, some of them quite close, but where the ghost is that of a man who comes to a woman,[24] not of a woman to a man. He accordingly classifies the tale with 'quest of the lost husband' tales cognate to *Cupid and Psyche*. This is one way round a tale which seems genuinely quite difficult to assign to any specific Aarne–Thompson category. On the whole I think it is closer to *AT* Type 307, where the gender is the right way round: Ranke's German tale 23 offers a similar outline:

> A girl is lying in a tomb, but comes alive each night to savage the guard. One night a handsome young soldier is due for the fatal task and he consults an old man about precautions. He hides from her in the church for three nights in a row, but at the end of the third follows the old man's instructions to bite her finger (an obvious sexual euphemism). She now becomes docile and the pair are able to marry.

Here again the tale is not a perfect fit, thanks to the happy ending. But there is a further variant, classified by Ranke as *AT* Type 407:

> A girl has become the bride of Death; he has taken her and she is lying in the tomb; a rose grows from the body and is plucked. The young man who plucks it notices that food disappears from his room; when he lies in wait, he sees that the rose has turned into a girl; after her further narrow brush with Death, he is able to marry the girl.
>
> (Ranke 1966: 27)

Once more a happy ending, but a better fit as far as it goes, despite the metamorphosis of the rose; this, too, might qualify as a parallel sexual euphemism to the pricking of the finger in the last example. Ranke notes the confinement of this version to Eastern Europe[25] – so that it would not be surprising for it to be told against a Macedonian background, as it is in the case of Philinnion. We might also note a number of cases where anecdotes about exorcisms refer to pairs, usually where the seducer, fiancé or husband has somehow been responsible for the death of the wife, and where the laying of the ghost of the one is related to the death of the other.[26]

A curious tailpiece to the idea of lovers beyond the grave is the occasional treatment of ghosts of fathers who disapprove of their offspring's love affairs; I point to one ancient and two modern examples. In Lucian's *Philopseudes* 14 the lover Glaucias' father Alexicles is summoned from beyond the grave by a professional Hyperborean necromancer to give his blessing to the match, which he does after some display of disapproval. There may be literary embellishment here, but the ghost of the angry father does occur in the popular tale: Squire Blount of Kinlet in Shropshire objects to his daughter's preferring a page-boy to a gentleman suitor, and continues beyond the grave to trouble daughter, page-boy and descendants;[27] or the ghost of Squire Boone of Norton Dawnay in Devon similarly disapproves of his daughter's marriage, and this time his opposition from beyond the grave culminates in her death.[28]

The Twelve Dancing Princesses (AT Type 306, The Worn-out Shoes)

The Grimms retold the story of a king who had either three or twelve daughters who strangely danced their shoes to pieces every night.[29] With the help of a cloak of invisibility, a soldier discovers that the girls enter an underground realm to dance with twelve bewitched princes. En route he is told by a mysterious old woman to take twigs from trees of silver, gold and diamonds as proof of his journey. He receives half the kingdom as a reward, and the hand of the youngest of the princesses. Afanas'ev prints a very similar version,[30] but the distribution of the tale is usually felt to be somewhat narrow and more or less confined to western Europe in the oral tradition. But once more ancient evidence will at least help to suggest otherwise.

What are we to make of the tale? At first sight there appears to be no ancient equivalent of the story, but one detail encourages further exploration. The hero has to pass on the way down to the underworld kingdom through a wood of gold, silver and bronze, and the breaking of branches alerts the girls he is pursuing. The Opies noted the bejewelled trees that meet Gilgamesh in the wonderland realm of Siduri after he has gone through the dark tunnel, but before he has crossed the waters of death;[31] but that is only one motif, and they were able to point to no classical version.

In fact the story *is* known, and in an only slightly elliptical early form: it is one of two stories told of the seer Melampous, and we might reasonably label this version 'the three revelling princesses':

A king, Proitos, offers Melampous a third of his kingdom for finding and curing either three or an indefinite number of mad princesses who roam loose on the mountainside under a curse from Hera or Dionysus. He refuses until the rate is raised to two-thirds, then he catches them in a cave above the Styx, purifies them and marries one of them.[32]

The underworld reference of the cave located specifically by Pausanias in the Araonian mountains above Nonacris and so above the Styx gives the story a proximity to underworld associations, as it has in the Grimms' version, though there is in this example no mention of the golden fruit or the helper. What is interesting is the way that roaming free under a Bacchic curse is translated into nineteenth-century terms as a 'secret ball'. The number of three rather than twelve princesses is also found in a variant reported by the Grimms.

But this is only a beginning. It is relatively easy to translate an underworld ball into a Bacchic rout. It is a more difficult leap, though, to translate the pursuit in the context of a ball or a wild romp into chasing an athletic girl in a race. Thanks to similarities of secondary detail, however, we can see the story involving the wild behaviour of the princesses presented differently in the story of Hippomenes or Meilanion (for the name itself, compare Melampous) and Atalanta.[33] Here, it is not a wild dance that the hero has to keep up with, but a footrace, although with the same penalties as in the modern fairytale – the losers die, the winner wins the princess herself. Propertius (1.1.9–14) alludes to a version in which the chase is through wild country rather than on a racetrack, and this detail offers a bridge between Melampous and Meilanion. In versions depicting Atalanta's footrace, the golden fruit are used again and interpreted slightly differently: an old woman tells the Grimms' hero to pluck the fruit from the branches as he goes past, and this holds up the princess; in the Atalanta story the hero is advised by Aphrodite and given three golden apples from her tree so as to distract the girl.[34]

The details of the Grimms' tale and the Melampous legend have an important bearing on a third and far more celebrated text: the sixth book of the *Aeneid*. There it will be remembered that Aeneas is a soldier who has to follow the aged Sibyl across the Styx, and that she, like the wild dancing women, is possessed by the god.[35] Aeneas has to pluck the Golden Bough as a passport into the underworld. Once there, he finds 'lost' women: dead heroines, including Dido (and he, too, will claim a kingdom and marry a princess after his expedition). If aspects of the *Aeneid* fit the story so neatly, what of the parallel episode in the *Odyssey*? Odysseus does not of course go to the house of the dead to meet lost women, but who does he find there when he arrives but a catalogue of women, *half of whom belong in some way to the Melampous legend*? The natural inference is that these three texts represent a variety of different angles on the theme of *Katabasis*, of which we can perhaps only piece together a partial version. It also reminds us that the catalogue of women in Book XI of the *Odyssey* may be an obvious interpolation in the return of a warrior from Troy, but the Grimms' form is a reminder that it might well be there because it belongs to a cycle of tales that fit a plucky and resourceful trickster like Odysseus.

A table will make clear the relationships so far:

Dancing princesses	Melampous	Meilanion/Hippomenes
Hero is set task:	Hero is set task:	Hero is set task:
he must find out where dancing princesses go (by following them)	he must rescue wandering princesses who go out and practice *machlosyne* (lewdness)	he must race running princess
unsuccessful suitors must die		unsuccessful suitors must die
He meets old woman who tells him to pick fruit from three metal trees		He meets Aphrodite who gives him three golden apples from golden tree
By plucking the fruit he holds up the dancers on three occasions		He holds the runner up by casting down the fruits

He goes down to the underworld	He catches up with them in a cave above the Styx	
He wins the princess and saves his life	He wins the princess and saves his life	He wins the princess and saves his life

There is a generally perceived sexual symbolism in an emphasis on 'wearing out dancing shoes'. This is a familiar euphemism for sexual activities over a wide range of popular literatures: girls may be doing even more than this and sleeping with demons or corpses in the underworld. The French version paraphrased in Andrew Lang's *Red Fairy Book* (no.1) has the sisters dancing in the underworld with the ghosts of their former suitors whom they in effect poisoned with their sleeping draughts. This would be parallel to the *machlosyne* ('unbridled behaviour') practised by the errant women in the Melampous tale.

One other connection arises out of the Melampous story and 'The Twelve Princesses'. The girls who go to a secret ball and leave the tell-tale traces of worn-out shoes come close to Cinderella characters. An important and imperfectly explored branch of the Cinderella complex is a group of male Cinderella stories ('Cinderello') in which the ball is a part of the story as usual, but where the hero breaks off twigs in woods of gold, silver and some third substance, and sacrifices (often a red) cow. Here Melampous prescribes the sacrifice of twenty oxen, and his analogue in the 'dancing princess' story breaks off these tell-tale distinctive twigs. Moreover Lang's French version has the hero grow the magic laurel trees and finally ask them for princely attire so that he can attend the underworld ball in his own person. We can suspect that the Cinderella story and the dancing princess complex overlap and once more may reflect different ways of relating the same basic material.

Rapunzel (*AT* Type 310)

The story of Rapunzel ('rampion') tends to be tied very closely to Grimms' *Fairy Tales*:[36] the chief characteristic is of a girl incarcerated in a tower from which a young suitor must rescue her, most characteristically by climbing up a ladder made from her hair. Frequently the sequel is an obstacle flight, and indeed it can be suspected that the story is only really a subtype of the obstacle flight tale-type itself. A more characteristic illustration than that of the Grimms' version would be Basile's, the tale of Petrosinella (*Pentamerone* 2.1). In making her flight with her rescuer, the heroine has first to gratify three animals – a dog, a lion and a wolf. The animals then repay their debt by helping the pair in the obstacle flight itself.

Once more we can point to an ancient version, and indeed one that is pre-classical in date. It is none other than the Late Egyptian tale *The Doomed Prince*,[37] a tale of which we do not have the ending, and which indeed requires the analogue of Basile and the Rapunzel type to show us what was likely to have happened.

The Prince of Egypt travels to the kingdom of Naharim beside the Tigris and woos the king's daughter, who is incarcerated in a tall tower. With a mighty leap he outdoes the opposition of other leaping youths. Despite the prince's supposedly humble birth, the king does eventually give him his daughter as arranged. But the prince was fated to die by a snake, a crocodile, or a dog. The snake is killed by the watchful wife; but the text breaks off just at the point where the dog has chased the prince into the custody of the crocodile, who instead of killing him enlists his support in the crocodile's battle with a water-spirit...(remainder lost).

This last incident would give the crocodile the same 'grateful animal' status as the wolf, the lion and the dog in the Basile tale. The story does only just edge itself into Greek literature as historical legend:[38] Diodorus (1.89) alludes briefly to the first king of Egypt, Menas, pursued by dogs (in the plural this time) to a crocodile, but does not offer us any more of the story.

Once enlisted tentatively into a tale-type, *The Doomed Prince* can help us with another modern tale discussed by Geneviève Massignon: 'the youth who was doomed to be hanged', to which she could assign no Aarne–Thompson number.[39] This tale, collected in French-speaking Canada and Madagascar, concerned a youth destined to hang at a specific point – which again seems to fall just after he has married; again, like the Doomed Prince, he dissembles humble birth. In this instance, the youth goes through the motions of being hanged, but only by angels who devise a kind of *Scheintod* after which he comes back to life and rejoins his new wife. This is not just pious hagiography – he has won his life by fervent prayer and devotion. It is none other than a survivor of the Greek tale of Protesilaus:[40] he too seems doomed, though our sources are not entirely clear about the nature of his fate. He incurs the wrath of the gods because he did not sacrifice at the building of his house; and the first man who jumped out of the boat at Troy was fated to die, a role for which he volunteered, and so he was killed; but his wife is able to persuade Zeus to allow him to come back for one night to rejoin her.[41]

We can see overall that a substantial cross-section of ghost- and underworld-related tales was already available in the classical world. Sometimes we can suspect that we have not quite the full picture: we are left wondering what fuller context might have surrounded the basic ghost-laying story, and we should like to know a great deal more about Melampous, Meilanion, and others of the kind. But on the basis of these and similar tales we are entitled to suspect that belief and local tradition about the interaction of the living and the dead would have been among the most resilient of popular traditions to survive the Ancient World. It is unsurprising in an area so dependent on conservative belief that the time gap should have made so little difference.

10

TWO HOMERIC TALES

The Cyclops and *Ares and Aphrodite*

The story of Odysseus and Polyphemus is the episode in Homer's *Odyssey* that is richest in comparative material, and its relationship to a number of folktale variants has now been examined thoroughly, if not always conclusively. But a number of issues remain to be explained: it is not so easy to see the larger context in which a Polyphemus story is likely to occur, while we are liable to lose sight of the literary aspects of Homer's handling amid a jungle of popular variants; and we might also wish to ask ourselves what some other such variants might look like when accorded more 'primitive' Epic handling than they receive from Homer.

In the case of this tale, *AT* Type 1137, we do not have to piece together spare parts of the tale from obscure mythographers: we have our fullest version at the very beginning of Greek literature in Homer's *Odyssey* (*c*. 700 BC). Hence there has been a long battle between those who see the Homeric tale as the fount of all other versions, or as at least a complicating influence on them because of its popularity, and those who see it as a specific and unusual telling of an already established tale.[1] And established it undoubtedly is in the repertoire of modern oral folktale at least: Oskar Hackman assembled 170 versions of the main tale and the story of the rarely related no-man type at the beginning of the twentieth century.[2] A handful of medieval literary and not-so-literary versions also provide rich comparative materials in addition to the oral examples.

It is worth noting that the tale of the Cyclops appears in certain specific contexts. There may be at least some significance in the fact that not only in the *Odyssey*, but in his next major appearance in surviving literature, the blinded giant appears in one adventure in a sequence of voyage narratives (as the third in the seven voyages of Sindbad the Sailor in the *Arabian Nights*). This in itself is a familiar fact, but one feature of the medieval Arabic narrative has not been stressed: the giant (here two-eyed) shares his island in the third Sindbad voyage with a tribe of hostile monkeys. That is a reminder that there is actually an intermediate text and rarely acknowledged version between the two renderings, seldom referred to in discussion of Polyphemus: Euripides' *Cyclops* (fifth century BC). As a satyr play this entails a chorus of sub-human, hairy, mischievous beings. If in Western tradition satyrs are more readily assimilated to horses or goats, their general appearance and mannerisms are not unlike those of monkeys either, and we are left wondering whether Euripides and the Sindbad author may not both be drawing on a context where the giant-blinding episode was combined with or juxtaposed to one involving satyrs. In the *Cyclops* tale, the satyrs assist Odysseus in his victory over the monster. One notes that Gilgamesh's companion Enkidu, who helps him with the slaying of the giant Humbaba, was also a mysterious satyr-like creature,[3] and that was long before our first Greek literature. It is well known that in the *Odyssey*, Athena is curiously absent from her normal role as helper, protector and companion of Odysseus; it may be that a less attractive creature was the traditional companion of the hero in this particular tale. We can be fairly certain that Homer's traditionally anti-magical, anti-fantastic presentation of stories that require magic or fantastic detail would have made such an option unlikely in the *Odyssey*.

The story also has further ramifications, appearing as it does in contexts other than those of the Homeric hero: it can be encountered in a Bellerophon-type narrative featuring a flying horse,[4] as well as in a sea voyage (*Odyssey* and *Sindbad*);[5] and the position of the Cyclopes in folktale needs in any case to be re-examined. The story of Galatea, Acis and Polyphemus, which emerges only in Hellenistic literature, is as much part of Greek tradition as the blinding of Polyphemus;[6] and we should ask whether there may have been a larger Polyphemus story overall of which we are only able to see separate parts. There was an alternative tradition in antiquity which makes the Cyclopes builders and skilled metalworkers,[7] and this latter at least would give rise to a tradition from time to time in surviving folktale of 'the Cyclops' gold'.[8] We should also test whether the blinding of the giant is related to the standard folktale accounts of 'giant-killer' stories.[9]

The outline of the modern popular tale can be set out as follows:[10]

1 A man encounters a cannibal giant in a confined space.
2 He uses what is available to blind the giant.
3 He escapes his confinement by means of a trick with an animal.
4 The giant nearly traps him by a counter-trick.

This is considerably more specific than the Aarne–Thompson summary of the story, but it underlines just how little is really needed to 'make the tale work'. The hero who blinds the giant does not actually need companions, and the giant does not need to have one eye only, though companions are useful to demonstrate in advance that the giant has cannibal intentions; and they are useful also to help with the blinding, which is considerably more difficult and less credible if the giant has two eyes. But two he does have in the Sindbad cycle, and elsewhere in oriental storytelling.[11] Wine is not necessary for the story either, and intoxicating the giant only helps the blinding; again it is dispensable, especially in cultures unfamiliar with or opposed to wine. (Hence it does not occur in *Sindbad*.) The No-man trick of the false name is not necessary either; it scarcely occurs outside the *Odyssey* and a curious group of Finnish variants, and is often invoked to show that Homer had combined tales into a version which has *not* generally entered the culture of popular storytelling.[12]

From time to time, too, in the modern tale the hero is able to free a prisoner or prisoners of the giant: his female princess captive may assist the hero in the blinding (Scottish, Frazer 1921: 3).[13] And many modern versions have a tail-piece in which the giant gives the hero a ring that identifies his whereabouts,[14] a motif naturally missing from the fairly natural colouring of the *Odyssey*, but itself very much at home in the normal world of fairytale, and perhaps just hinted at later in antiquity in a textually corrupt passage of Petronius.[15] But we could argue that the tailpiece in the *Odyssey* is actually an equivalent of just that component of the tale.[16] Instead of accepting a talking ring that will identify his whereabouts to his pursuers, Odysseus is tricked into giving away his real name, and into keeping the ship too close in to the coast; this then renders him liable to persecution by the Cyclops' father, Poseidon, as well as to the more imme-diate risk of the Cyclops' rock swamping the ship. This would be a good example where the *function* and position of a motif determines what it is parallel to, rather than its content. One notes, too, a variation which is deter-mined by whether the story has a land- or a sea-based setting: the Cyclops may be drowned when the talking ring is thrown into a river.[17]

The analogue to Polyphemus that has been most thoroughly studied is the tale of 'Basat and Goggle-eye' which forms the eighth narrative of the Oghuz tales in the medieval Turkish *Book of Dede Korkut*.[18] This, like all the other narratives in this Turkish collection, is a land-based version. It demonstrates better than most modern versions I have seen the capacity for fairytale horror: the monstrous one-eyed giant demands an enormous tribute of men and sheep, and has cooks to deal with it; blinded, he has a Samson-like attempt to bring his cave down about his tormentor (cf. the death throes of the Virgilian Cacus). Oddly, he turns out to be the foster-brother of his slayer Basat, and the foster-son of the Oghuz hero Uruz, whose name seems related to that of Odysseus himself (cf. Ulysses). His parentage, from a fairy and the lustful Oghuz shep-herd who raped her, makes him a local phenomenon, in contrast to Polyphemus, child of Poseidon, or the Hesiodic Cyclopes, children of Gaia and Ouranos. There is oddity, too, in the movement of the hero: there is more about the ring in the sequel episodes, which are very considerably extended into heroic slapstick: the Cyclops traps Basat in his treasure vault; the Cyclops' sword splits the hero's into two; Basat beheads the Cyclops with the latter's own sword.

As for the Homeric handling, it should be remembered that the essentials of the tale can be realised in a matter of a few lines: to fill most of the book the reciter can, or indeed must, adopt a leisurely approach. In much of the prelimi-naries the Homeric account is able to build up suspense, and yet still take any first-time listener off guard: first a mysterious note is struck with the sea mist over the area, causing the ships to beach blind on the neighbouring island, and the crews glimpse the smoke and hear the voices of the Cyclopes and their flocks (*Od*.9.142–148; 166f.). But any sense of foreboding is then relaxed; the neighbouring island is free of hunters, and goats roam freely; the primitive nature of the Cyclopes is inferred, in that we are told they do not build ships, or farm, and have laws only at family level (*Od*. 9.125–129; 108–115). Odysseus seems to drop a hint of foreboding on his own account, but when he addresses his crews he manipulates his fears in a more ambiguous way: his own crew will ascertain whether they are arrogant, wild and unjust or hospitable and god-fearing (*Od*.9.173–176). The crews themselves have forebodings about waiting for the Cyclops (as had Odysseus himself), but his hopes of a gift are not so misplaced: the organisation of the Cyclops' cave and pens is meticulous, and there is not the faintest hint of cannibalism – everything is neatly pastoral; only the size and noise of the Cyclops and the closing of the cave is ominous (*Od*. 9.213–249).

The idea of the men hiding under the bellies of sheep or disguised in sheep-skins is only necessary or possible where the context of the Cyclops is pastoral. Odysseus has himself clinging to the underbelly of the ram; often in the modern tale the hero and any companions put on sheepskin;[19] this too may go some way towards explaining the presence of satyrs on the Cyclops' island in Euripides *Cyclops*: if the Cyclops has prisoners who wear animal skins (goatskins would be more appropriate) then we have one possible explanation of how the prisoners can be 'read' as satyrs – shaggy goat-footed creatures, at least in later classical literature. Again the Odyssey naturalises by having Odysseus' crewmen bound to the underside of sheep rather than actually wearing sheepskins: it is quite an operation to flay a sheep in a confined space when trying to avoid the clutches of a blind giant – though Odysseus' solution would really work best where the sheep were perceived as gigantic as well (in fact he binds three together).

As to the giant-slayer aspect of the tale, we do have a case where Cyclopes are killed, not by a hero, but by a god: Apollo kills the Cyclopes who forged the thunderbolt that killed Asclepius, and is about to be thrown into Tartarus when Leto his mother intercedes: and the god has to mind the cattle of Admetus for a year.[20] The Cyclopes in that case were three earth-born giants released from imprisonment in Tartarus by Zeus (one notes a Basque version where the Cyclops is called Tartaro).[21]

Hackman emphasises the fact that Homer's tale seems to be compounded of two separate tales, a one-eyed monster-blinding tale, and one where the hero eludes vengeance by giving himself a trick name: the usual form is not Homer's No-man, but rather some permutation on the word 'self' ('Who is hurting you?' 'Myself is hurting me'...). It is useful to note the most frequent context of the 'Myself' folktale, Hackman's B form of the tale. It often occurs where a small boy sits at the fireplace and accidentally causes a spark which burns his fairy playmate, who has called herself Self, a name repeated by him; it may sometimes be down to her carelessness rather than his cunning that the confusion over the name occurs. When she shrieks, other fairies do not respond because of the ambiguity of the name, or the offender's apparent identity to her own. Sometimes the hero is roasting a duck on the fire, a context still closer to that required by the Polyphemus story. It should therefore be obvious enough why Homer, or any other storyteller, might be drawn to blend the two stories: the context of both tales is that the hero is hurting a supernatural creature by or with fire, and this coincidence would naturally encourage the two strands to converge.[22] The puzzle might rather be why this variant has apparently occurred so seldom. It is also of interest that the B form of the tale has a water-sprite or the like attracted by the hero: one might be tempted to think of the story of Galatea attracted by Acis, the enemy and victim of Polyphemus in his other appearance much later in classical literature.

The context of the Polyphemus story

There is some degree of consensus that the Polyphemus story must have existed independently of the *Odyssey*. It is therefore useful to note other contexts where it does occur as an episode or an inset tale as opposed to a single orally inspired story. We have already suggested the natural context in which the A and B forms of the tale would converge and overlap: stories where a defenceless but resourceful hero comes across a supernatural creature while in an enclosed space by a fire (with or without food to roast), and where the supernatural creature comes to be injured by fire.

We should note the obvious reason for the inclusion of the story in 'The Adventures of Sindbad' in the *Arabian Nights*: it seems easy enough to incorporate the tale as an episode in any string of voyage episodes by simply assigning the Cyclops a cannibal island. But there is nothing in the mechanics of the tale itself to imply or demand a maritime setting: it can look equally at home in the *Book of Dede Korkut*, set entirely in inland Turkey. We might note, however, that the traditional classical locations of the Cyclopes tend to be beside the sea, whether on the island of Sicily (for the Galatea episode) or on the mainland coast of northern Asia Minor (in the *Argonautica*).

We should note, too, a certain degree of resemblance between the overall 'package' of other-worldly episodes in the Sumero-Akkadian *Epic of Gilgamesh* and the *Odyssey*: both heroes encounter goddesses capable of transforming humans into animals (Ishtar and Circe); both are involved in the killing of divine cattle (Gilgamesh kills the Bull of Heaven; Odysseus's men kill the cattle of the Sun); both are somehow unhappy in the company of a voluptuous lady in an other-worldly paradise (Siduri and Calypso) after an underworld journey; both reach the home of a master mariner (Utnapishtim, Alcinous); and both 'miss' immortality (Gilgamesh fails to keep the plant Utnapishtim's wife had helped him to find; Odysseus rejects the offer from Calypso). One might reasonably suggest the same limited parallel between Odysseus' blinding of Polyphemus and the encounter of Gilgamesh and Enkidu with the giant of the cedar-forest Humbaba. He too is blinded, but only temporarily by the winds, and he is actually killed, as Polyphemus is not. But it is noteworthy that other Middle Eastern ogres *are* slain in the context of Cyclops-type stories. In *Dede Korkut* the Tepegoez is indeed killed after being blinded; a modern Armenian version likewise insists on such a detail; in *Sindbad* the murder of the monster is at least threatened, but not actually carried out. Mundy suspected that the overall context of the *Dede Korkut* version is really a giant-slayer tale (*AT* Type 300). Again there seems a natural degree of overlap and a natural tendency for such a group to assimilate the story.

At the other end of the chronological spectrum we can look briefly at the modern Armenian version just referred to, which has still clearer affinity with the giant-slayer type:

> A supernatural agent warns a young boy how to capture a magic horse which will take him to find the princess of his dreams, captured by a one-eyed giant Tapagoez. He masters the horse, finds from the girl that the only way to kill the giant is by taking out his eye, takes the girl to a kingdom where he insults the king, then marries the girl, now restored to her own royal father.

The natural affinity of this version is with the story of Bellerophon, whose tradition is firmly anchored in Asia Minor, and again with 'giant-killer' tales. It is interestingly padded out in much the same way as the *Dede Korkut* version with a string of slapstick episodes after the actual death of the monster, in a genuinely folk manner.

We might note the general laxity of a wide range of versions over just how confined the hero actually finds himself. In the *Odyssey*, the idea of a confined space is absolute and carefully insisted upon. There is no way that Odysseus and his remaining men can get out of the cave except by blinding the Cyclops. On the other hand, Euripides' *Cyclops* has Odysseus conveniently *outside* the cave, and the cannibalism against his men inside; he has to go back to save his men. We could argue that this unusual arrangement is really dictated by Greek staging conventions rather than by the internal dynamics of the story itself. The *Arabian Nights* goes to the opposite extreme of carelessness (among many other ineptitudes): Sindbad and his men seem to be able simply to walk out of the giant's palace, in spite of its formidable security door, but just come back again because they can find no shelter anywhere else on the island! The Armenian text has the hero so endowed with strength that he can roll and unroll the Tepegoez' great stone at will, and there is no real reason why he should bother to kill the giant at all as he can whisk the girl away on his magic horse apparently without fear of pursuit.

Lastly, we might point to the natural association of the Cyclops story with other cannibal tales. The medieval Latin in the *Dolopathos* collection (with the ring and the giant blinded by eye salve) is set as one of three robbers' tales, the other two concerning how the resourceful robber, having blinded the Cyclops, saves a mother and child from three ape-like monsters by masquerading as one of three thieves' corpses. They take a slice from his thigh, and are about to take more when driven off by a storm. One thinks of a ghoulish child sacrifice in Lollianus' *Phoinikika*; in both situations there is a complaint that the flesh is not right, but the Lollianus papyrus is far too fragmentary to establish whether this is 'our' story. Once more the presence of ape-like creatures in the vicinity reminds us of the monkeys in *Sindbad* and the satyrs in Euripides' *Cyclops*. And of course one notes that Homer's tale of Polyphemus is close to that of the cannibal Laestrygonians in *Odyssey* 10 (only the tale of Aeolus intervenes).

To sum up, literary and sub-literary compilations of tales will seize on the Cyclops story for any one of a number of reasons: as a travellers' tale, as a heroic giant-killing tale, as a cannibal story, as a story of encounter by the fire, or as a story connected in some elusive way with satyr tradition. We should not pretend to have exhausted or finally got to the bottom of its affiliations. One tell-tale detail will often serve as an indication of how the storyteller wishes us to view the tale. Euripides' *Cyclops* is the first version to imply some pecking order in which the giant eats his victims: he will go for the fleshiest and stoutest first; Sindbad's account follows suit. But Homer, with his need to insist from time to time on the heroic brawn of Odysseus, is silent and seems to give the Cyclops an entirely random choice.

Two modern Greek versions of the Cyclops story have a unique interest in that they do appear close enough to the *Odyssey* itself to have been derived from the same branch of oral tradition, or simply to have been reworked from a text of Homer in comparatively recent times; both do contain the unusual link between the blinding of the Giant and the No-man tale. The value of such exhibits is not of course to help in tracing the form of the tale back before Homer, which, if derived from Homer, they cannot possibly do, but to illustrate in the same way as the *Dede Korkut* version the differences between popular and literary values.

The Kerasund text translated by Dawkins (MGF4a) first appeared in a rare Pontic periodical in 1884. Here the Cyclops' opponents are only two in number, and they are genuinely shipwrecked sailors (the Homeric Odysseus only claims to be such). This makes for a very good motivation for waiting for the Cyclops: the pair are hungry, whereas Odysseus' crews have already been able to help themselves to sheep. The contrast in narrative approach from the *Odyssey* itself is immediately apparent:

> At last they found a cave. 'Let us go inside', they said, 'Perhaps we shall find something there.' Then they went into the cave, and what did they see? A great big bowl full of porridge and another still bigger bowl full of milk. Eagerly they rushed up to the bowls to eat something, but presently they said, 'And what if we eat and the man who owns the cave comes and is angry with us? What if he is an ogre and

129

devours us in his fury? Come, let us wait a little and then perhaps he will come, whoever he may be.' So they waited and waited and no one came, and they were so mad to eat that their eyes started from their heads. 'Come,' said they, 'let us eat just a little, and then we can again wait for a while, and if anyone comes, we can ask his pardon, and he will not do anything to us.' So said they. 'And then if there is any rain to fall, why, let it fall. Is not this better than to die of hunger?' So presently they ate a little porridge and drank a little milk and satisfied their hunger. How much did they eat? The bowls were enormous. Then they sat there and waited for the man who was the master of the cave.

This account of the waiting for the Giant would have been at home in *The Three Bears*, or any children's tale built round the idea of 'maybe just a little taste...'. But it contrasts very notably with the rather muddled motivation in Homer, where the logic of the situation demands a hasty retreat, but Odysseus' curiosity to see the Cyclops and the (characteristic) hope of gain delay himself and his crew against their better judgement. We could say that the Homeric version does deepen the character of the protagonist: he is naturally curious and avaricious; the two shipwrecked sailors are simply hungry and desperate. But Homer may have offered character development at the expense of the naive plausibility of the popular telling.

The popular version slips up, however, on the problem of where the action takes place: they are still outside the cave when they meet the giant, and yet after announcing his cannibal intent he seizes both and drags them in. The Homeric telling is much more convincing, with the crew trapped inside the cave before the Cyclops so much as sees them.

The popular version is constructed to highlight the issue of the name: one gives his real name, the other the name 'Nobody'; the Cyclops eats the one with the real name first, underlining the principle that to give one's actual name gives any evil force power over one; to give a false name or a name amounting to nothing denies such a power. This, too, is normally the point in the tale where the Cyclops will feel victims and select the fattest, leaving the cunning protagonist till later because he is thinner (as in Sindbad, for example); here it is as if the real name has somehow more substance than the false name. After the trick has been put into operation and the now blinded giant has summoned the fellow Cyclopes, there is an interesting embellishment: we are told 'The Cyclops would say no more to them; he was afraid too that they might find the man and devour him themselves.' This is good thinking on the part of storyteller and Cyclops alike: I suspect that it has arisen directly from the rather basic instincts of popular narrative, where who gets how much of what food looms larger than it does in Homer. Gluttony is more a matter for popular narrative than for Epic.

The rest of the version is unremarkable. The other text from Kerasund (Dawkins MGF 4b) does not contain the No-man episode, but abounds in folk-mannerisms of other sorts. It resembles the Nièvre *Red Riding Hood* (of almost the same date) in having the man-eating monster try to insist on the victim drinking blood; the older and wiser of the two companions surreptitiously disposes of the flesh he has pretended to eat – before the ogre starts cooking a dead man's hand on the fire. He creeps up on the pair in their sleep and slits the throat of the younger, a far cry from announcing his cannibal attentions in advance, before being blinded by the survivor in the usual way. Folk narrative does not spend time on simile, and therefore we have no carpenter with his adze to compare with Odysseus drilling the giant's eye: again folktale can have a vividly no-nonsense approach: 'Yerikas (cf. Ulixes) went up to him very quietly and squish! drove the spit into the ogre's eye'. Because there is no No-man story, there is no need to involve the other Cyclopes. But this version does, in a manner worthy perhaps of satyric drama:

> The ogres shouted to Yerikas: 'Come and let us have a dance and make merry.' The ogres made merry and so did he, but he was saying: 'O God, I hope they won't come near me!'

Dawkins gives no further context for this intriguing ending. It has the flavour common in Slavonic tales, among others, of involving the hero in festivities of some description, which often result in an avowal of truth/falsehood ('Some of the beer went down my face but none went into my mouth'). But the bizarre detail should leave us in no doubt of the tale's resilience in popular hands.

Ares and Aphrodite and an Egyptian magical variant

Although we have no direct literary ancestor of the blinding of Polyphemus, we do have a clearly earlier version of the story of Ares and Aphrodite in *Odyssey* 8 in an Egyptian Middle Kingdom story from no later than 1600 BC. The action is the stuff of novella rather than fairytale – an adultery detected and punished; but both versions have a strong magical element which justifies its inclusion with the latter. In both cases the tale is inset in a court entertainment containing a sequence of stories: the bard Demodocus recites the tale in the hearing of King Alcinous and the guest Odysseus himself; the Egyptian story is told at the court of Cheops by one of his sons, as the second of an indefinite number of wonder-tales.[23] The adultery is described in both texts as taking place on the property of the absent husband (in Hephaestus' house; in a pavilion in the official Ubainer's garden). The adulterer and the husband are contrasted in both texts, but in different ways: the contrast between the cripple Hephaestus and the handsome war-god Ares is implied in the first instance; the Egyptian tale has Ubainer contrasted in social status with the lover, a mere commoner. The informants are different: since the characters in the Greek tale are themselves divine, there is nothing odd in having the Sun himself as the informant to Hephaestus; in keeping with the realistic flavour of the Egyptian text it is Ubainer's steward who notices and tells his master. The adultery itself is handled in a carefree, matter-of-fact way in both texts:

> Ubainer's wife sent to the steward who looked after the [garden],
> To say, 'Have the pavilion in the garden made ready!
> Look, I'm coming to relax in it.'
> Then the pavilion was made ready with every good thing.
> [They] then went,
> and they made holiday with the commoner.
>
> (Parkinson 107f.)

> And (Ares) came into the house,
> and took her hand and called her name and spoke to her,
> Come here, my dear, let us take our pleasure on the bed.
>
> (*Odyssey* 8.290 ff.)

In both cases, too, the trap is magical or supernatural: Hephaestus contrives invisible bonds round the bed to hold the guilty couple until he can call the gods to witness. Homer exercises characteristic reticence about the details, in keeping with his general lack of interest in magic. But here the Egyptian interest in magic and magicians comes into its own. The adulterer is in the habit of bathing in a pool after the act, and Ubainer contrives a magic crocodile, made out of wax but animated into a real beast, which holds the adulterer under water for as long as seven days until the master is sufficiently free of official duties to expose him to the Pharaoh and call off his magical pet. In the Greek text reaction is light-hearted and mixed: Hermes suggests to Apollo that he would gladly change places with Ares beside the naked Aphrodite; there is considerable financial haggling over the dowry and the question of the adulterer's fine, while Aphrodite discreetly retires to suitable privacy on her release. Nothing worse can in any case threaten the gods, who are immortal and indestructible, but highly susceptible to ridicule. The Egyptian climate is much more unequivocal: the crocodile is animated once more to claim its victim, the lower-class lover, this time for good, and presumably he simply eats the offender without further ado. And Ubainer's wife is burned, with no further fuss.

Once more the Egyptian story underlines what has long been felt in the case of the Polyphemus story: that magical operation is minimised in Homer; and that the Homeric poems reflect or adapt material that is much older. The Middle Kingdom text belongs to the first half of the second millennium BC, over eight centuries before the supposed date of the *Odyssey*. It also underlines the difficulty of categorising these episodes along modern generic lines: the Egyptian text seems to lie tantalisingly between adult fairytale and novella; Homer's version is much closer to the latter.

11

SOME MORAL PARABLES

*The Pied Piper, The Three Wishes, Rumpelstiltskin,
The Singing Bone*

Some magical tales are clearly constructed to articulate simple moral messages
rather than to further the fortunes of a hero or heroine; and such wisdom tales
are almost by their very nature destined for migration. Traces of two of the
following types have been noticed in antiquity; the others, so far as I am aware,
are presented for the first time.

The Pied Piper (Christiansen 3061)

There has been little attempt to treat this tale as other than a migratory legend
of limited distribution: it is customary to think of the Pied Piper as being 'of
Hamelin' even in the title of the tale and hence there has been no incentive to
trace the origin back before the year 1284 AD to which local Brunswick tradition assigned a mass exodus of children.[1] The one British instance known to
Briggs seems at least in part derived from Robert Browning's nineteenth-
century literary verse version (1842), though it has a significant divergence in
that its piper leads the children off through the woods, not into a cave in the
mountainside, and there is an alternative subtype with the piper ridding a
locality of snakes, not of rats (*ML* 3060). The two variants can be presented as
follows:

> A locality is suffering from an infestation of animals; the authorities call
> in an outsider to rid them of the menace, but renege on the bargain;
> the professional animal-charmer rids them of their children in revenge
> for their treachery.

At least half the tale, or rather parts of the two halves, are indeed found in
antiquity. The first tale in Lucian's *Philopseudes* (11–13) relates to a Babylonian
'Chaldaean' called out to cure a snakebite. In addition he summons all the
snakes of the locality and causes them to disappear, but one snake is too slow
from age and has to be summoned separately. Here we have the cure of a
plague of snakes, and we are reminded of the detail in Browning's version of the
Piper where one little boy does not disappear because he is too slow and does

not catch up. But there is no fee, and no 'second strike' against the children of those who default on paying it. These are simply ingredients of the tale.

An alternative approach is to look at pied pipers or other musicians in antiquity who take revenge for a broken bargain. The obvious candidate is Apollo, who contracts with King Laomedon to assist with the building of the walls of Troy (to his musical accompaniment). When Laomedon defaults on the payment, Apollo retaliates with an unspecified plague; this is to end if one of the Trojans' daughters is sacrificed. The Trojans send their children off to avoid selection (Servius on *Aeneid* 1.550). Heracles rescues the eventual victim, Hesione, but is likewise cheated of his reward and kills Laomedon and all but one of his sons. If we look further into the plague, we note that previously Apollo has been associated with a plague of mice on the initial site of Troy.[2] Apart from a minor rearrangement in the order of events – the contract was for building work, not for pest control – we have everything here: the musician-worker who also controls mice punishes a broken contract by getting rid of most of the children – and we have the little boy who gets away and lives to tell the tale. Traditions differ on the survivor: either he wished to honour the broken bargain, or he was very young. Either way 'the one that got away' was the future King Priam. We should also note that there is *something* odd about Apollo's costume: Hyginus has him sneered at by Niobe for a *vestem deorsum* – a 'down-below outfit'? – but unfortunately at a point where the text is damaged (*Fab.* 9.2). In Grimm, the piper is actually given the name 'Brightman' on account of his coat: the term naturally fits Apollo regardless of costume.

A further less precisely attested candidate for pied piper would be Dionysus in one of several adventures of at least the right pattern. The eccentrically dressed roving musician is initially rebuffed and, in retaliation for a rebuff (usually against the acceptance of his rites, rather than pay for pest control), will contrive fatal mischief of unpredictable kinds; and his appearance is sometimes presented as parti-coloured. He is the first deity attributed with the wandering through the woods of the daughter of King Proitos, an incident sometimes multiplied into the wanderings of all the women of Argos. One notes the tradition in Apollodorus in which the price is not right for Melampus to cure the plague and the condition spreads to more women, so that the high fee has to be paid after all. But that, we might argue, is not quite the same as having the King of Argos default on a promised payment. Euripides' *Bacchae* might also be invoked: following Pentheus' rejection, Dionysus takes the women off with him to the woods and the mountains, though of course that is the least of the punishment in store for the recalcitrant king. It would certainly be typical of folktale tradition to expurgate the exodus of loose women into one of children. But the whole story is found encased within the circumstances of the biblical Exodus narrative (*Ex.* 5.1–12.30), of an indefinite date BC. Moses is asked by Pharaoh to call off a plague of frogs in return for allowing the children of Israel to sacrifice in the wilderness. The Egyptian king reneges on the bargain (the pattern is repeated many times for a variety of other plagues). In retaliation

Moses calls down a plague against the firstborn, and each Egyptian family loses a child. There is even an introductory snake-removing episode, like that in Lucian: Aaron's rod can turn into a snake; Egyptian magicians turn their rods into snakes; but Aaron's rod eats up all the rest. We can hardly object that Moses is neither pied nor a piper.

The Three Futile Wishes (AT Type 750)

The Opies trace this tale back beyond the modern period and manage to take a version of it as far back as the Indian *Panchatantra*,[3] but they make no reference to classical versions, of which we can trace a considerable variety within a relatively small number of texts.[4] The modern fairytale generally entails the granting of three wishes by a supernatural agent in return for some act of kindness; the wishes are then used up accidentally or foolishly, the last wish being required to restore the mischief done by the first two:

> A poor woodcutter obeyed the wishes of a fairy and did not cut down her tree: she granted him three wishes. He fell asleep by the fire, but on waking wished for a pudding. This was granted and his wife wished it stuck to his nose; he now had to wish for the pudding to be detached from his nose, and so was only a single pudding better off.
> (Briggs *DBF* 2.309f.)

The instance from the *Panchatantra* entails a poor weaver who foolishly wishes for an extra pair of hands and two heads in order to work faster – only to be killed as a monster; and so is based on a single wish. The classical version par excellence is the tale of King Midas and the Midas touch:

> King Midas of Phrygia does a good turn to the god Dionysus by returning his old slave and tutor Silenus, whom Midas had caught by the stratagem of drugging his drinking water. He is offered a wish, and chooses that everything he touches will turn to gold. Dionysus reluctantly consents, and Midas finds that because the wish works so well he cannot eat as his food solidifies whenever he touches it. He has to ask the god to take away his gift, so that he is the same as before.[5]

Here we have a more aristocratic version: kings unthinkingly wish for gold where peasants wish for puddings. Dionysus plays the part of the supernatural agent, and so here is the equivalent of the grateful fairy. The mechanism is actually identical, though the terms are put differently: in terms of the fairytale, it is as if the god grants the king two wishes rather than one, so that the second has to be used to cancel the ill effects of the first. Midas is also attributed with the punishment (by Apollo) of ass's ears for wrongly judging a musical competition; these are permanent in Ovid's version (a separate but contiguous story).[6] On

135

the analogy of the modern tale, it could just as readily have been a part of the
'foolish wishes' story: if Midas were to receive three wishes from Dionysus, he
might ask for gold; his angry wife, like the peasant's wife, might in anger wish
him a pair of ass's ears. The third wish would cancel the Midas touch but leave
the ears intact. But I can find no trace of such a version.

There was also a popular variant, still to be seen in the context of fable. In
Appendix Perottina 4, preserving materials from the first-century fabulist
Phaedrus, we have a Latin verse tale in which Mercury offers a wish to each of
two women who have offered him shabby hospitality: the first wishes her baby
to grow a beard as soon as possible – which he proceeds to do immediately; the
second, a prostitute, asks that whatever she touches may follow her. She touches
her nose and draws it out to an impossible length, like the sausage on the end
of the wife's nose in modern examples.[7]

The irreversible wrong wish: *The Sibyl in the Bottle* (*AT* Type 555)

The sibyl was granted immortality but not eternal youth (Ovid *Met.* 14.130ff.)
as a bribe by Apollo in turn for sexual favours (which were refused). We find
Petronius' Trimalchio describes how he saw a sibyl in a bottle, saying 'I wish to
die, I wish to die' (*Sat.* 48.8). Smith *ad loc.* quotes two modern folktale
versions already known to Frazer:

> A girl in London prayed to live for ever, and still hangs in a basket in a
> church and eats a roll every St John's day.
> A merry woman with all she could desire still wished to live for ever
> and, after a hundred years, began to shrivel, but could not die. She is
> placed in a glass bottle and hung in the church of St Mary in Luebeck,
> and stirs once a year.

The latter tale, in particular, corresponds to a festival described in Ovid *Fasti*
3.523ff. and celebrated on the Ides of March: the common people pray for as
many years as they drink cups, and would live as long as Nestor or the sibyl if
the charm only worked. Ovid adds the picture of a drunk old woman dragging
home a drunk old man (543). The implication is that for all their vain wishing
they revert to the wretches they started out. None of these cases mentions the
agency of supernatural granters of wishes. But these too occur: a fairy in an
English tale known to Briggs ('The Old Woman in the Vinegar Bottle'); or a
wish-granting fish in two of the Grimms' tales (1992: 19 and 85).

The English version has an old woman in a vinegar bottle wishing improve-
ments in her lot, till the fairy granting the wishes refuses to make her pope, and
has her revert to the bottle. How she came to be there in the first place is not
explained. What we see here is a version where the wishes are extended and the
opening truncated, or indeed lost altogether; the German version (Grimm

136

1992: 19) omits the bottle altogether, but has one more wish, that the greedy woman be like God and make the sun and moon rise. The former ambition should be an allusion to the ultimate ancestor of the story, that of Tithonus, once more granted immortality but not eternal youth by Zeus, to be eventually shut up in a room by his lover Eos/Aurora, mumbling unintelligibly or changed into a grasshopper. Tithonus did indeed cause his lover to rise every morning, she actually being the dawn itself.[8]

Castles in Spain (AT Type 1430)

This tale-type involves a complex sequence of futile wishes in a short compass, and each dependent on an initial stroke of luck. Usually a poor man acquires a genuine possession, and proceeds to daydream of all the others it will bring him; but at a point where his dream brings out his own greed or arrogance, he does something (a sudden movement, a kick, or the like) which destroys the basis of his wealth for good. Briggs cites an English ballad version:

> A foolish boy boasts of the wealth he will gain from putting eggs he will buy under his hen to hatch and so transforming his fortune. His mother asks whether he will be too grand to know her. On his saying that he will be too grand to know himself, the angry mother gives him a blow which spills the milk he was to sell to obtain the eggs.

In *Aesop* 77 Jacobs already has a close version:

> A foolish milkmaid dreams of the beautiful clothes she will buy with the profits from her milk pail. A careless gesture, as if of already wearing the imaginary clothes, upsets the milk pail.

There are a number of other examples in the context of popular moralising which feature 'the broken dream' (Lucian, *Hermotimus* 71):

> Those who fabricate an unreal blessedness for themselves have just the same experience, surrounded by wealth, digging up treasure, kings heaven-blest for some other reason – all this the goddess Wishing (*Euche*) easily manages, great in her gifts and never saying no, whether you want to fly, to be as big as a Colossus, or to discover whole mountains of gold; and if a slave interrupts their reverie with a question on day-to-day necessities – with what he is to buy bread, or what he is to say to the landlord who has been waiting ever so long with a demand for the rent, they are so angry with him for taking all those good things away with his troublesome questions that they come near to biting off his nose.[9]

Three Futile Wishes: Lucian, *Navigium* (*AT* Types 1626, 1920)

As we have noted above, foolish wishes easily lend themselves to organisation in the popular format of groups of three. There is a more complex popular story in which:

> Three men going on a pilgrimage possess an object of food in common (such as a loaf of bread). Rather than divide it, they agree that it should go to the one who has the best dream. The first dreams of going to heaven, the second of going to hell; the third dreams that the other two will not come back from their respective destinations, and so eats the bread anyway.

On such a formula Lucian offers in dialogue form the following story:

> Three philosophers who are walking from the Peiraeus to Athens agree to reveal their respective wishful daydreams. No reward is specified for the winner. The first wants a corn ship laden with gold (and a beautiful boyfriend aboard thrown in); the second, a military career outdoing that of Alexander the Great; the third, a set of magic wishing rings like that of Gyges. Their waggish companion Lycinus pours scorn on the absurdity of all three dreams: the ship will sink; the great world conqueror will die; the man who is clever enough to wish in effect to be god is no more than a greedy fool. Lucian is wiser than all of them, since he does not indulge in stupid dreams.

There may also be an element here of the contest in lying (*AT* Type 1920), a subject on which Lucian is elsewhere expert.

Rumpelstiltskin (*AT* Type 500)

The story-type officially known as 'The name of the helper' seems not to have been sighted before the Renaissance, and only with the Grimms (no. 55) does the familiar and fairly standard form of the tale emerge:

> A strange mannikin performs spinning for a young girl forced through an idle boast to spin yarn into gold for a greedy king. The mannikin does so on condition that he shall have her first child – unless in three days she can find his name. The name is overheard at the eleventh hour, and the girl is able to confront him with it: 'Rumpelstiltskin'. Recognising the trick, he stamps his foot with disastrous consequences, splitting himself in two.

A number of variations are found, mainly on the name itself, often given a jingling quality ('Tom Tit Tot' in most English versions), but not always

('Whuppity Stoorie' in Lowland Scotland). The Grimms themselves had an animal name in the sixth of their seven versions, *Flederflitz* ('batflit'). But other variations are found in the structure of the story. A more risqué version reported from Cornwall has the stranger's condition for helping the squire's wife Duffy, that after three years she *herself*, not her child, is to be his;[10] and it emerges clearly enough later in the tale that he is the devil – or rather the chief devil, since his name is neither Lucifer nor Beelzebub but their more powerful colleague Terrytop. In this version the squire to whom the wife is married goes out to a witches' gathering to overhear the name, and other versions also multiply the little people who help with the spinning. A characteristic structural feature not noted in Aarne-Thompson's analysis is that the crucial information on the name is overheard sung in interspersed verse.

Carl von Sydow produced two contributions using the modern European versions and concluded, first, that the tale had originated in Scandinavia, then, that it had spread from the British Isles.[11] Whatever the direction in the West and North European spread of the tale, the employment of a stratagem to hear a supernatural creature's divine name is not new, and neither is this tale.

The crucial information is contained in a single passage of Dio of Halicarnassus' *Roman Antiquities* (1.68) that the wife of King Dardanus of Troy, Chryse ('Gold-girl'), had been instructed in the mysteries of the *Megaloi Theoi* and brings the gifts of Athena consisting of their *hiera*, including the heavenly talisman the Palladium, as her dowry to the king. He institutes the worship of these gods in the mysteries of Samothrace (renamed Dardania),[12] *but keeps their names secret*. The *Megaloi Theoi* were identified as early as Herodotus with the Cabiri, usually a pair of deities of non-Greek origin, and their rites were (at least by Hellenistic times) equated with those of the Cretan Curetes or the Salii: the implication would be that they practised wild dancing including leaping and stamping. We have just about all we need in this information alone. Here we have a wife whose name itself seems to carry the promise of wealth at the point of her marriage; she is already acquainted with mysterious outsiders *with secret names* (conveniently known to us thanks to a scholiast on Apollonius of Rhodes). The leaping and stamping appears in the fairytale when Rumpelstiltskin is spied upon leaping at his secret den (again appropriate to the context of mysteries); and stamping occurs when in his rage at the guessing of his name the Grimms have him stamping the ground so as to split into two. As so often, we have the right sort of context and what looks like half the story: a 'goldwife' and her mysterious helper with the ineffable name. As the Cabiri were fertility deities, it is not absurd that they should claim the first-born child of Chryse, for which their own services might have been responsible; and we should certainly have the motivation for Dardanus' wishing to accommodate them in a special sanctuary if they look after his 'Goldgirl' (the folktale form of this is that the 'goldgirl' is locked up in a room and required to produce the golden yarn). Where the *Megaloi Theoi* are equated with Greek deities, the equation is with Pluto (Axiokerses) and Hermes (Kadmilus) – just right for the

SOME MORAL PARABLES

devil connections of the villain. What is lacking is the vital mainspring of the story: the pressure on Princess Chryse to guess the name of her demonic deities in return for their part in securing her marriage.

We have a second, much less satisfactory 'take' of what seems, as far as it goes, to be a second version of the same story. A girl, Chryse ('Goldgirl' once more), is the goddess of the island of that name. She is in love with Philoctetes ('Possession-lover'), the Greek hero, and he sustains a foot injury from the snakebite at her shrine. A further version of the injury, contained only in Servius, has the snakebite connected with Philoctetes' stamping the ground as a way of divulging the secret of where his master Heracles' ashes are buried. Without the version in Dio of Halicarnassus, we should probably not even try to make sense of this one. But with the plausibility of Dio's materials as most of a Rumpelstiltskin tale, what have we here? A girl of the same name, a greedy fellow betraying his own unique secret and damaging his foot by an ill-advised stamp on the ground. There is something of the fairytale here, too, though we hardly know enough to make sense of it. It is only when we come to a third ancient version that we can connect the girl, the snakebite and the ineffable name with any real confidence:

> Isis wishes to increase her powers and needs to know the secret name of the sun-god Ra. She finds it out by making a poisonous snake bite the god; he treads on the snake and his pain is such that he has to agree to disclose the secret name to her alone, so that she heals him, but in so doing comes into possession of the power she seeks.[13]

We can best see how the versions are related from the following table:

Chryse has contact with Cabiri with hidden names	Chryse meets Philoctetes, the only man who knows where Heracles' ashes are hidden	Isis needs to know the secret name of the sun-god Ra
She has palladium and sacred objects associated with the Cabiri		
With these as dowry she marries Dardanus		
Dardanus accepts the Cabiri mysteries		
He does not disclose their names		
	She sends snake to bite foot of Philoctetes	She sends snake to bite foot of Ra
In their dances they leap and stamp the ground	Philoctetes stamps the ground and is poisoned	
His city of Troy is safe so long as Chryse's dowry the Palladium is there	The Greeks gain the power of Heracles' ashes to sack Troy	She gains the magical power of Ra's name

140

What the comparison seems to tell us is that Servius' tale is a trace of some lost Graeco-Roman version where not Heracles' bow and arrows, but his ashes, have to be found to bring about the fall of Troy. If we can regard the two versions of Chryse as one and the same, we have nearly the complete tale. But as matters stand we should perhaps be content to remain as puzzled as we are by the mysterious Cabiri themselves.

The other version that can be recognised from antiquity is partly submerged in anti-philosophical satire in Lucian's satiric dialogue *Fugitivi* (mid-second century AD). As so often, it requires a slight adjustment of angle, but almost all the required data of the fairytale is there in some form.

> A man is 'sallow, with a close crop and a long beard, with a wallet hanging from his shoulder and a short cloak, cantankerous, uneducated, strident, and abusive' (*Fugit.* 27). He belongs to 'a pestilential tribe of men, for the most part slaves and labourers, who...[in childhood] spent their time slaving or labouring away, or learning the sort of trades you would expect such fellows to learn – leatherworking, building, having to do with fuller's tubes, or *carding the wool to make it easy for women to work and wind, and easy to draw off when they twist yarn or spin thread* (*Fugit.* 12). He is received as a guest in the house of a married couple, masquerading as a philosopher, and runs off with the wife of his host. The husband goes in search of her and meets Hermes, out in search of such rogues. In order to get the missing wife back they have to raise a hue and cry against the villain *by name*. Hermes tries a few names suggestive of greed or wealth (including Polyctetes, 'Much-gain', cf. Philoctetes), but without success (ibid. 26). By chance the searchers meet a slave-owner who *does* know the name, and they also overhear the captured wife singing about him in Homeric verses (he is a Thersites, a threefold dog, etc.). The villain is captured and says little more than the jingling *Ototoi, Papapaiax*. When he is found his purse is examined: it contains gold instead of bread or lupines. The odious creature is sentenced to death by torture, and the wife restored to her husband.

Is this 'our' Rumpelstiltskin? It is a little difficult to unravel the action from a dialogue so heavily laden with rhetorical diatribe, but the plot is indeed close to that of the Cornish version noted above. The wife herself, not her first child, is the prize to which the stranger has already laid claim. And she cannot be found again until the offender who has claimed her can be named. The name is of the animal variety (Cantharus 'Beetle', compare the Grimms' sixth variant, 'Bat'); but his one line of speech is largely made up of jingling lament *Ototoi, Papapaiax* (*Fugit.* 33). We might suspect, though there seems no way of proving it, that that is more likely to have been his name in some more popular version of the story. But it is the standard description of the Cynic philosopher that coincides very neatly with what we might expect for the other-worldly stranger: he is not said to be little or old, but is bearded and disagreeable; he is later described as a Thersites, the proverbially misshapen Homeric misfit. We even have the god Hermes, an appropriate fairytale figure, to fail to guess his name.

We might still feel entitled to be less than convinced: the tale has to be awkwardly unscrambled, and we do not find Cantharus actually helping the woman or producing the gold from the spinning, though he seems to have a slave's training in helping female tasks. In spite of the divine machinery in the story, every effort seems to be taken to keep the human actions at the level of the realistic and commonplace rather than the fantastic and magical. But there is an important clue in the name Cantharus itself. The Cantharus was the Egyptian scarab beetle, a symbol of the sun and its capacity for resurrection and regeneration. And this points us directly to the mythological Egyptian story already cited where the 'secret name' is central: Isis has to know the beetle-god's secret name, and poisons his foot to obtain it. And in the Graeco-Roman world, cantharus/scarabus would have overtones of Egyptian magic and there-fore of sinister un-Hellenic activity. But Hermes would indeed not know the name of a creature who represented an 'ineffable one'. It can therefore be said with some confidence that the tale of Rumpelstiltskin *did* exist in the ancient world, and that Cantharus is indeed the secret name in one Greek version of the story. We should perhaps suggest that in a good many of the other cases there is some consistency about the name. If the senior of the *Megaloi Theoi* is equated with Pluto, then his name has overtones of wealth, as has Philoctetes, and Hermes' guess for Cantharus' name Polyctetes. The first name to appear in modern tradition in a complete tale is Madame L'Héritier's 'Ricdin-Ricdon'. Jingle aside, we can translate it as 'Richgift', yet another version of the same.

We should, of course, point to a partially parallel case where a curious crea-ture demands the answer to a supposedly insoluble question to spare the life of a child: the riddle of the sphinx that forms part of the ancient Oedipus legend *does* provide the vital mainspring missing in the Chryse story. And the sphinx itself curiously corresponds to the riddling identity of Cantharus overheard in Lucian's story just noted (a threefold monster, consisting of dog, she-goat and lion, in this case *Fugit.* 30). The circumstances differ in that the sphinx in the Oedipus story has not provided any services in exchange for the lives of the young men of Thebes; her attack is usually presented as a punishment for a transgression of Laius. However, the speed with which it self-destructs when Oedipus solves the riddle corresponds to the promptitude with which Rumpelstiltskin meets his end. Again, there is a significant foot injury in the tale, but attached to the propounder of the puzzle in Rumpelstiltskin, to its solver in the Oedipus tale. We are left, as so often, with the feeling that we need another piece at least before we can get an overall view of the puzzle.

The Singing Bone (*AT* Type 780)[14]

In some cases, a folktale or folktale element has been partially rather than fully recognised in an ancient example. The Grimm version of *The Singing Bone* has the following outline:

> A king promises his daughter in marriage to the man who could kill the wild boar that is laying waste his country. A simple kindly boy kills the boar, but his older brother murders him, buries the body, and lays claim to the princess. Years later a shepherd makes a flute from a bone he has found in the sand, and it sings a song that reveals the murder. The shepherd takes the singing flute to the king, and the older brother is executed.
>
> (Grimm 28)

The opening of this sequence is quite clearly identical with the Greek legend of the Caledonian hunt. There the hunt leads to murder and a quarrel over a woman. Meleager usually murders his uncles (as in Ovid *Metamorphoses* 8.437–444), not his younger brother (but in Hesiod Fr. 25 MW Toxeus is a brother); and the quarrel in Ovid is over Atalanta's share of the booty, not her hand in marriage. What seems to clinch the resemblance is, oddly, the point where the versions seem to differ. The folktale murderer is punished by a magic hidden stick-like object of whose effect the criminal himself can have no knowledge; similarly, in the Meleager tale, the murder is punished by a magic stick, in this case put in the fire by his mother Althaea (8.451–525). Both endings clearly rely on folkloric devices: a 'cranes of Ibycus' motif in the folktale, an 'external soul' in the classical legend.[15] Grimm has a little man giving the innocent brother the advice on how to kill the boar; the guilty party is punished by being put in a sack in a river.

Crane offers a widely differing modern Italian version: two brothers kill a third for a griffin's feather to heal the king;[16] there is no princess. Here we have a reminder of how soon a related tale can become unrecognisable; the interesting point, however, is that the guilty brothers when found out are burned, as Meleager is by the sympathetic magic of the firebrand.

The more general history of Meleager in Greek mythology emphasises the similarity to the murderer role: Meleager is a son of Ares and Althaea. In *Iliad* 9 he kills the brothers in a war after the hunt; the Grimms' version tends to presuppose a private hunt rather than a public war or a public brawl over the boar-hide. Ovid's treatment of the moral balance is different: in particular he exploits the pathos of the murderer Meleager's death, rather than the justice of his punishment.

We should note a degree of resemblance between the Meleager tradition and related material to the earliest Egyptian *Two Brothers* story, and its analogue, the tale of Peleus. The brother Bata has an external soul, like Meleager, housed in this case in a pine-tree; when Bata's divine but treacherous wife finds herself a more royal match, she asks her Pharaoh to have the tree cut down.[17] Kakridis cites a further example in which a sister-in-law in love with the brother kills her husband by having the log put in the fire.[18]

The tale has been assigned a tentative origin in Belgium in the monograph treatment by Mackensen, who recognises the possibility of polygenesis for so simple an idea.[19] Stith Thompson endorsed this view, emphasising the possibility of an independent tradition in central Africa.[20] It is difficult to see Meleager's murders as unconnected to *The Singing Bone* tale: the inclusion of the boar-hunt in Grimm links the modern European to at least one ancient version, and makes it difficult to claim any more than a local subtype for modern Belgian examples. But again we cannot claim to have established an obvious archetype. The story of 'murder will out' may be nearly as old as murder itself, and does not need a tell-tale object. The voice of the murdered Abel's blood already 'cries to God from the ground' in Genesis 4.10, with yet another cause of jealousy, a superior form of sacrifice.

These examples, then, serve as a reminder that fairytale mechanisms extend beyond the fortunes of individual heroes or heroines and their quests to simple and indeed not-so-simple 'wisdom' tales. The antiquity of the types seems beyond doubt, though both the moral meaning and the reconstruction of *Rumpelstiltskin* must remain elusive. But it does seem clear, if only from Lucian's odd version, that women would resort to the help of cantankerous bearded assistants long before the industrial revolution gave new meaning to this ever more intriguing tale-pattern.[21]

FAIRYTALE INTO ROMANCE

In a number of chapters on the ancient versions of fairytales we have noticed that some of our clearest and some of our most complex examples turn up not in short mythographers' summaries, but in tales long enough to be described as romances in their own right. Several of these we might most conveniently describe as novellas; others seem long enough to be advanced as full-blown novels. Our first example was quite unexpectedly *Joseph and Asenath*, which no one had suspected hitherto of being a Cinderella, but which is generally now accepted as a novel or novella. Equally clear is the case of *Chaereas and Callirhoe*, which we have seen as an exceptionally full instance of the *Innocent Slandered Maid*. We have also vindicated the claim of the central tale of Apuleius' *Golden Ass*, *Cupid and Psyche*, to its characterisation by the author himself as an *anilis fabula*. We have found that one ancient novel, that of Chione ('Snow-girl') actually carries the very name of a fairytale heroine. Yet even where scholars have translated the title as *Snow White*, they have not expected to find the fairytale and the problem has been allowed to go without investigation. We have found that three out of the four fragments substantiated or suspected have thematic connections with one or other of the two principal Snow Whites. And we have noted that Xenophon of Ephesus' story, though much more problematic, has the names of principal characters and a substantial part of its plot convergent with the same tale of *Snow White*.

On the basis of these examples alone we should already be noting the high proportion of our existing small collection of ancient romances that show plot affinities to well-known fairytales. But when we turn to the remainder of the ancient novels, we find a similar picture. The longer the novel, the more complex the relationships tend to be, as we might reasonably expect; but they are almost always there.

Two further Cinderellas: Longus and Heliodorus

Longus' *Daphnis and Chloe* and Heliodorus' *Aethiopian Tale* present relatively uncomplicated variants of Cinderella, though in neither case with the transparency of *Joseph and Asenath* or Aelian. Longus (second/third century AD) offers us the version of Cinderella *par excellence*, in the sense that it contains the broadest possible cross-section of the Cinderella folktale materials:

> A girl, daughter of 'Rose' (Rhode) is exposed in a cave, but is nourished by a sheep. A man called 'Oakman' (Dryas) fosters her and names her 'Young Shoot' or 'Grass-girl' (Chloe). She pays respects to nymphs in whose shrine she was found. In the course of a dance, she is pursued by her would-be lover, an as yet unidentified aristocrat, Laurel (Daphnis), from whom she hides in a wood. Her foster-mother 'Glen-lady' (Nape) keeps her indoors spinning in winter; when the time for her marriage arrives, she wants to exploit her marriage prospects to help her own child. But the nymphs secure the discovery of a dowry beside the corpse of a dead dolphin; Oakman receives it. When she discovers that Laurel is an aristocrat, she flees back to her flocks. But a token test reveals, inter alia, by means of a pair of golden slippers, that she too is an aristocrat and she marries Laurel forthwith.

The heroine is exposed in infancy and sees herself as under the care of the nymphs whose images she worships and cares for; they and Pan provide the element of supernatural helper (with some assistance from the ancient worthy Philetas). She is suckled by a sheep, giving us the helpful animal, and is seen 'at a church' (the cave of the nymphs) by the hero. She runs away from 'the prince' – the aristocratic Daphnis – once his true parentage has been discovered. When the tokens are produced they contain golden slippers. There are some interesting surprises, as when the corpse of a rotting dolphin guards the dowry that a lucky shipwreck has provided for the couple. In a modern oral version, the dolphin would no doubt have been a helpful fish instructing the heroine to process its corpse – with the same result.

Not only is Chloe recognisable as part of a Cinderella mechanism, but Daphnis has also some of the features associated with the much less well-explored male Cinderella. Chief features of this are protection by a sometimes red ox and a suggestion of trespass, and an ability to pick an inaccessible apple from a tree; Daphnis is saved by the red-haired oxherd Dorcon (talking animals are not possible in a novel); he is accused of trespass when his goats nibble a rope after wandering from their normal grazing, and picks the apple from the tree at the point when marriage preparations can begin in earnest.[1] We thus have the prospect of an interlocking 'double Cinderella' tale, where not only is the heroine a Cinderella, but the hero is the complementary Cinderello figure as well.

All sorts of secondary Cinderella characteristics appear in this complex texture. For example, a recently noted male Cinderella published by the School of Scottish Studies, *The Finger Lock*, has the hero unable to compete at a music competition till an old man gives him a set of magic pipes (not available to his rival brothers). We are not surprised to find that Daphnis receives a much finer set of pipes than his own from the ancient Philetas once the wooing of Chloe is under way.[2]

Heliodorus' very long and convoluted *Aethiopian Tale* (third/fourth century AD) offers us a different realisation of Cinderella again:

> The modest Charicleia is persecuted at birth: her mother realises that as a white child of black parents she would have been rejected by her father as proof of her mother's infidelity. She is brought up as the foster-child of Charicles at Delphi, and herself discharges sacred functions as priestess of Apollo. She and the hero Theagenes meet at sacred games, and are kept on course by Calasiris, who by cunning ensures that the girl is provided with her birth tokens, including a royal Ethiopian robe and belt, which the couple take on an elopement back to her father's kingdom of Ethiopia where production of the two objects establishes her parentage and the couple are able to marry.

Here Calasiris plays the part of the fairy god-person. The heroine is typically reticent about wearing the 'bride-show' outfit until the very last minute (10.13) and, as in Longus, the tokens establish parentage rather than identity as such. There is also considerable resemblance to some features of the Sanskrit *Sakuntala* version.[3] Numerous interludes intervene to delay the pair, but the Cinderella skeleton is there and is effectively highlighted, especially in relation to Charicleia's belt (4.8).

A part Snow White: *Apollonius of Tyre*

Apollonius of Tyre has been regarded as an 'odd one out' among the ancient novels on account of its very late date, its combination of literary aspirations and basically popular style, and its focus on parental rather than amatory relationships.[4] But, like Xenophon, it also shows some of the standard characteristics of a *Snow White*, close to the form used by Xenophon himself:

> Apollonius leaves his infant daughter with foster-parents Dionysias and Stranguillio before embarking on a fourteen-year voyage. Meanwhile the daughter Tarsia grows up far more beautiful than the couple's own daughter, and the jealous foster-mother decides to have her killed; again there is a compassionate executioner, who at least delays till she can say her prayers. She is then snatched by pirates and placed in a brothel, where she retains her chastity through the charity and compassion of her customers until she recognises her father and marries the most eminent of her restrained clients. The foster-parents are then stoned (the more scrupulous Stranguillio with less justice than his wife).

This version would have the brothel clients as the unlikely protectors of the chaste heroine, and indeed there is a similar brothel scene in Xenophon himself. What is lacking here is the characteristic element of the heroine in a coma, which does occur in Xenophon's brothel scene; it may be that the priority of interest given to the recognition of the heroine's father takes precedence, or the scene may have been displaced: Tarsia's mother has already undergone a most elaborate *Scheintod* in the first half of the story, and the author has at least enough literary awareness to avoid so blatant a repetition of motifs.[5]

Three convergent tales: Achilles Tatius and the tale of Leucippe

The long novel by Achilles Tatius, most probably written in the second century AD, is generally assumed to contain a story that is entirely the creation of its author, with perhaps a general backward look at the plot of Euripides' *Iphigenia in Tauris*. I wish to show that the story is much more complex than that, and that the author shows a knowledge of a number of folktales which in any case overlap: it is a sophisticated retelling of a fairytale complex which is very strongly 'Snow White related'.

We have a considerable repertoire of mythology round the name Leucippe itself, which, so far as I am aware, has gone unnoticed in attempts to understand or explain the story. There is a usefully long 'alternative' account of the romantic adventures of a girl called Leucippe in a myth recounted more than a century earlier by Hyginus (190):

> The prophet Thestor had a son Calchas and daughters Leucippe and Theonoe: the latter was playing by the sea when pirates seized her and brought her to Caria. King Icarus bought her as his concubine. But Thestor, at the loss of his daughter, set out to find her: he went to Caria, and was thrown into chains at the very place where Theonoe, too, was detained. Leucippe for her part, now that she had lost her father and sister, asked Delphi whether she should search for them. Then Apollo replied: 'Go from land to land as my priest, and you will find them.' When she heard their fate, Leucippe cut her hair and went forth from country to country disguised as a young priest. When she arrived in Caria, Theonoe saw her and, thinking her to be a priest, fell in love with him/her and ordered (the supposed youth) to be brought to her so that she could sleep with him/her. But Leucippe said she was a woman and that this was impossible. Theonoe was enraged and ordered the priest to be shut up in a cell and gave orders for someone to come from the prison to kill her. It was the aged Thestor who was sent to kill her; completely unaware of events, Theonoe did not recognise her father and gave him a sword, telling him to kill the priest. When Thestor came in with the sword, he said his name was Thestor,

148

that he had lost two daughters Leucippe and Theonoe, and had come to this dreadful disaster that he should be ordered to commit a crime. When he turned the sword against himself, too, and threatened to kill himself, Leucippe heard her father's name and snatched the sword from his hand. She asked her father Thestor for help to kill the queen; when Theonoe heard her father's name she revealed she too was his daughter. And so King Icarus recognised him and sent him home with gifts.

There are points of contact here with the Leucippe novel. The Leucippe here loses a sister captured by pirates on the seashore; Achilles' Tatius Leucippe loses a cousin Calligone under similar circumstances just before the beginning of her own adventures. Both Leucippes are threatened with being killed, in Achilles at the direction of an oracle, in Hyginus by the heroine's own sister with an oracular name Theonoe ('divine mind'). Both are ultimately rescued at the point where their father intervenes in the plot.

But there is also what appears to be a new element here: in Hyginus' story, Leucippe disguises as a man, the nearest equivalent to a sex change. This is authentic mythology: where we have independent accounts of a myth of Leucippe, in Antoninus Liberalis and elsewhere, it is in accounts of a boy brought up as a girl, and changed in response to prayer so that he can conform to the demands society has been tricked into expecting.

We should stress that there is otherwise no immediately obvious connection between Antoninus' account and that of Hyginus. All we might feel able to say at this stage is that sex change or cross-dressing seems coincidentally associated with the distinctive name Leucippe ('White-horse'), for no apparent reason. So much, then, for what mythological materials and the classical materials connected with the name Leucippe can tell us. They cannot on their own tell us anything about why a girl connected with change-of-sex should be called 'White-horse'. It is only when we apply comparison with a sequence of interrelated fairytale types that the novel and the seemingly unrelated mythological extracts can be seen as different aspects of an overall tale-complex. We can look at a modern Armenian version of *AT* Type 884B:

A girl is brought up by her mother as a boy. She finds a king's lost daughter and, as a reward, the king gives her his daughter and a magic horse called 'Pearly-face' (Lulizar). The daughter asks for her 'husband' to be executed, as he is a woman; instead the king sets three fatal tasks: he/she is to find the twin horse to Lulizar (by drugging his drinking water); to collect seven years' taxes from devils;[6] and to steal a rosary belonging to the mother of the devils. The devils' mother curses the heroine with a change of sex: she now becomes the hero and can marry the princess and keep the pearly-faced horse.

149

The tale is also found in modern Greek folktale (Dawkins *MGFT* no. 46) with only one task this time: stealing the Cyclops' gold. These modern variants combine the elements in the unconnected mythological tales: the girl changed to a boy, the search for the sister who wishes to execute her 'woman' husband that occurs in the other Leucippe version (Hyginus 190) and, above all, the motif of the white horse. But does any of it occur in Achilles Tatius? We also note that for a long stretch of the text the heroine Leucippe behaves like a man towards her fiancé, while he for his part is obliged to behave to her like a woman: Leucippe does not sleep with Clitophon at the behest of Artemis (she does not actually pretend to be a man or even disguise as one, but in practical terms the sexual effect is the same). And much more explicitly, Clitophon behaves towards Leucippe's rival Melite as a womanish husband; only when the white-horse girl turns up (i.e. the recovered Leucippe) does he 'become a man' with Melite. In other words, both lovers renounce their sexual identities during most of the plot.[7] We should also notice that in the contiguous type *AT* 884 a man's true fiancée is restored to her rightful place by the gracious withdrawal of a more temporary liaison – one thinks of Melite's giving way to Leucippe in Achilles.

The animal brothers-in-law (*AT* Type 552)

This tale-type is notoriously difficult to characterise because individual motifs seem to be employed so freely even within the same tradition area. Yet it can be related to two major cycles of ancient material, the cycle surrounding the life of Agamemnon's son Orestes and the novel by Achilles Tatius. It also serves as an illustration of how folktale versions of a story tend to differ from those preferred in more 'elevated' literary genres. The outline of the folktale is as follows:

> A young prince has three sisters: they are married off to unlikely bride-grooms either by their father's whim or under duress. The bridegrooms may be animals or birds, or men in control of animals such as swineherd, huntsman and gravedigger, or mutilated figures who are also robbers or Draks. Their brother-in-law, recovering from the separation from his sisters, is infatuated with a beautiful girl (Florita, Beauty-of-the-World, or the like), of whom he goes in search. He smuggles himself into her bedroom by a ruse, and she tells him of tasks her father will set for marriage: he has to distinguish her among a crowd of identically dressed women; create a wonderful garden full of birds; and provide a two-year-old child that recognises its parents overnight. Or the tasks may assume a more mundane character: clearing an orchard of fruit (with the help of the swineherd brother-in-law's pigs), or eating a huge meal in a day. Or again they may be supposedly exotic, such as 'finding the centre of the earth';[8] in any case, one of the brothers-in-law has to help with each of the tasks.

There may be a rival who kidnaps the princess, in which case the rival has to be removed by gaining access to his external soul and causing his death. After all this there is a general reconciliation, and a disenchantment of the animal bridegrooms where appropriate.

The resemblances to Achilles Tatius cover a considerable swathe of the territory of the fairytale. The relevant parts of Achilles' plot may be summarised as follows:

Animal brothers-in-law[9]	Achilles Tatius
A young prince has three sisters	A young aristocrat has a half-sister, an effeminate cousin and a maid
They are contracted to unlikely bridegrooms either by their father's whim or under duress	They contract unlikely lovers
The bridegrooms may be animals, or men in control of animals, such as swineherd, huntsman and gravedigger	The half-sister is kidnapped by a pirate bridegroom; the effeminate cousin becomes lover of pirate and gravedigger; the maid is lover of 'Goatman' Satyrus
Their brother, recovering from the separation from his sisters, is infatuated with a beautiful girl (Florita, Beauty-of-the-world, or the like), of whom he goes in search	Their brother, recovering from the separation from his sister, is infatuated with a beautiful girl
He smuggles himself into her bedroom by a ruse, such as putting guards to sleep with a magic wand[10]	He smuggles himself into her bedroom by a ruse, drugging the guard Conops
She tells him of tasks her father will set for marriage:	
he has to distinguish her among a crowd of identically dressed women;	He distinguishes her among a large entourage of women (1.4)
create a wonderful garden full of birds; or disguises as a beautiful bird	He woos her in a wonderful garden full of birds
He uses a 'honey-on-the-lips trick'[11]	He uses a 'honey-on-the-lips' trick (2.7)
Tasks may assume a more mundane character: clearing an orchard of fruit (with the help of the swineherd brother-in-law's pigs), or eating a huge meal in a day; or they may be supposedly exotic, such as 'finding the centre of the earth'	He finds the centre of the earth (Alexandria)
In any case, one of the brothers-in-law has to help with each of the tasks	One of the partners has to help with each of the tasks
There may be a rival who kidnaps the princess	A rival, Gorgias, takes control of the beautiful girl
In which case the rival has to be removed by gaining access to his external soul found in the egg of the firebird, causing his death	The company await the firebird (phoenix)[12]
The bride and/or the groom wage a dramatic military campaign against attackers	Clitophon is on the winning side against the pirates
After all this there is a general reconciliation, and a disenchantment of the animal bridegrooms where appropriate	After all this there is a general reconciliation; the pirate bridegroom is forgiven and taken into the family

What is happening is that instead of having animal brothers-in-law as such, Clitophon has three unorthodox companions with unusual liaisons. The maid Clio has a lover Satyrus (a goat or horse-like creature); his cousin Cleinias has a homosexual lover Menelaus who is also a gravedigger and a pirate/herdsman; and his half-sister Calligone has the pirate and wastrel Callisthenes. Like the hero of the folktale, Clitophon too gains access to his beloved's room. The three helpers save the day at strategic points in the plot.[13] Some of the more unusual – and unusable – features in the fairytale tradition are recycled as detachable insets (descriptions, digressions, and the like). One notes a conspicuous ecphrasis of the sufferings of Prometheus in Achilles; in a Russian version printed by Afanas'ev (*Maria Morevna*), the hero feeds an imprisoned demon dying of thirst who escapes with the bride.[14] Or again there is an ecphrasis in Achilles of Andromeda and the sea-monster; one of the more exotic brothers-in-law that the hero of the fairytale encounters is an enraged whale to whom the king is forced to make over his last daughter.[15] In Megas 34, proving that one has found the centre of the earth requires that staple chthonic task of bringing back leaves of a jewelled tree and gold from a presumably underground river. One thinks of the curious digression in Achilles 2.14 where Libyan women bring up gold on pitched poles driven into mud. Most striking perhaps is Clitophon's disquisition on the 'erotic' powers of magnetic stones. The Dodekanese version has stone steps talking to the princess, telling her how the hero took care to sweep them.[16] There are far too many instances of this sort of free recycling to put down to coincidence: a fuller study of the sometimes inaccessible versions of this tale would doubtless reveal more. We can never predict exactly how the literary and sub-literary traditions are going to correspond on any particular point, but correspond they do: Achilles is not randomly digressing or inventing.

Leucippe as a Snow White tale (*AT* Type 709)

In the first instance, the name Leucippe may have served as a synonym for Chione in any case: on one occasion Ovid treats the name Leuconoe as interchangeable with Leucippe, and some genealogies present Leuconoe as a variant of Chione (they are both attributed with the parentage of the musician Philammon).[17] This leaves us at face value with the probability that Leucippe and Chione were understood as one and the same figure under two different names, though obviously there are other possibilities, such as simple error or confusion; these should be eliminated if the evidence converges in other respects.

Indeed, the basic plot outline of the main story in Achilles can be seen as that of an extended Snow White (*AT* Type 709): the early description of the heroine Leucippe is of a girl with the familiar Snow White colour-coding white-red-black.[18] The girl is in effect driven from home by her mother Pantheia (on a technically wrong charge that she has been ruined by a rapist). She falls into

the hands of pirates who consign her at the behest of an oracle to a compassionate executioner, who substitutes the inside of an animal for the flesh of the
heroine; and she lives with (giant) robbers who have a title with peasant connotations (*boukoloi*, herdsmen). On the next murder attempt the heroine is put
into the statutory coma and laid out in limbo for days on end before coming
round. There are further death-and-recovery episodes, and the familiar 'substitute bride' episode well established in Snow White texts, before the couple are
reconciled: Melite succeeds in treating the reluctant hero Clitophon as her
husband, and Leucippe reappears in disguise to reproach him and bring him
round so that the original couple can at last be properly married.

All that is really missing from this is the jealous female relative to motivate
the killing of Leucippe, which is done in Achilles simply at the behest of an
oracle. But when we look at Hyginus' earlier version above the *other* Leucippe
story, we *do* have her sister Theonoe ordering the heroine's execution.[19] This
gives us exactly the missing piece: the jealous love-driven prophetess seeking
vengeance. Leucippe, in Hyginus' version, is to be sacrificed by her own sister
Theonoe (both are sisters of the diviner Calchas, and Theonoe's own name
means 'Divine Mind'); in this version of Hyginus, Theonoe has already been
captured by pirates and has become the lover of King Icarus (another bird
metamorphosis) in Caria. When Leucippe, here dressed as a man, refuses to
submit to her, she commands an outsider to take a sword and slay her. How this
accords with Xenophon, Achilles and 'Snow White' can be suggested as follows:

Snow White	Xenophon	Leucippe novella	Achilles Tatius
Snow White outshines even step-mother	Anthia outshines even Artemis		Leucippe outshines her cousin Calligone
		Leucippe's sister Theonoe is captured by pirates and lives with king Icarus	Her cousin Calligone is captured by pirates
Snow White is to be killed by order of step-mother who demands to eat her liver	Anthia is captured by pirates, and pirate chief's daughter Manto demands that she be killed	Leucippe is sold to the pirates and Theonoe commands that she be sacrificed by a third party	Leucippe is captured by pirates and is to be sacrificed by a third party (at will of Artemis); her inside is to be eaten
This is avoided when kindly ally substitutes animal innards	This is avoided when her kindly ally, a herdsman, refuses	This is avoided when her kindly ally among the herdsmen/pirates substitutes an animal's inside	This is avoided when her kindly ally among the herdsmen/pirates substitutes an animal's inside

One loose end in Achilles does call for further comment in the light of
Hyginus' information about Leucippe. There, Leucippe was to be sacrificed by
her sister Theonoe, already captured by pirates. What we *should* have expected
in Achilles Tatius was *Calligone*, Leucippe's cousin captured by pirates, giving

orders for the sacrifice of Leucippe. Does this happen? In fact the reader loses sight of the fact that both the kidnapper of Calligone and the slave-dealer who sells Leucippe are called Callisthenes.[20] Callisthenes will have been with the pirate abductor Chaereas when Leucippe is sacrificed for the second time. Achilles has not really produced two identically named pirate chiefs, as is often assumed; he is much more likely to have chosen to gloss over the piratical activities of someone he chooses at the end to whitewash as a hero. In other words, Achilles would seem to have abridged the tale of Callisthenes and Calligone very considerably, bringing it in only at the beginning and the end, when the paradigm of the fairytale shows it quite clearly in the middle as well. The loose end seems to point to a version of the story that corresponds to Hyginus' version of the Leucippe story.

In exploring these relationships we can quickly arrive at a view of what the story told by Achilles is actually recounting. In a general way, it is a normal 'romance of love and adventure'. But it is fairly specific in its handling of relatively uncommon family relationships: there is a major sub-plot featuring the abduction of the hero's half-sister (also his fiancée); this feature and its implications relate the plot to 'the search for the lost relative' type tales, such as *AT* Types 451, 552 and 884. There is also considerable prominence for the notion of helpers and protectors who are humble or have animal connections: there is a prominent part in the plot accorded to a character actually named *Satyrus*, with its sinister and goat-like implications; and the latter and Menelaus are engaged in an intrigue in rescuing the heroine while attached to *boukoloi* – both 'herdsmen' and 'pirates'. There is also a connection through the heroine's very name to a version of Leucippe's story told by the mythographer Hyginus, in which Leucippe disguises as a man, and looks for a lost sister captured by pirates.

We begin to suspect that the four different tale-types are really sub-types of the same story, and that that story is also in its essentials the template of the story of Iphigenia and Electra. At its fullest it would entail Clitophon's loss of Calligone to a pirate, her cousin Leucippe pursuing her, and *Calligone* actually issuing the oracle that demands the death of Leucippe. There is then the scenario of 'unlikely brothers-in-law' to the rescue: Satyrus (goatman) and Menelaus (herdsman) are 'married' to Clio and Cleinias respectively; they rescue Leucippe/Chione from execution and double as the dwarfs/animal brothers-in-law of the Snow White story and of the lost-brothers story (*AT* Type 451).

An *exampli gratia* version of a folktale version of *Leucippe and Clitophon* would run as follows:

> There were three sisters called Clio, Calligone and Cleinia. Clitophon is told by his father to allow them to marry whoever they please, or the first person to take them. A goatman (Satyrus) takes Clio; a pirate takes Calligone; and a herdsman Menelaus takes Cleinia. Meanwhile

Clitophon falls in love with the superlatively beautiful Leucippe. He gets into bed with her, and hears of tasks her father Sostratus has set for her successful suitor. While he is pursuing her, the brothers-in-law assist him: the goatman helps him in a beautiful garden; the pirate sells on Leucippe; the humble herdsman Menelaus brings her back from the grave (he is a gravedigger as well as herdsman).

This is a substantial proportion of Achilles' outline, with only occasional adjustments to the scheme (Clio is a servant, Cleinias a homosexual cousin; the two Callisthenes figures are identified as one; the garden task and the bedroom scene are in reverse order).

It is no less instructive to move Achilles' cast list through the plot of Hyginus' Leucippe story:

Leucippe loses her sister Calligone in a pirate raid. She consults an oracle (at Delphi) which tells her to disguise as a man and search for her sister. She finds her at the court of the King of the Birds (Icarus) (at Ephesus?). The sister falls in love with Leucippe in her masculine guise, but then tries to have her killed when her advances are rejected; as a result she finds both her lost sister and her father.

Here, Calligone would be the sister, not the cousin of Leucippe; there is no complication from a Clitophon figure, who is as it were cut out of the story.

What can we learn from these various popular approximations to the story of Leucippe? That it is a 'Snow White' goes almost without saying: there is an ancient connection between the names Leucippe and Chione (both are credited with being the mother of Philammon); Florita is connected with the Anthia tradition of Snow Whites; and Snow White is applied as a name to Rapunzel and obstacle-flight narratives. The reason for this is not that these are common heroine's names randomly applied. It is rather that all these stories interlock because all of them simply represent different selections from, and different angles of viewing, the same chain of events.

The full story, of which each of the folktales represents a convergent cross-section, would run something like this:

A brother has three sisters/a girl has three brothers; the blood-relatives are forced to go away and live among distant and hostile people; the hero/heroine searches for them and enjoys their protection/looks after them during a period of their animal enchantment; the heroine is threatened by a jealous rival and has a long period of incarceration/silence/coma before being able to make a prestigious marriage. There is much emphasis in the folktale versions on release from enchantment.

155

Conclusion

What we have to take into account is the high proportion of extant fictional texts that can be connected, in varying degrees of closeness, with identifiable folktale types. That is to say, instead of dealing with a series of specially invented plots, we seem to be dealing with extended literary versions of folk or traditional narrative. The table of resemblances can be set forth quite specifically:

Chariton	Type 882/883	Innocent slandered maiden; wager on the wife's chastity
Xenophon of Ephesus	Type 709	Snow White
Chione fragments	Type 709/451	Snow White/Search for lost brothers
Tatius Achilles	Type 709/552/884A	Snow White/Search for lost brothers-in-law/White-horse girl
Longus	Type 510/511	Cinderella
Heliodorus	Type 510/511	Cinderella
Joseph and Asenath	Type 510/511	Cinderella
Cupid and Psyche	Type 425A	Search for lost husband
Apollonius of Tyre	Type 510B/709	Cinderella/Snow White
Preclassical:		
Doomed Prince	Type 310	Rapunzel
Dumuzi texts	Type 510/709	Cinderella/Snow White
Telepinus complex	Type 425A	Cupid and Psyche (parts)
Enlil and Ninlil	Type 900	King Thrushbeard

There are a large number of difficulties in sustaining this view: the most obvious is the long gap in time between our ancient examples and the modern oral specimens classified over the past century. The next is the flexibility of the types themselves: for example, a Snow White may look very different in the oral cultures of Iran, Spain and Albania, and it may be quite genuinely difficult to arrive at hard-and-fast definitions of at least some of the types. But there is a certain consistency in the picture: if one or two of the novels were clearly based on folktale, and the others quite unequivocally on historical events, we might be sceptical. But there is a certain consistency in noting the similarity of the plots to each other and to a really quite narrow band of tales. Moreover, it is now possible to point to evidence outside the novelists that these tales did exist in antiquity: short notices in the mythographic tradition and elsewhere can be combined, overlapped and shown to imply the existence of most of these types outside the novels in antiquity itself, and in some cases much earlier than the classical period of Greek and Roman literature.

The differences between the novels and their folktale counterparts are no less important than their similarities. It is a commonplace that Homer and, to a lesser extent, Herodotus tend to edit the amazing and magical out of the tales – to the extent that Homer forgets to tell us in so many words that the Cyclops has only one eye. The novelists compromise in a similar way: they may have an eye on the marvellous and the exotic, but not quite at any cost: on the whole, they wish, at the same time, to avoid forcing the normal human but aristocratic hero and heroine into doing the impossible or acting out the routine impossibilities of mythology – or for that matter carrying out 'folktale' operations that ought to be beneath their aristocratic dignity. Hero and heroine may, at a stretch, change into rags or wear animal skins; they do not change into fawns. They may act in an effeminate way, but may not undergo a sex change. They may fight pirate chiefs with almost comic frequency, but they may not take on one-eyed cannibal ogres. A good deal of the time we have to apply some lateral thinking in order to translate our image of a fairytale into a classical one. If a classical author were to write 'Pyrrha went into the wood and met an evil man called Lycus', it still takes us some time to see the possibility of Little Red Riding Hood and the Wolf, partly because the story would be expressed in another form, but partly also because we are unlikely to be expecting it.

Also, the novelists tend to practise romantic symmetry: where, for the most part, Cinderella- or Snow White-type fairytales concentrate on the individual heroine, the novelists will tend to treat the pair as parts of a single organism.

It may come as some surprise to those looking for – or trying to avoid looking for – the origins of the ancient novel to confront the relationship of these texts with modern fairytales. But we have a good parallel in the history of fairytale itself. We can point to a parallel phenomenon in seventeenth-/ eighteenth-century France, when a version of *Beauty and the Beast* could run to well over 300 pages. It is unsafe to assume that there were no oral versions of this tale before that time, or assert that the type had a literary origin, as we have seen in discussing *Cupid and Psyche*. It is rather that there are logical steps in the history of literature when subject matter will dictate its own expansion for a different audience from short mythical or fairytale narration to full-blown romance. It is not a matter of the first novelist writing the first novel on a Tuesday afternoon in July: it is rather a matter of telling the full story of Cinderella or Snow White, or some similar figure, to a public receptive of a longer luxury literary account. Those who venture to read Madame L'Héritier's version of *Rumpelstiltskin* of 1696 (*Ricdin-Ricdon*) could be forgiven for thinking that they were reading a compressed form of Heliodorus.[21]

13

FOLKTALES AND SOCIETY
Some reflections on ancient evidence

So far we have looked at ancient folk- and fairytales in terms of their resemblance to modern tale-types, as explored by the Aarne–Thompson system by the beginning of the 1960s. But folklore scholarship has moved in other directions, as has classical scholarship itself; both disciplines have opened hitherto forbidden doors into the bloody chambers of psychology, sociology and anthropology,[1] and have looked at the relationship between oral and written cultures,[2] the socio-historical contexts of literature and sub-literature, or the relationship between psychology and literature – and a broad variety of interdisciplinary explorations is to be taken for granted in both. What is lacking is the connection in the writings of classicists between *fairytale* – as opposed to myth – and social history, psychology and anthropology.[3] I am content to suggest a few lines of approach prompted *en passant* by the materials we have examined. Within reasonable compass, I could not attempt anything like comprehensive coverage of the explosion of folklore studies in these directions, but it seems proper to note the implications of a whole range of new, if often imperfect, ancient examples for the kind of theorisings that have taken place over the last four decades or so.[4] It should be emphasised that very often a new ancient example will tend to confirm what is generally known or suspected about the nature of its tale-type; but it may equally well caution us against premature generalisation about the presumed origin or primary purpose of any given tale.[5]

Enough has been produced from socio-historical, anthropological and psychological viewpoints, and from emerging feminist scholarship drawing on all three,[6] to point to some common ground: that traditional fairytales are particularly inclined to reflect the life crises and problems of social self-identification of adolescent girls.[7] The most convenient way forward is to discuss briefly the implications of new versions of each individual tale. Where we have a fairly continuous chronological sequence of literary texts, as we have for *Little Red Riding Hood* from Perrault to the present, we can trace variation tendencies that are historically and socially coloured (if not necessarily 'determined'): the girl can reflect peasant sewing practices in French oral versions ('will you choose the path of pins or the path of needles?')[8] of what is most probably the earliest modern form of the tale. The objects she brings to her

158

grandmother will themselves reflect the social standing and viewpoint of individual versions; and the tale can be made to carry the anti-Semitic ideologies of the Third Reich, portraying the evil Jew as the wolf;[9] or it can be presented as a moral parable against rape,[10] or (especially in the hands of illustrators and advertisers) be angled to imply a flirtatious nature on the part of the girl herself.[11] The sheer variety of presentations and 'readings' of the story say something about the resilience of a simple tale about a girl who is confronted with and trapped by a wolf, who may join it in bed, and either escapes or is saved, with the death of the wolf either by a stone- or water-related fate.

When we extend the range of the tale by adding several ancient versions our picture is no clearer. But it is noticeable that it is no less varied, despite our much smaller and more diffuse sample from antiquity. The figures we have suggested as Red Riding Hoods may be passive figures rescued from dark ghostly wolf-spirits – or the feisty feminist nymph Thetis who turns a wolf-figure to stone on the spot, changes to fire in wrestling with a future husband, or sends her son under the pseudonym 'red-girl' to seduce a wolf-king's daughter. Or we have a male child victim who survives dismemberment by the werewolf figure, a fact which should act as a warning against gender stereotyping.[12] If we accept the analogues offered from antiquity, it becomes very risky to generalise about the 'meaning' of the tale, or be any more than highly speculative about its possible origins. And we also have a form of social regulation in antiquity quite foreign to those of a post-Renaissance Christian culture: the Delphic oracle in Pausanias' tale simply *orders* young girls to be exposed for seduction by the wolf-spirit (as an alternative to his wholesale murder or expulsion of a whole community).[13] Clearly, institutionalised rape is an issue present in ancient forms of the wolf/girl confrontation; and when the victim offers to marry the athletic icon Euthymos ('Courageous') to escape the clutches of the amorous wolf-figure, she is about as Disnified as any modern stereotyped bourgeois heroine. This accords very well with Zipes' summation from an entirely different perspective and without the ancient examples to hand:

> 'She is projected...as an object without a will of her own...in such an inscribed and prescribed male discourse, the feminine other has no choice. Her identity will be violated and fully absorbed by male desire either as wolf or gamekeeper'. Zipes sees her tale 'in the light of Lacan's psychoanalytic theories as a conservative male fantasy conditioned by socio-cultural conventions.'[14]

Except that it was no fantasy; whatever rite went on at Temesa, a real and historically attested prize athlete put a stop to it – to his own advantage, and the girl had little choice in a tight corner but to promise him a permanent relationship.... But again the modern fixation with a sexual motif as the driving force behind *Red Riding Hood* has to be set against the occurrence of male Red Riding Hood figures both ancient and modern.

It is probably in recent views of Cinderella that we find the greatest degree of consensus. The modern tale tends to project the view that the underprivileged girl can triumph over adversity and possible sibling rivalry, armed with proper respect for superior divine or demi-divine authority, and make a good marriage against difficult odds. This is what girls in a male-dominated society are expected and conditioned to do;[15] and there is a strong emphasis, ancient and modern, on the element of modesty alternating with 'bride-show'.[16] Where there are tasks imposed by a stepmother or sibling rivals, we are looking at the girl proving herself by domestication, and thus initiated into an adult world, and the domestication motif is already seen in our earliest attempt at a 'take' of the tale, in Inanna's complaint to Enki about her household and pastoral tasks in contrast to the privileged occupations of her sisters.[17] Again, we see an unlooked for religious dimension in the *Joseph and Asenath* versions: the purpose here is the social control of endogamous marriage, where Asenath must be a Jew to marry Joseph. The siblings are not rivals, and no more does Asenath need to do a hand's turn around the house. She is a privileged aristocrat (like a fair number of Cinderellas since), but she is as pious to the gods before conversion to Judaism as she is to Yahweh afterwards; and in her wallowing in the ashes she shows the oddest blend of initiative and determination on the one hand and vulnerable passivity on the other; and it might almost be a race to claim the right to wash Joseph's feet and so subjugate herself to looking after her future husband.[18]

Aelian's version contains fewer surprises, but it concurs with the variants where the prince humiliates the heroine and then has as it were to be trained by absence to value her: Cyrus learns very early that she is not his sexual property, and may not be sexually harassed by him; yet she is the first to acknowledge the primacy of her *de facto* mother-in-law, a culturally determined trait no less in *Cupid and Psyche* than here.[19]

A similar picture can be drawn for *Snow White*. Here the core of the story seems to be the preservation of chastity in a male environment, and survival in hostile contexts, coupled with skill in domestic tasks. This, as noted, is actually hard for ancient aristocratic societies to take on board: aristocratic young women are expected to protect their chastity, but are once more not expected to do a hand's turn in the household. The glass-case segregation may well mirror a period of segregation at puberty, as it has been held to do in the modern tale.[20] Social and family loyalty is uppermost in the search for lost brothers' variants, and there may be some hint of matriarchy in the girl's problematic succession to the kingdom which occurs in that tradition.[21] But here there is a particularly piquant difference between our own assumptions and those of a society where the heroine is twice raped by gods and punished by the jealous female for boasting about having the offspring of two gods.[22] This seems to draw on an ancient view of the honour entailed in carrying divine offspring: it is seen in a much modified form in the New Testament treatment of the honour accorded to the Virgin Mary for being the carrier of the Son of

God, while the rape element is echoed at least as late as Basile's version of *The Sleeping Beauty* – the prince makes love to the girl without having been able to wake her, and attempts are made by his lawful wedded wife to murder the princess.[23] It is not difficult to see how a post-reformation Christian world order, and in particular societies increasingly critical of rape, have toned the story down and changed its social meaning out of recognition in this case. But once again we should emphasise how varied and variable is the ancient Chione tradition, and how hazardous is generalisation dependent on it; while the story of the girl among dwarfs is the least understood tradition in the ancient remains of the story, and we should be well advised to keep an open mind on it.[24]

Cupid and Psyche tends to emphasise a similar set of social values: the bride is expected to obey forced marriage on demand, and submit to the attentions of an unseen monster of snakelike aspect. Phallic reference could scarcely be more evident. Separation of husband and wife results in infertility; and the penalty for seeing the snakelike monster – visual intimacy between husband and wife – carries domestic responsibilities for the girl, and duty to a taskmistress mother-in-law-to-be, with its water-carrying, wool-collecting and grain-sorting.[25] The Hittite precursor of the story seems to have been used as a birthing text; this accords well with the relief of Psyche's extended pregnancy in Apuleius' version.[26]

The *Innocent Slandered Maid* belongs broadly to the same group of 'wifely expectation' texts. An extreme instance of the 'wager on the wife's chastity' version, Livy's account of the rape of Lucretia, has the girl dying rather than face the world after having been raped.[27] The social values of *Chaereas and Callirhoe* are much toned down: young wives must endure any amount of calumny and humiliation to preserve their marriage, and even endure another partner to save the husband's child; but Callirhoe faces the King of Persia's threats and seduction techniques with the same self-possession as Aspasia faces Cyrus.[28] And retribution is to be expected of marriage wreckers (though in *Callirhoe* the real perpetrators of the conspiracy against the heroine are still at large by the end of the tale). We should indeed be inclined to emphasise the defining quality of the very label 'innocent slandered maid' for a wide cross-section of folk- and fairytale. The ancient examples both here and in the ancient novel should prompt us again and again to ask why this should be so.[29] Is it because female vulnerability has a subconscious psychological appeal which is fundamental to gender differentiation, stimulating voyeuristic instincts on the one hand and cautionary reflexes on the other? There is certainly no difficulty in detecting the former in Ovid or Achilles Tatius, but it cannot be excluded entirely from Christian Apocryphal Acts and martyr-literature either.[30]

One notes the marked contrast between the resources of Medea in the tale of 'The girl as helper in the hero's flight' and her relatively docile counterparts in the modern folktale versions. The latter will tolerate the husband's 'wrong bride' in a way that Medea does not tolerate Creon's daughter Glauce for supplanting her, and will simply find a way of bringing him round, while not herself actually sleeping with other men as she has evidently promised to do. But we must also distinguish a divide between 'tragic' and 'happy' outcomes to the story, as well as the values of Greek myth and modern popular narrative: tragedy thrives on horrific revenge and the dangerous woman pushed beyond endurance in a way that is foreign to the conventional values of fairytale, which cannot cope with the situation of the heroine as wicked witch.[31]

By contrast, we might see the purpose of *Bluebeard* tales as to warn and emphasise the need for quick-wittedness and resilience in the face of danger: brides must pay the penalty for destructive curiosity, or should resist exotic but ominous strangers. Bruno Bettelheim was quick to see the whole business of the forbidden chamber as a sexual symbol: the bloody key is the male member involved in defloration, the bloody egg represents female sexuality, and the whole test is less of a curiosity test than a female fidelity test.[32] Tatar has reservations about any such possibility, emphasising female curiosity, as the Opies had done.[33] But when we look at the career of Procris we can see that her sexual infidelity to her husband is immediately followed by the episode with the Bluebeard figure, Minos. This might be taken to incline the balance of evidence towards a psychological explanation, but does not necessarily do so decisively.[34] We could just as readily argue that in this ancient version at least, sexual temptation and female resourcefulness are compartmented in different episodes. But we should also note a long-neglected interpretation in that most learned and commonsensical of comparatists, Alexander Heggarty Krappe, who noted the strong inclination of Balkan variants towards the idea that the new wife must be made a bride of death by having to eat the flesh or pick the bones of the previous victims, so that Bluebeard emerges as a kind of Dr Death with the wife who can perform the unsavoury task as his deserving wife and companion in crime.[35] Freudians do not have a monopoly on symbolic interpretation. We should certainly be tempted to see in Procris the type of the resourceful lover, taking precautions against the dreadful fate that normally befalls lovers of Minos, just as we note the wise precautions taken by Bluebeard's last wife against the 'egg test'. But, yet again, the legends surrounding Minos are so eccentric, prolific and contradictory, like those surrounding Procris and her sisters themselves, that we should once more be prepared to accept our lack of perspective on the tale as a whole.

We have spent most of our time on folk narrative and little on the rituals connected with them. On the whole this is an accident, since few if any of the tales discussed are related to the kind of ritual evidence that we have in such authors as Pausanias and the Elder Pliny; and also because relationships of myth to ritual remain problematic.[36] But again there are exceptions, and much to be done. Psyche's tasks turn up as apotropaic rituals in the Hittite text to which I have sought to relate it.[37] And we have the strange case of the ritual honeycomb in *Joseph and Asenath*, which is difficult to explain but turns up occasionally in other Cinderella workings.[38] A more general observation should be made about the frequency with which heroines are required to perform semi-ritual tasks, appease supernatural forces, and the like. This is a reflection of social conformity and socio-religious control: worship Aphrodite and you will marry the prince; stay chaste and do not boast, and Artemis will let you survive the wedding. We might also note, on the classical side, the emphasis on 'withdrawal' rituals such as women's initiations and suchlike, especially at puberty: Dowden has related these on the whole convincingly to the stories connected with Iphigeneia, Leucippus/Leucippe and Callisto, and we find usual suspects like Melampus and the Proetides occurring in connection with both.[39] We have seen the first two of these stories connected one way or another to ancient 'Snow White' related material, and it would not be difficult to see Snow White's seclusion with the other-worldly dwarfs before her re-entry into civilised society in the marriage with the prince as a learning experience: only when the young girl has been away from home and put her back into housework, and has learned the dangers of taboos against strangers, can she cope with marriage to the prince.

When we turn to hero tales, the same pattern of disadvantage triumphing over adversity to reap social advantage is generally prominent. The 'obstacle flight' is a reminder that the hero figure is dependent on specialist experts, and also on a resourceful wife, who will triumph over a false bride.[40] The Argonautic tradition diverges quite significantly, as it happens, from the popular norm of the tale. Here, the economic prize, the gold in the golden fleece, is more prominent than in the tale as a whole, where the primary object tends to be to gain a wife, rather than steal the material goods of the bride's father. There is certainly a plausibility in relating the golden fleece to the economic plight of the Mycenaean Greeks, reduced to little more than opportunist piracy to replenish the coffers of the mainland settlements;[41] and gold-panning on the rivers of Colchis is still practised. But the overall ancient tradition, encompassing the trick of Pelias in forcing Jason himself to define the impossible task, places the hero in the normal league of underdogs who have to prove themselves against all odds with any help they can get.

Other male heroes again can be subsumed under the general motif of the disadvantaged trickster who will repay humiliation. 'Demicoq' tales are of this order, though our example from Lucian is much toned down in this respect. There is much to link this type with the kind of adventures we associate with the infant Hermes or Tom Thumb, a kind of impertinent and irrepressible roguish rudeness, resourcefulness and indestructibility that can be allowed to speak for itself.[42] The roles of Odysseus in the Polyphemus story and Hephaestus in *Ares and Aphrodite* also emphasise resourcefulness against the odds as a matter of course.

We can also note a number of tales where the central emphasis seems to be a variant of simple survival wisdom, rather than the necessary adjustments for young brides or the proving of young bridegrooms. 'Be sure your sins will find you out' is an especially succinct characterisation of *The Singing Bone* tale (though Ovid's handling of it in *Metamorphoses* 8 emphasises rather the emotional conflict of the hero's mother and the pathos of his magically induced death).[43] And *The Pied Piper* has indeed given the proverbial stamp to the phrase 'paying the piper': debts are to be honoured, or a worse price has to be paid. The change in political power from King Laomedon in Troy to the mayor and the corporation of Hamelin is not in itself significant for the meaning of the tale, but one notes in passing that Laomedon fails to learn the lesson twice over, and ultimately pays with his own life. *The Three Wishes* is perhaps the ultimate wisdom tale, though doubtless there will be those who will try to insist that the sexual variant in *The Arabian Nights* ought to offer the underlying drive.[44] But the simpler the structure and essential motifs of a tale-type, the easier it is to recast in almost any social situation.

Other instances in our sample concern the cautionary wisdom necessary in dealing with death (and its avoidance), and with the world of the dead. Many of the ghost stories emphasise the ambiguous area between the living and the dead, the widespread taboo of thieving from the dead, or the dangers of dabbling with the underworld and its agents: outwitting the devil is the ultimate trick, and there is no lack of pre-Christian devil figures (contrary to popular assumption), to fulfil the role.[45]

Not all views of the sociology of fairytale rely on an instinctive view of developmental psychology and its responses to the major crises of life. It is a matter of record rather than dispute that the French *Précieuses*, the Grimms and the Disney industry represent a series of social slants on the tales, importing aristocratic, bourgeois and 'great-American-dream' views of the texts respectively.[46] But a number of individual details are open to challenge. I should like to point to three cases where the sociology of sub-literature has a bearing on the texts examined. Zipes, in particular, has pointed the way over several decades to a socio-political basis for fairytale. He notes, for example, that the traditional first date of *The Pied Piper of Hamelin*, 1284 AD, can be related to the possibility of mass emigration from the region in search of employment, and suggests that this humiliating circumstance explains the connection with the story of 'paying the ratcatcher'.[47] He further suggests that popular French post-Perrault handlings of the *Red Riding Hood* story point to an origin connected with 'choosing the path of pins or the path of needles', when young girls would be divided according to their sewing ability,[48] and that *Rumpelstiltskin* looks at the relationship of young girls to the increasingly mechanised production of textile manufacture contemporary with the Grimms' treatment in the nineteenth century.[49]

I have no doubt of the substantial truth behind all three observations to their respective tales, and in particular the importance of a knowledge of traditional crafts for the interpreter of folkloristics. But I doubt whether any of the three can be used to explain the *genesis* of the tale, as opposed to its cultural and socio-economic colouring at the time of each of Zipes' 'takes'. Assistance with domestic women's tasks already occurs in the Lucian passage dealing with Cantharus as, arguably, a 'Rumpelstiltskin' figure in the second century AD, and it might in any case be argued that Madame L'Héritier's *Ricdin-Ricdon* stands up as a Rumpelstiltskin tale in its own right long before the nineteenth century could interpret the tale in terms of the industrial revolution. On the other hand, the archaic detail of 'choosing the path of pins/needles' is far from universal in *Red Riding Hood*, though it is doubtless rooted in the oral tradition. It seems to require more demonstration than Zipes offers that it is quite so central, and we should feel entitled to assume that an explanation such as 'fear of were-wolves', or simply of being swallowed, is much more essential to the tale and is as clearly attested in antiquity as it is in the late medieval world. As to *The Pied Piper*, Zipes' own acknowledgement that there may be two tales here, with the specific conditions of Hamelin only later attached to the tale of the ratcatcher, may serve to weaken his case.[50]

In all such instances the existence of an ancient analogue poses a problem: do we have to sacrifice a plausible and immediate socio-historical explanation for the late appearance or nuancing of a specific tale when a version turns up, say, from 1,500 years earlier? Or do we save our socio-economic explanation by somehow redefining the earlier analogue as only similar, or belonging to a different, and perhaps even extinct, branch of the tradition, rendered virtually unrecognisable as a result of totally different cultural conditions? We might play out such a circularity against the background of each tale in turn; I content myself for the moment by noting that as early as the Sumerian Inanna texts dealing with Cinderella, the proud young girl is trying to shirk demeaning and humdrum domestic tasks – and her father Enki is as good as telling her to get on with them.[51]

It is on the whole in psychological explanation that this author finds the most promise, and yet the most disappointment with currently available materials. The viewpoint of the practising clinical psychologist seldom seems to offer explanations of a tale that can commend themselves to students of literature and sub-literature except at the level of common sense.[52] It is easy enough to agree with Bettelheim that Cinderella will encourage young girls to be self-reliant, and that the tale contains sibling rivalry, but it is a great deal less easy to find a psychological justification in Freudian or Jungian dogma that will appeal to anyone outside the sect: explanations that rely heavily on the incestuous variant of Cinderella cannot necessarily be used to explain the tale as a whole,[53] and the proliferation of appeals to oedipal desires or penis-envy so characteristic of Freudian psychoanalysis seems as ill-matched to the actual texts as Christian allegorical explanations of Ovid.[54] All too often it can result in 'meaning' imposed at the cost of common sense and plausibility.

Often greater plausibility can be obtained from the psychological implications of comparative anthropology, which, by its nature, encourages the investigator to penetrate the cultural thought world of a subject whose world is different from his own. The psychoanalyst who seriously entertains penis envy as an explanation for any aspect of Cinderella should ponder the significance in an Iranian women's version of the tale of inscribing an ass's member on the cheek of the bad girl in Type 480![55] The greatest service of anthropology to folktale is to encourage us to think in terms not of basic biological or behavioural truths behind fairytale, but rather to empathise with pre-scientific folk wisdom. Where storytelling is a form of wisdom – often indeed almost the only such – then an appreciation of the nature and limitations of wisdom can serve to take us a long way along the road to understanding the fairytale and its teller.

Nor should we allow ourselves to forget that fairytales are storytelling in the end, and that the individual teller's input is critical. Once more, the past four decades have seen an increase in interest in 'how you tell it' in the live oral tradition.[56] Those who know Oedipus only from Sophocles should reflect on the following formula tagged on as the epilogue to a modern Finnish oral version of the complete story in which the hero is eventually granted absolution:[57]

> The boy [i.e. the Oedipus figure, now pardoned for his crime] then took himself a wife from the village and they had a big wedding and celebrated for three days, and I was there too. And afterwards I had a bad hangover and found myself sleeping with a kitchen maid. The young couple were sleeping in the bedroom. In the morning the maid got up to make coffee, and I asked if I could have some too. The maid said: 'You will have yours in a minute, I have to serve the young couple first.' And she opened the door and peeped in, and there they were in their bed and very busy. She waited a while and then peeped in again, and there they were at it again. And that is why I never got my coffee.

Such an ending is a well-attested technical device for equivocating on whether the story took place or not: the 'witness figure' never actually gets his drink. It strikes the right note for a fairytale treatment in which even Oedipus experiences a truly happy 'happy ending'. But again we might have a very different reaction to such a conclusion from those whose interest is the study of scopophilia.

14

CONCLUSIONS

It should be clear from the foregoing chapters that a substantial number of the folk- and fairytales that have been recognised since the Renaissance as the basis of the modern repertoire were long in evidence in antiquity. About such favourites as *Cupid and Psyche, Alcestis*, the Cyclops story or the slipper-test in *Cinderella* there has never been any doubt; and wherever there are traces of medieval examples, there is the reasonable presumption that the history of the tale is one of normal transmission and diffusion, and not a matter of polygenesis from a series of entirely separate 'reinventions'. To such a core of ancient popular tales, however, we should now seriously consider adding an ancient (and in some ways disturbing) tradition of *Snow White*, an *Innocent Slandered Maid*, and even the makings of a *Red Riding Hood*.

On the other hand, the difficulties in matching *The Frog Prince, Puss-in-Boots, Rumpelstiltskin* and others to such ancient analogues as we can offer are considerable, and each case has to be judged on its merits. Where there is no hitherto identified medieval tradition of a tale to bridge the gap between the Ancient World and the fairytale collections of the Renaissance and beyond, the difficulties quickly mount, but again the case for polygenesis is itself difficult to sustain where there are no obvious barriers such as enormous oceans or permanently closed frontiers to prevent the normal movement of a tale, at least in oral tradition if not popular wisdom books as well. The capricious distribution of surviving evidence is likely to leave room for reasonable doubt for the foreseeable future: even in the study of fairytale the magic helper to reveal all has yet to be found.

But we should be content to have made a beginning in shifting the balance of evidence. There are now several more candidates than Rhodopis for an ancient Cinderella and some, if not all, of the modern branching into subtypes may well have already taken place; we also have an earlier analogue for large components of *Cupid and Psyche*, and most of the ingredients for a *Master and Pupil* tradition. I suspect we have scarcely edged open the door of Bluebeard's forbidden chamber, or the no less chilling institution that forms the centre of attention in the story of *The Dancing Princesses*. But even where an obvious classical story is not apparently in evidence, Near Eastern narrative tradition, mythological or otherwise, tends to provide a further cross-section, as it does for *King Thrushbeard, Rapunzel* and others.[1]

In spite of the difficulty of constructing a continuous tradition from few and isolated examples, it should be clear enough that the variants we encounter in an ancient context are not really exceptional when seen in the larger context of international folktale. None of the tales considered has been transformed completely beyond recognition, though a Christian context tends to transform any theological implications of tales quite considerably: gods and goddesses may have to become powerful magicians if they are to survive in a compulsory monotheist culture – it is no longer a privilege, if it ever was, for mortal women to be seduced by gods, and some rather different way now tends to be found of expressing an oracle's direction that a heroine be sacrificed. We should emphasise that time and again it seems apparent that *our* first version of any given tale is unlikely to be *the* first. This is as true of *Polyphemus* as it is of *Cupid and Psyche* – as it was seen to be true of *The Poor Man of Nippur* long ago by those studying master–thief-related tales. There are one or two surprises: many of the tales which could have been the individual creations of Lucian, in particular, now seem a good deal less likely to be his, rather than ingeniously cultured variants on very basic folktale material. But we can be much more specific than the classicists at the turn of the nineteenth century who could only vaguely see a popular colouring in such literary versions. We should also add that the possibility of resuscitation from literary versions is seldom to be suspected in practice, even when in theory it can never be ruled out entirely.

At the same time, it is clear that some of the conjectures of historic-geographic folktale scholarship are in need of revision. It is not much help to think of *Demicoq* or *Rumpelstiltskin* as modern tales with a mainly west European distribution pattern when literary versions of both seem to turn up from the pen of a Greek-speaking Asiatic under the Roman Empire; nor can *The Pied Piper of Hamelin* be seen as mere local legend, as it has so often been assumed to be, when the basic ingredients can turn up in the neighbourhood of Laomedon's Troy. Three such examples do not shake one's confidence in the method as a whole, but they certainly serve to underline just how inadequate it remains when so many of the oral variants of such tales under the Roman Empire are lost for ever.

We should note the degree of consistency with which modern well-loved fairytales have attempted to remove the sexual element that is so uninhibited throughout most of their classical predecessors. The Grimms stand convicted of compromising their originally scholarly enterprise by constantly endeavouring to tone down references to pregnancy or incest, in spite of a tendency to retain or even intensify the violence in the tales.[2] We note that there is little trace in modern versions of the idea in Herodotus and Strabo that Cinderella was a highly paid courtesan; and only very little trace of the double rape of Snow White. There is little trace too of the value system which punishes the latter for boasting about its consequences; and there is no trace of the rape of Alope in

Puss-in-Boots, or of the rape of Amymone by Poseidon in *The Frog Prince*. Scholars have rightly suspected sexual elements in *Little Red Riding Hood*, but she only has to take her clothes off for the wolf, where in Pausanias' tale of Lykas she had to surrender her virginity. And in modern parody she is allowed to shoot the wolf, but she may not rape his daughter. Naughty sisters may vomit frogs and snakes from their mouths, not from their private parts; and Bluebeard cannot dispatch his lovers in anything like the manner attributed to Minos in Antoninus Liberalis. If indeed the story of Cantharus is a 'Rumpelstiltskin', it is no surprise that he actually seems to have succeeded in seducing the wife of his host, no more than an unpalatable prospect in the modern tale. Even in antiquity we note that Lucian may well have toned down what happens to the villains at the end of his version of *Demicoq*: with equal prudery Dawkins refused to disclose such details in the robust Graeco-Turkish peasant version he published in 1916. It is still only through the mouth of characters like Aristophanes' Philocleon that we can recover the Lamia's belch. On the other hand, violence in the tales has proved a good deal more resilient than rape or any other sexual activity; Dickens' *Captain Murderer* bakes his victims in pies, and Cinderella's sisters can still undergo savage mutilation.

In some cases the addition of ancient materials should make some difference to the balance of interpretations imposed on the modern versions available up to now. On the whole they confirm suspicions rather than upset them, especially on the sexual and gender-related side – at least as far as modern European tales are concerned. No doubt increasing interest in Near Eastern materials both ancient and modern will fill many gaps in our picture, but again we should not perhaps be inclined to look for radical change: Sumerian Cinderella fragments may not look too much like Disney, but they do have a disconcerting closeness to the world of Basile in the seventeenth century.

We should perhaps be asking whether the confrontation of ancient fragments and modern variants by the armful tell us anything about folktale methods as such. It confirms what has always been generally felt, that the Aarne–Thompson index is a helpful tool for locating variants and, in particular, we should emphasise the need for those outside the circles of professional folklorists to use this indispensable resource. The persistent avoidance of it by specialists of the eminence of H.J. Rose is in part responsible for the climate of dismissiveness that still surrounds the study of ancient folk and fairytale in the UK.[3] Anyone handling the material at all is likely to do so through the channels of literature, or ancient religion, or anthropology, or the editing of Near Eastern texts. There is simply no adequate access to enough comparative material except through the tale index (*not* the motif index) to enable a story to be given a context, and desperate rearguard actions against conceding the possibility that a story in Ovid is based on a folktale rather than the origin of it should be seen to be misconceived. Once it has been shown that much of the standard modern canon of fairytales existed in antiquity, then the pre-existence of popular materials should be assumed without the need for this to be demonstrated in every case.

CONCLUSIONS

That said, any index remains only an approximate way of characterising tales once it has found them. The use of the supposedly revolutionary Proppian functions is much closer to Aarne–Thompson motifs in practice than its proponents are inclined to claim, and the ultimate implication of Propp that all fairytales are really selections from a single tale remains as unlikely as it was surprising to Propp himself. But we are certainly left with a sense that some tales *are* closely and persistently connected from the very outset at a level we cannot easily probe. Thetis, in particular, seems a seminal figure in whom several strands of apparently separate modern tales seem to converge: different selections of the 'facts' of her tale can be selected to read as *Cinderella* or *Red Riding Hood* or the witch in *The Two Brothers*. I do not presume to explain this particular case, but there is certainly an object lesson in the adaptability of the Sumerian goddess Inanna, who seems at times to double as Medea, Snow White and Cinderella, with a contribution to *Jack and the Beanstalk* for good measure.[4] More Near Eastern texts and more classical papyri may help to fill in the picture. But we are unlikely on present experience to arrive at the origin of any particular story.

We should be inclined to regard such investigations as a beginning, and much more needs to be done: the folklore in Aristophanes in particular calls for further investigation elsewhere. Moreover the preoccupation with genealogy that characterises ancient mythographers can be used to present some unlikely and intriguing possibilities. One of our ancient Snow Whites in the person of Chione is attributed with a son Eumolpus – one of the less well-explored possibilities for an ancient Bluebeard. The wife of the more glamorous brother in the ancient Greek *Two Brothers* story is also a front runner for *Red Riding Hood*. Oedipus seems to have played the part of the huntsman in a less well-known *Red Riding Hood* story, that of the Teumessian Fox, to say nothing of the parallel between the Riddling Sphinx and Rumpelstiltskin. The picture begins to emerge of a shrinking and increasingly incestuous fairytale community where everyone knows or is related to everybody else.

But we should now at least begin to ask whether the study of ancient variants tells us any more about the 'meaning' of individual fairytales. As I have suggested in the previous chapter, they tend instead to warn us against 'monolithic' interpretation of any supposed meanings; and against the assumption that tales were always as they are in the Grimms until liberated by feminists, psychoanalysts, and other revisionists. We can see in antiquity that many heroines of tales are a good deal less vulnerable than their much later counterparts: we should not give Thetis much chance of being swallowed by the wolf, and Medea has her own all too positive way of dealing with her forgetful husband. I cannot begin to imagine what Angela Carter would have made of Ovid's Chione: not content with having the girl twice raped by gods answerable to no one, he kills off the heroine without prospect of resurrection for her arrogance against Artemis. It is all a far cry from 'Mirror, mirror on the wall...'.

This last point should lead us to another. While the skeleton of a number of

170

tales has survived intact, the nursery rhyme or jingle effect of the punch lines has scarcely survived at all. Lucian has his counterpart to Rumpelstiltskin's victim citing a pastiche of Homer: but even this is again a far cry from a rhyme entailing 'Tom Tit Tot' or the like. But I suspect that we should not be too hasty to suggest that such jingles and punch lines as 'All the better to eat you with' did not exist in antiquity: it is rather that we have in every single case adult transmissions of the tales, which are on the whole interested in different things.

One of the major differences in point of view that our subject raises is that between 'myth', on the one hand, and folk- or fairytale on the other – or rather, between the perspectives of the mythographer and the teller of fairytales. We have found Hyginus, in particular, an invaluable source for the unusual variants of mythographic material from which fairytale can be quarried; but time and time again an invaluable detail will be sacrificed in the pursuit of genealogical detail, following a tradition that stretches back at least to the Hesiodic *Ehoiai*. In fact mythographers' genealogies can yield invaluable connections in themselves: we should be able to say that one of the two brothers of the *Two Brothers* tale was married to an ancient *Red Riding Hood*, and that Snow White and the Whitehorse girl are one and the same. Tracing other such connections, and proving beyond reasonable doubt that Snow White and Cinderella are really two different aspects of the same girl, is once more a task for the future.

We should, in particular, note the role of fairytale in the content of a variety of genres, from Epic right down to fable. It should be no surprise at all that such a text as Menander's *Dyskolos* discussed in Appendix 1 can be so readily brought within the net, and new ancient texts of any length ought routinely to be tested as far as possible for their popular affiliations. In particular, we should note the role of popular storytelling in the formation of romance, and the extent to which romantic treatment is able to absorb and transform fairytale – not to mention the implications of so much fairytale content in the romances themselves for the problem of the 'origins of the novel'. Bruno Lavagnini made a good case for local legend as evidenced in Hellenistic poetry and its prose ingredients as a likely basis for fiction. But for 'local' we should expect to read 'international'. When both a selection of Sumerian Dumuzi fragments and *Daphnis and Chloe* can be related *independently* of one another to the Cinderella story, it is hardly surprising that there should be some degree of resemblance between the Daphnis and Dumuzi tales themselves. Those critics who wish to minimise or dismiss the latter now have at least a larger context which explains both the similarities and the considerable degree of variation, natural enough in different regional variants of popularly transmitted tales.

Lastly, we are left asking about the nature of fairytale itself. When we look at a sacred novella about Asenath or a pair of anecdotes about Rhodopis, each embodying its Cinderella story, are we really talking about the same phenomenon as we find in Basile, Perrault, or the Grimms? It is always open to students of the modern genre to find some way of cutting it off from its chronologically remote predecessors. Zipes invites me to see the changes in terms of a mutating biological organism,[5] a metaphor I find more attractive than many classicists, conditioned as we are by B.E. Perry's famous rebuttal of 'biological' literary history in *The Ancient Romances*.[6] We are certainly looking at *something* that is growing, changing, and still adapting, as it clearly has done over the short time when its history has been open to detailed scrutiny. I prefer however to see the problem in slightly more familiar terms: we have been trying to look at Snow White and the Sleeping Beauty *before* they were lost in the glass case or the magic thicket of the post-classical centuries. And what is beginning to stir is even more fascinating than what survived these magical preservatives.

One recent anthologist opened his work with an Elizabethan complaint of 1596 by Thomas Nashe about the fatuous pedantry and triviality of fairytale research:[7]

> O, 'tis a precious apothegmaticall Pedant, who will find matter inough
> to dilate a whole daye of the first invention of Fy, fa fum, I smell the
> bloud of an Englishman.

I presume to carry that pedantry a stage further by citing a similar sentiment a millennium and a half earlier by Quintilian:

> *Nam qui omnes etiam indignas lectione scidas excutit, anilibus quoque*
> *fabulis accommodare operam potest.*

> For the person who investigates every single page, even if it is not
> worth reading – such a person is capable of giving his time and trouble
> to the investigation of old wives' tales.

(1.8.19)

APPENDIX 1
Some difficult cases

The tales in this sequence are not selected for any thematic connections, but rather for the fact that the traces of them in antiquity present special problems because of the eccentric way our surviving sources present them. There is no pretending that any one of them is easy to recognise or disentangle at first glance in the limited ancient forms in which we have it; yet once the blueprint of the tale is established, the ancient versions are difficult to explain away as only vaguely or incidentally resembling their modern counterparts.

Puss-in-Boots (AT Type 545)[1]

This well-loved and widely-known tale has totally eluded identification in any ancient source. One reason for its familiarity, at least in Western Europe, is no doubt its early inclusion in Perrault; another may be the apparently 'defining' detail of the cat's boots, which are in fact no more characteristic of the basic story than is the glass slipper of *Cinderella*. In the first instance, we can trace the tale back as far as a story in Straparola (2.1) as early as 1553, where a poor third son, Constantino Fortunato, is supported in what can only be called massive criminal deception by his resourceful cat, culminating in his receiving a whole kingdom and king's daughter; a doublet follows some eighty years later in Basile's tale of Gagliuso (2.4). This latter has the cat presenting herds of partridges and other game to the king in the name of his young master, as part of the initial strategy of setting him up as a client of the king. It is worth noting a New Kingdom British Museum papyrus of not later than *c.* 1200 BC in which a cat is herding a clutch of geese, though without a further context it is risky to relate it to this tale; the cat carries a stick, but most disobligingly is not given any footwear.[2]

The relevant parts of the Aarne–Thompson pattern (*AT* Type 545) are as follows:

I   The helpful cat (or fox):
(a)   A boy inherits nothing but a cat (fox);

II   (b) The cat (fox) tells the king that the boy is a dispossessed prince;

III (a) The king is to visit the boy's castle;

     (b) The cat (fox) goes ahead and has peasants say they are working for his master;

     (c) He goes to a giant's castle and through trickery kills the giant and takes possession of the castle for his master;

IV   (a) The cat (fox)'s head is cut off and it becomes a princess.

The most promising line of enquiry is through the alternative animal, the fox: a number of oral versions in the Mediterranean and the Near East still retain this alternative as the typical 'cunning animal'; and although the cat or near equivalent does figure in ancient fable, cat lore in Graeco-Roman literature is relatively sparse. As it turns out, the fox is very sparsely represented in mythography, and only one story concerns the misfortunes of one, Alope ('Fox-girl', 'Vixen'). Hyginus (*Fab.* 187) gives us the only continuous surviving account of the fox-girl whose son acquires a kingdom:

> Alope ('Miss Fox') is a beautiful girl raped by Poseidon, and she exposes her child with a royal robe; the child is suckled by a mare and found by a shepherd. A dispute arises with a fellow shepherd who is willing to bring up the child but wants the robe, withheld by the original shepherd. When they go to Alope's father, Kerkyon, he immures her alive and has the child once more exposed; it is once more reared by the mare, and this time the shepherds recognise the divine protection for the child, now called Hippothoon ('Swifthorse'). Now the evil Kerkyon ('Animal-tail') kills strangers who fail to beat him in a wrestling match. Theseus does so and Hippothoon petitions him for his ancestral kingdom as a son of Poseidon; as a descendant of Poseidon himself, Theseus grants the request. It is too late to save Alope, but Poseidon changes her body into a spring.

At first sight there is nothing whatsoever in the story other than the name Alope itself to connect the story with 'our' tale. Yet most incidents in the story can be inferred automatically from Alope's two acts: her bearing of a child to Poseidon and her exposing a royal robe with the child. The shepherd boy inherits not the fox itself, but the birth-tokens left by 'Miss Fox'.[3] These enable him to be recognised as a prince, and at length to lay claim to a kingdom, which he is able to claim from a wicked grandfather with some animal connections (Alope's father's name Kerkyon relates to *kerkos*, the tail of an animal). One of the most stable elements of the modern story is the stratagem where the cat/fox tells his young charge to bathe in a stream as a means of borrowing a king's robe (when his clothes are reported stolen). In Hyginus' story the equivalent would be that thanks to Fox-lady's sleeping with Poseidon, he can claim not just to be prince but son of a water-god as well (and he has also been suckled by Poseidon's animal, the horse). Usually the fox instructs the peasants or shepherds to claim that its protégé is their master; once the shepherds in Hyginus' version have shown the robe to the king and it is authenticated as a royal robe, they are entitled to regard Hippothoon as their master, and claim as much when Theseus arrives. Normally the last trick is for the fox to frighten an ogre, drak or other monster into believing he is threatened by the approach of a superior force. Here the advent of Theseus should have this effect on Fox-lady's father, himself with some strange animal-tailed nature. The hero is expected to claim the monster's territory – which he does, as son of Poseidon and grandson of Kerkyon himself. Aarne–Thompson do not include in their analysis the final motif: that the fox sometimes feigns death in order to test the hero's piety. Here Alope is genuinely killed (by the immuring normally reserved for the monster in the third episode). We are not told whether Hippothoon honours her or not (he has some reason for not doing so, having been exposed in the first place). In some versions the fox *asks* for its head to be cut off, and turns into a beautiful girl; here she already is such. Pausanias duly confirms that there was a tomb for Alope near the wrestling-ground of Kerkyon (1.39.3). The whole question of the animal's burial is certainly a feature of the end of the tale.[4]

We can see the basic outline and identity of Hyginus' tale a little more clearly if we strip it down to its basic implications:

> Fox-girl leaves a king's robe for Hippothoon, who thinks he is only a shepherd's son. As a result:

> an ogre-king recognises that he is royalty;
> the peasants realise that he is related to a god;
> a greater king accepts his claim to the ogre-king's kingdom;
> Fox-girl dies, but receives a tomb and a commemorative spring.

We do not normally expect a horse in *Puss-in-Boots*, and we might explain the suckling mare in Hyginus' tale as sent by Poseidon; but cat and horse *are* connected in Grimm (1992: 106), where the cat promises the poor miller's youngest son a horse after seven years in return for obedient service; and where the resemblance of setting and overall effect to *Puss-in-Boots* itself is clear enough. There is no campaign of deception, but rather the ordinary fairytale of a 'magic helper'; kingdom and princess accompany the horse in the usual way. We seem to be dealing with yet a third angle on the same tale-complex.

The most puzzling detail about the tale from Straparola onwards has always been its apparent immorality: it seems to glorify trickery and give a worthless and ungrateful peasant a status to which he has no right, and to underline his unworthiness with his shabby treatment of the cat or fox. But Hyginus' version of the story gives us a very good reason why: the reason for the hero's servile status, as the illegitimate child of a rape, could not be told; or rather could not be easily told to a modern children's audience. The opening preferred from Straparola onwards is that the cat is simply bequeathed to its humble owner, or that the fox is caught in a trap and offers his master wealth and marriage to a princess as a way out.[5] Once more, as in the case of *Snow White*, we have considerable transformation and rearrangement of the tale depending on whether the motif of rape and divine human birth is made explicit or allowed to drop out.

The Frog Prince (*AT* Type 440)

We began with the reference to a frog prince in Petronius 77.6: 'the man who was (once) a frog is now a king' (*qui fuit rana nunc est rex*). In the light of so many instances where familiar fairytales have turned up in antiquity, we should at least search for any further traces of this one. As usual it is helpful to begin with the general outline of the modern tale. The version most frequently cited is as often the misleadingly untypical one of the Grimms, in which the princess loses a golden ball in a well and has to get the frog to retrieve it.[6] But from British sources we can recover the following:

1   A girl is sent to a well,[7] or to 'the well at the world's end'[8] to draw water usually in a bucket, but sometimes in a sieve.[9] She may be sent by a step-mother (with the sieve making the task impossible),[10] or for water to cure her sick father,[11] or for no stated reason.
2   She is confronted by a frog (or a snake, or a crab) or a kelpie or bogle,[12] who offers her the water in return for marriage.
3   In spite of what is usually her reluctance, the creature insists on going through with the marriage.
4   He is revealed as a handsome prince once enchanted and now freed from the spell.

There is some further scope for variation: in one version, classified as *AT* Type 1180 by Briggs, a bed on the spot is sought by a kelpie, who has to be fobbed off by different diversions all night long, and from whom the girl manages to escape in the end. She sets him the task of fetching a drink of water in a riddle and 'an rivven dish', courtesy of a helpful dog.[13] Sometimes there is more than one girl, with the possibilities of an overlap with a 'kind and unkind girl' tale (Type 480): (one girl will allow the creature intimate contact, the other two refuse it).[14] Sometimes the marriage proposal is missing, and the tale ends simply with the girl obtaining the water in her sieve from her unlikely location. And in one Flemish version noted in Bolte–Polivka two of three girls are confronted by the would-be animal bridegroom, who then drops out of the tale, while only the third encounters the handsome prince.[15]

What girl in classical literature, we might ask, would be drawing water in a sieve from a well at the world's end, encounter an unseemly amorous creature, and end with a prestigious marriage? I can point to only one candidate. The forty-nine obedient daughters of Danaus of Argos were punished in the underworld with drawing water in leaking pitchers for eternity. The lake of the underworld fits well the description 'at the world's end' (the Homeric location is beside the stream of Ocean surrounding the earth). But one of these daughters, Amymone, was sent a great distance in the upper world by her father to draw water at a distant stream (from Argos to Lerna), Poseidon having dried up the nearby rivers. On this errand she was waylaid first by an amorous satyr who wanted to rape her, then by Poseidon, who drove off the satyr and seduced her himself, in exchange for providing streams of water by striking a rock with his trident.[16] As the frog's attention is presumably attracted by the girl's throwing of the golden ball, so the satyr's attention is drawn by her throwing a javelin. She was also expected on another occasion to kill her cousin-husband, the son of Aegyptus, on her wedding night (with a dagger); his name is given in a notably corrupt list in Hyginus as Midamus.[17]

We have to decide how the sparse and slightly ill-assorted strands of the story of Amymone fit the modern tale. The general setting is right – a search for distant water, and a sexual relationship in exchange for water; the sieve points to the impossible task later visited on the Danaids (but on no one else in antiquity, so far as I am aware). The episode with the unsuccessful satyr fits the modern story of the kelpie ('sprite') who fails to seduce the girl. The problem is that we have no tradition of Poseidon changing into a frog, though he is a practised shape-shifter and can even pass on the gift to others: we should expect him, if anything, to manifest himself as a horse, his 'own' animal. The nearest to a marine metamorphosis we get is the presentation of him in a miniature mythological sketch by Lucian,[18] who has him hurrying to the planned seduction riding on a dolphin. It may be that the idea of transformation into a frog is a variant not found in Greek local tradition in antiquity (but Aristophanes' *Frogs* confirms the association between frogs and the underworld lake). It may be that Poseidon astride a dolphin offers us the equivalent in function to the frog – an encounter with a grotesque marine creature. An alternative is that the amorous creature and the 'handsome prince' are here represented as two separate characters throughout, one *succeeding* the other,[19] rather than transforming into the other, so that the satyr is to be equated with the frog-character in function, Poseidon with the prince. We may also be dealing in our materials with two completely different versions: the sons of Aegyptus were regarded by the Danaids as dangerous and even sub-human,[20] and Amymone is on record as having murdered one of them;[21] in some versions, the princess does actually kill the frog before the transformation can take place. It seems plausible that we *are* dealing with an only slightly unusual version of the frog-prince tradition in the Amymone story, but with the most characteristic mark of the modern tale still missing, rather than with the mere possibility of ill-assorted similarities. If we had Aeschylus' lost satyr-play *Amymone* we might be a good deal the wiser – or puzzled even more.[22] The most useful version in the modern folk tradition is

Bolte–Polivka's first Flemish version mentioned above: two sisters reject the unseemly frog-suitor, but when the third sister comes to the pool she finds instead the handsome prince. This gives us the possibility in the folk tradition of detaching the frog and the prince. It is an easy step from this version to one in which a girl goes to the well and recoils from an amorous satyr, then in reward for her virtue encounters the king of the sea himself and marries him in return for her rescue. As so often, part of our difficulty is that we see Poseidon as the successful rapist succeeding the unsuccessful one, the satyr. But the general outlook of mythology is that a powerful god whose embrace promises a child is the equivalent of a handsome prince offering marriage. (Indeed marriage *is* on offer in the one surviving fragment of Aeschylus' *Amymone*, from whatever quarter, the satyr or the god.)

There is one intriguing tailpiece. The delicate detail of the frog in bed with the prince is passed over in Chambers' nineteenth-century presentation with a 'here let us abridge a little'. When Philostratus purports to be telling the story of Amymone to a child (*Imagines* 1.8), he abridges in much the same manner in the corresponding place, simply noting that a wave is already over-arching the marriage, and tactfully diverting the child audience's attention....

The Kind and Unkind Girls (*AT* Type 480)

We are accustomed to notice the role of ugly sisters in Cinderella tales, or the princess's two jealous sisters in *Cupid and Psyche*. Very often such tensions are simplified into a conflict between a good and evil pair, and this is the usual basis for 'the kind and unkind girls'. In the case of this particular tale (*AT* Type 480), we have an excellent chance to look at the historic-geographic method against unusual circumstances. The American folklorist Warren Roberts published his monograph treatment of the tale-type in 1958.[23] In the very same year, the text of a near-complete new comedy by Menander, the *Dyskolos*,[24] was published for the first time: the play was not known from normal Byzantine manuscript sources or available to Renaissance scholars: in other words, there was no possibility that a printed literary source could have fed the oral tradition or served as its base, at least after the end of antiquity. We therefore have an opportunity to look at the presentation of an ancient literary version of a story and a modern oral tradition that runs the least possible risk of having been influenced by it.

The modern folktale tradition of *AT* Type 480 extends over Europe, the Near East and as far as isolated examples in Japan, as well as in the colonial Americas.[25] The popular tale runs as follows:

> A young person goes down a well or visits a hermit or hermits to recover a lost object; the hero/heroine obliges a nasty old creature at the bottom of a well, who confers blessings which may include a wedding and a dowry; a second, less pleasant sibling finds herself unfavourably treated.

A wide range of secondary motifs occur in the various tradition areas, including an oven that needs bread taken out, a tree that needs its fruit to be plucked, or a flight from a fiendish pursuer.[26] All these the good girl helps and the sibling does not; and the structure of the fairytale is strongly balanced around the contrast between the two and their respective rewards and punishments for their contrasting behaviour. It often, but not invariably, runs into a Cinderella variant, usually with one ugly sister rather than two; and it is not hard to see that it is really a chthonic version of Cinderella itself: the helper comes from below, usually from a well, rather than above, and has specifically to be obliged if not humoured first. The modern tale has been traced as far back as a Latino-Czech version of the fourteenth century, with no fewer than three variants in Basile, one in Perrault, and an early English drama by Greene.[27] Its celebrated versions are *Diamonds and Toads* (the blessed girl vomits the former, the accursed the latter), and *The Three Heads in the Well*, where three creatures convey the blessings and curses. It often incorporates the tale of the caskets, in which the accursed sibling chooses the wrong object: it is already familiar from the casket scene in *The Merchant of Venice*.[28]

When the full rigours of historic-geographic method were applied to the tale, Roberts constructed an archetype as follows:

> A stepdaughter and real daughter meet a woman or witch who assigns tasks and gives rewards and punishments; the heroine pursues an object that falls down a well (or is carried away by a river); the step-daughter comes to a house where she meets the old woman. The girls meet three animals, plants or things (fruit tree, cow, oven only in North Europe); the girls are asked to do household tasks; the heroine is offered a choice between a large and attractive box and a small and ugly one; the real daughter chooses the large and attractive box full of snakes.

As to the place, the epicentre of the tale was located in the Near East; and its origin is necessarily before the first literary version, and so before 1400. How right was Roberts, in the light of the *Dyskolos*, and any other ancient remains?

A mythological variant is available in the story of Cecrops' daughters, though mythographic sources report or allude to the story in a very scrappy and inconsistent manner.[29] Ovid's account in *Metamorphoses* 2 adopts the following order of events:

> Athena entrusts the three girls with the box they are forbidden to open, containing Erichthonius and a snake. Herse and Pandrosus are obedient to the goddess, but Aglauros opens the forbidden box (without immediate consequence). Mercury then falls in love with Herse, and anticipates 'marriage'; Aglauros is greedy and demands a bribe of gold for access to her sister. Athene now consults Envy, who

feeds on snakes, and the latter fills Aglauros' breast with the venom and fire of envy. Mercury comes to visit Herse and turns the obstructive Aglauros into stone.

In this account the simple balance and logic of the folktale sequence of events has been lost, and one suspects that the poet or his source has tried to combine more than one version of the basic tale. We should expect Herse to have had to choose a box which would have contained gold; while Aglauros quite clearly does have the infection by snakes, toads or the like implied in her being smitten in the breast by envy. The modern Greek version given by Dawkins in *MGAM* of the two girls suggests a simpler form of the tale:[30]

> Two girls are set tasks by an old woman; the obedient one is told to open her lap, but not to look, and receives gold coins in her lap; the other, being greedy and envious, receives snakes after a repeat operation.

Note that one of the features of the modern tale is action towards the fruits of a tree the girls pass on the way to their test. This would fit the olive provided by Athena; but there is no hint of it, at least in Ovid's version. The operation of opening one's lap to receive a reward strongly suggests a sexual euphemism: Herse's reward is 'marriage to a handsome god' and the inevitable child; one thinks of Danae and the shower of gold, in which tale it clearly indicates or prefaces a sexual encounter.[31]

The Dyskolos

The late appearance of a uniquely complete Menander play in 1958 made it too late to be incorporated in Stith Thompson's index. The plot can be summarised as follows:

> The heroine Myrrhine lives with her disagreeable father Cnemon next door to her half-brother Gorgias and Cnemon's estranged wife. She is pure and good-hearted, performing menial tasks and devoted to the nymphs, to whom she brings garlands. Sent to draw water from the well, she encounters the wealthy suitor Sostratus there and charms him with her demur simplicity. Pan causes the hero Sostratus to see and fall in love with her at or near the shrine of the nymphs. He sends a messenger across forbidden territory belonging to her father Cnemon. The messenger he sends is driven off, pelted by Cnemon with clods, stones and *pears*. Sostratus' mother brings a sheep to be sacrificed to avert a dream that Sostratus will be enslaved without reward: the sheep eats the leaves off branches; the sheep is killed; the slave Getas who tries to beg a small container from Cnemon, the gruff old man, finds him to be a hoary snake instead. The cook tells Getas that the old and

gruff have to be flattered with politeness. Two objects are dropped down the well by Cnemon's aged housekeeper, the crone Simiche; and the gruff old man falls down in his efforts to recover them. Sostratus and his son Gorgias rescue him from the well and revive him, despite the fact that public opinion wishes him dead. As a result Gorgias receives a talent for his sister Myrrhine's marriage to Sostratus. Others try to get things from the gruff old man, but still find him very disagreeable.

Even the moral essence of the story is quite literally quoted by one of the characters: when the cook Sikon explains his technique to Getas (too late, since Knemon has just torn a strip off him) (*Dyskolos* 492–497): 'The person who wants something has to be a flatterer. If an older man answers the door, right away I call him "father or Daddy – or an old hag, mother"; if a middle-aged woman, "my dear madam" (lit. priestess); if it's a youngish slave, I say "my good fellow".' This is the mainspring of the fairytale: that the heroine and her rival will have contrasting standards of politeness to a forbidding stranger.

Not only is the general outline of the heroine's role correct in the *Dyskolos* (it is covered in the prologue), but some of the rather odd incidents in the flight are covered as well. It is very odd for Cnemon to use pears to pelt his tormentors,[32] since he is not really likely to run out of clods and stones. But the tree that needs stripping in the folktale is thus 'worked in'. The sacrifice of a sheep is found instead of a cow in a number of Roberts' versions;[33] the motif is shared with some versions of the Cinderella tale, where the cow protects the heroine and is killed by a jealous stepmother. The unkind girl often receives a box full of snakes:[34] her counterpart, the rude slave Getas, asks for a *lebetion* ('just a tiny kettle') and finds Cnemon *himself* a snake (*echis*);[35] this is an odd choice of expression unless Menander was familiar with some form of the tale.

A further counterpart to the 'casket' motif is found in Gorgias' unselfish attitude. He sees himself as too poor to get married. Yet he cannot accept the sister of the rich Sostratus as a wife, precisely because this would be a wealthy match.[36] His modesty and reticence is of course all the more reason why the blessing is forced upon him.

Clearly Menander's version could not have been the first. He seems to be dramatising an extant story, as New Comic dramatists would normally have been expected to do.[37] The plot uses the kernel of the story, but the basic contrast here – between the good girl and her thoughtful suitor and the unthinking slave – has been sidelined in order to highlight the character of the *Dyskolos* himself: he is a realistic solitary misanthropic farmer,[38] rather than one of three dwarfs in the woods or a magical creature down a well in the other world. But in fact he fulfils the roles of two variants: the action takes place at his well nigh solitary house; but when he falls down the well he embodies the 'obliging old person down the well' form of the tale. Two other ancient examples seem to give a much clearer view, at least of parts of the story.

Here, then, we have an illustration of how much can be extracted out of how little. In the case of *The Frog Prince* Petronius' allusion is probably enough to guarantee that the tale already existed. But the version in Grimm misses the critical clue of 'the well at the world's end', which points much more obviously at the involvement of a Danaid in the story. In the case of *Puss-in-Boots*, the defining motif is really the animal's setting the poor man's son as a dispossessed prince, and that is provided very clearly; the motif of infant exposure skews Hyginus' handling of the tale, but should serve as a reminder that an ancient version may preserve something unsuspected in the familiar versions of the modern tale. In the case of *The Kind and Unkind Girls*, Menander's dramatic technique complicates the identification of the story considerably, but the motif of the curmudgeonly old man down the well being won over by courtesy is once more enough in itself to identify the tale-type.

APPENDIX 2

Two ancient hero tales

The Two Brothers (*AT* Type 303)

As early as Frazer's Apollodorus it was noticed that certain aspects of the tale of Peleus, father of Achilles, looked like a fairytale.[1] But what fairytale? The basic story pattern in modern folk/fairytale that most consistently fits is that of the *Tale of Two Brothers* (*AT* Type 303), itself of considerably greater antiquity than extant Greek literature, since parts of it are clearly present in an Egyptian New Kingdom tale of the same name. The outline of both the ancient and the modern tale is one of considerable complexity, and it may not be surprising if parts or aspects of the basic fairytale paradigm resurface in Epic or Fiction under better-known names. The paradigm for the modern tale can be put as follows:

> Two brothers are born with a strong connection with the sea (through their mother having been fed magic fish, or the like). One or both leave home, leaving a life-token such as a bottle of water or a knife which will change if his life is in danger. One kills an ogre or a dragon and marries a princess; but on seeking a castle of no return, he is held under a spell or petrified by a witch. The token reflects his peril and the other brother sets out to rescue him. The other brother comes to the princess and she expects to sleep with him as her husband; he places a sword between them, or otherwise refuses the duties of a husband; and next rescues his brother. When he recounts his sleeping with her, the princess's husband slays his brother before he can find out the truth. On establishing from the princess his brother's loyalty, he brings him back to life.

In both the surviving ancient forms of the tale, the suspected unfaithfulness of one of the brothers precedes the encounter with the perilous lady that requires the token and the rescue. We can establish the parallel between the Greek and Egyptian versions of the tale as follows (I have compounded the modern incident pattern from several overlapping examples):

Peleus saga	*Two Brothers* (Ancient Egyptian)[2]	*Two Brothers* (modern)
Brothers' father is a master-builder		Brothers' father is a bricklayer
The two brothers have killed a third, a seal (Phocus)		Two brothers devour a crab belonging to their uncle
Peleus receives a suit of gold armour from the gods		Two brothers are 'Gold-children'
Peleus kills a man in a hunting accident		One brother kills a king's son in a hunting accident[3]
Peleus resists the blandishments of his host Acastus' wife	Bata resists the blandishments of his brother Anubis' wife	One brother resists the erroneous advances of his brother's wife
	Brother sets up a life-token	Brothers set up a life-token (tree, flower, bottle, dagger)
He hunts for a living	He hunts for a living	
He cuts out tongues of the game he conquers and so exposes false claimants to them		He cuts out tongues of the serpent/giant he kills and so exposes false claimants to them
He is rescued by a half-horse (Cheiron) from his host's revenge	He is rescued by a talking cow from his brother's revenge	
He helps Heracles in the capture of Troy; Telamon obtains wife Hesione from Troy		One brother involved in giants' siege of stronghold; given princess from the stronghold[4]
The gods reward his probity by giving him an immortal wife Thetis	The gods reward his probity by giving him an immortal wife, containing the seed of all the gods	He wins amazing princess by completing impossible tasks:
He has power over ant army (Myrmidons)		wrapping army in rug/enjoying power over ants[5]
He wrestles with water-nymph changed into cuttlefish and other shapes		wrestles with princess changed into blackman;[6] with water-fairy[7]
Their union is ill-fated, and Thetis attracts the attention of Zeus and Poseidon	Their union is ill-fated and his wife attracts the attention of the sea and the Pharaoh	
Princess has power to change into stone		Witch changes hero to stone
Thetis appears to get rid of her children by Peleus	She tries to get rid of her child by Bata	
She is pregnant by Peleus but quarrels and leaves him; she is pursued by the sea god Poseidon	She is made pregnant by Bata, but is estranged from him, and accepts the pharaoh from across the sea	
	She makes three attempts to kill her husband	
She goes to live in the sea		
	Their son wins the favour of the Pharoah Pre-Harikhti	
but reconciliation with her mortal husband is in prospect		

There are some motifs missing in what we have of the Peleus saga; Telamon is not prominent in the surviving versions after the single adventure in which the two brothers kill their half-brother Phocus, and the 'life-token' consequently has no need to surface in any recognisable form in the Peleus tales that survive. The prominence of Cheiron is no surprise: frequently in modern versions each of the brothers has a horse and/or dog companion who acts as his protector. A modern Greek version recorded by Dawkins (*MGAM* 489) has an obvious counterpart to the motif of Peleus wrestling with Thetis: this is tied into 'Two Brothers' with the motif that the hero has to rescue the second brother from the princess; this would be tantamount to having Telamon as the hero immobilised by the witch, and requiring to be rescued by Peleus *from Thetis herself*. There are some other curiosities along the way: the temptress wife of Acastus in the Peleus tale is sometimes called Hippolyta; and both brothers help Heracles obtain the girdle of Hippolyta, queen of the Amazons; one wonders whether she, in turn, is in some sense a doublet of Thetis, with whom the hero has to wrestle and whom he has to conquer?

There are also unexpected connections to link the Peleus saga to the modern tale: one thinks of the instance in the version of the latter in Megas 21 where the hero has to wrestle with his bride changed into a blackamoor, like Thetis changed into a cuttlefish; or the Graeco-Italian tale (Calvino 146) where the brothers are bricklayer's children; one thinks of the circumstance in the Peleus saga where the father, Aeacus, helps in the building of the walls of Troy. Basile's first modern version (1.9) actually retains one of the hunting-accident episodes to motivate the departure of the first brother away from home; or the motif of one brother's capacity to change into an ant resurfaces (Crane no. 6), with the obvious connection to Peleus and the Myrmidons. One notes the prominence of magic weapons, given to Peleus by the gods on his marriage to Thetis, and hinted at in Ranke no 29; cutting out of the tongues (of giants, other son cuts off dragon-heads, Ranke 29); and the idea that Telamon's child should be as strong as the Nemean lion: one of the brothers is allowed to wish himself the strength of a hundred lions (Crane no. 6). The brothers share in Heracles' conquest of Troy and of the Amazons, as echoed in Ranke 29. The killing of the third brother, Phocus, is not present in any of the modern variants I have seen; but something of it or its motivation is certainly hinted at: in several modern forms the children are 'gold-children' because they have eaten part of a golden crab that predestines one of them to be a king, the other to be fabulously wealthy. Phocus (seal) may well be a variant of the crab, and have to be killed to start the whole mechanism going. The boys' mother is given as Endeis ('Needy') in the Peleus saga; we find the heroes' father's wife as 'a needy fisherman's wife' or the like in the modern tale. The general reason why the hero is put in danger is that he is lithified by a witch. In the Ancient Egyptian version this is because of the wiles of his unfaithful supernatural wife, the counterpart of Thetis; we note that Thetis herself does indeed have the power to ossify,[8] though she does not use it on Peleus in the extant Greek tradition.

APPENDIX 2

The Jealous King and *Peleus and Thetis* (*AT Type* 465)

In addition we can note that a different tale-type reflects the Peleus story in modern fairytale through a different perspective on the story, emphasising this time the powerful suitor of the hero's evidently reluctant wife.

> A jealous king is out to take over the wife of a poor man. (The woman has amphibious connections: she has the skin of a fish, a turtle, a frog, or the like). The husband incurs his wife's wrath by burning her animal skin in the fire. The king sets the poor man tasks which the marine connections of his wife help him to accomplish; either the king is killed, or after some kind of showdown he desists and allows the couple to continue in peace.[9]

Various forms of the modern tale seem to draw on other folktales: in particular an Armenian tale (Hoogasian-Villa 23) incorporates almost an entire Cinderella adventure into that of the heroine who starts off as a turtle which a poor boy insists on marrying. Another incorporates strong elements of 'six against the world' (Hoogasian-Villa 15) (to assist in the impossible tasks). Closer targeting of ancient forms of the story allow us to probe the reasons behind these curious and apparently random connections.

It should be almost immediately apparent that the modern tale *AT* Type 465 presents a different trajectory through the tangled career of Peleus and Thetis:

> Peleus marries a creature from the sea, and incurs her anger over a burning incident (her child rather than a skin); Zeus wishes to marry her himself but desists only after a powerful warning that the consequences will be his downfall.[10]

Peleus is also an Argonaut, which accounts for the connection with 'six around the world', of which the Argonautic story is one of the first two known versions, as we have seen. But he is also a key player in the *Two Brothers* story; the earliest known version of *that* tale entails a king three times trying to kill the junior of the two brothers (Bata in the New Kingdom Egyptian tale). We should remember that Peleus has a deceased brother Phocus ('Seal'), who turns up as the animal helper in some modern versions of the tale,[11] in spite of the criminal intent generally given to Peleus and Telamon in the Greek legend.[12] The impossible tasks set for keeping his wife include tasks like finding a carpet that an army will fit into half of.[13] Since, of course, Peleus is the commander of the Myrmidons ('ant-men'), that is easily done. He is also charged with providing an amazing banquet too big to eat, or lasting forever, or suchlike; the celebrated wedding feast of Peleus and Thetis which all the gods attend might be felt to correspond to this,[14] though few details of it other than the infamous apple come down to us.

Jack and the Beanstalk (*AT* Type 328)

This story is reported by the Opies as appearing first in parody form in the eighteenth century, before surfacing as a chapbook version in 1807.[15] The general pattern is as follows:

(a) The hero, Jack, acquires magic beans and these are used to plant an enormous tree.
(b) The hero climbs the tree and encounters an ogre and his wife; the wife offers Jack limited hospitality.
(c) The hero steals three objects from the ogre: a bag of gold, a hen that lays golden eggs, and a harp which turns out to be a fairy.
(d) The pursuing ogre is killed when Jack cuts down the tree.

I know no close Greek or Roman parallels, but a much older literature does offer an important one. The Sumerian tale of Bilgames (*sic*) and the Nether World contains the following episode:[16]

The goddess Inanna plants a willow tree: it acquires a monstrous infestation by a snake, a Thunder-bird and a Demon-woman. Inanna calls on the hero Bilgames to free the tree, and it is cut down to provide precious objects, while the enemies are driven off.

This handling gives the story a different focus: the tree is part of the preparations for Inanna's marriage. But as so often in the comparison of fairly disparate versions, there is a tell-tale detail in both texts which does not seem obviously accounted for by reinvention, just because it seems so arbitrary. In the fragmentary beginning of the Sumerian text there is a description of Inanna's father Enki's ship caught up in a storm; such a detail occurs in the first chapbook edition of *Jack and the Beanstock*,[17] and is often dismissed as part of a clumsy moralising of the story (how the giant had once cheated Jack's father out of his inheritance by murdering him when a storm at sea had distracted most of the servants...). We should perhaps be less hasty in ruling out a storm scene as a very old part of the tale.

APPENDIX 3

Thrushbeard and The Starmaidens

At present it might be assumed that both these tales are of fairly recent origin, and indeed Stith Thompson himself saw the latter as a local tale of the New World. But once more we can cast the net further both in time and area.

King Thrushbeard (AT Type 900)

This tale, which occurs both in Basile and Grimm, is represented all over Europe, and has a scattering of variants also in the Near East. A study by Ernst Phillipson collected late medieval variants onwards,[1] and concluded by historic-geographic method that the tale originated in Germany, a view not shared by the originator of the method, Karl Krohn, who thought it had spread from Italy. The futility of the method without a much wider chronological spread of examples will become apparent. The basic story looks like this:

> A princess treats her ardent suitor with disdain, in spite of his princely status; he contrives revenge. He goes to the princess in disguise and contrives to make her pregnant, and they move away from home. In disguise he contrives a number of humiliating situations and insults against her, before revealing himself and marrying his now humbled and contrite partner.

Whatever the details, we are dealing with the resourceful revenge (including rape), on the part of a disappointed suitor, and tricks to conceal his identity.

There are quite a number of differences in detail, as can be seen from a comparison of the versions in Basile and Ranke themselves:

Basile 4.10	Ranke, *The Baron's Haughty Daughter*
Princess Cintiella rejects the prince of Sulco Longo	Baron's daughter rejects king by giving insulting dismissal (by letter)
He goes off and disguises as a merchant, and offers her a cloak if he can have access to her garden, her rooms, and finally her bedchamber	He disguises as juggler, and is able to win the favour of the girl and seduce her
There he rapes her	
She is now pregnant and goes off with him	She is pregnant and goes off with him
He arranges with co-operative servants to have her treated insultingly	He instructs staff at his various castles to be rude to her (three times). She has to be kitchen maid, tavern keeper, etc.
	At last she is allowed to change her menial roles for that of his bride

This story already exists in a Sumerian myth of *Enlil and Ninlil*.[2]

> Young Enlil makes advances to young Ninlil; she rejects him, because, she says, she is too young for sex. He has his ship brought, and seduces her aboard ship. He makes her pregnant, is exposed and disgraced, and goes off; but she follows him. He comes to the 'man of the gate' and the captain of the ship and tells them in the same words to tell her that 'their lord has not spoken graciously to her'. He disguises as the 'man of the gate' and the 'man of the ship' and sleeps with her, so that she has two more children. Eventually they are reconciled and restored.

Here we have rape as in Basile and seduction as in the Baron's daughter. We have no disguise at the outset, and Enlil's disgrace is a good deal more deserved than in the folktale. But the tale is the same: especially in respect to the three episodes where he must be with her in disguise. The alignment is slightly different: the disguises are only after the rape, and the disgrace is really as a result of it.

As to the three pregnancies, these occur in what is really a reciprocal of *AT* Type 900, where, in a text collected by Dawkins (*MGF* 292), it is the girl who does the trickery rather than her husband:

> A girl marries a man and each time he goes off she follows, to Salonika, Aigina and Venice, gets ahead of him, and tempts him in a disguise so that he makes her pregnant three times without ever having knowingly slept with his wife: the children are marked with the star of morning, the moon, and the sun on their respective foreheads and are brought up in a room below the earth, with suitable complicity on the part of servants (just as Ninlil provides heavenly-body gods for the under-world, by similar highly formulaic procedures in *Enlil and Ninlil*).

Here, the trick is by way of answering the challenge to give her husband 'three measures of salt'.

Is there a classical Thrushbeard? The equivalents of *Enlil and Ninlil* in the Greek Pantheon would be Zeus and Hera, whose stormy relationship is a constant throughout mythological texts from the *Iliad* onwards. In fact, three isolated pieces of information about their marriage circumstances fit this outline well. First, Zeus seduces Hera without the knowledge or permission of his father Cronos, and the pair run off to Naxos, where she can have a child. But they quarrel, and Zeus plays the trick of leaving her behind while he arranges a bogus wedding, disguising a log of wood as the *daidalon* of the bride. Hera panics and runs to join the procession; she becomes the real bride, as in the folktale (Plutarch, *de Daidalis Plataeensibus* 3 apud Euseb. *Prep. ev.* 3.1f.). These indications would offer us the watery background of the Sumerian tale, and the 'marriage trick' of the European versions. There is also a curious scholiast's suggestion that Zeus seduced Hera in the guise of a cuckoo (*Schol. Theocr.* 15.64). This might be a reference to some insult where she has called him 'cuckoo-beard' to correspond to the Thrushbeard of the Grimm version; or it might refer to his coming to her in a jester's guise in a bird costume, as a sort of Papageno figure. At all events we can be confident that King Thrushbeard, if only sketchily present in Greek myth, is already available as a romantic narrative in the earliest known literature.

The Starmaidens: a tale between the Old World and the New?

In 1953 Stith Thompson documented a fairytale which he claimed to have no counterpart outside the culture area of the North American Indians:[3]

Two sisters stay out in the open air and wish themselves husbands among the stars. They find themselves married to two stars in the sky. They disobey an instruction not to dig, and discover a hole in the sky. They let themselves down from the sky, with various consequences.

There are, however, a number of analogues to just such a story in European and related folktale. Often one of the sisters is married to an old star-husband; often, too, such a maiden kills herself in the fall into the lower world. We might note that marriage to an old husband and falling to death from a cliff is what happens to Psyche's sisters when they aspire to her heavenly bridegroom in preference to the old husbands they have got themselves.[4] One form of the American tale has the star-husband enticing the girl up to the sky in the guise of a porcupine, thus adding a 'beauty and the beast' element often present in versions of the Psyche tale.[5] One thinks, too, of the affair of Endymion and Selene, which entailed some form of taboo-breaking during his stay in the sky, and appears to end in his eternal sleep, whether or not on the earth.[6]

Add, too, the fact that some of the versions have the partner enticing the girl up a tree to the sky;[7] that there is a dispute between the sun and the moon, or between their wives;[8] and that the girls find themselves swept up to the sky on a whirlwind. These conditions prompt us to look at one of the two main episodes of Lucian's *True Histories*, where we find the following:

(a) a preliminary episode in which two of Lucian's crew are enticed to make love to two tree-women (1.8);
(b) an immediately following episode in which Lucian's ship is swept up into the sky by a whirlwind (1.9);
(c) a war between the sun and moon (over territory) (1.12–20);
(d) the moon-king is Endymion, snatched up to the moon to the sky (1.11);
(e) Lucian is offered a marriage on the moon, which he declines (1.21);
(f) there is a well-hole and mirror on the moon by which one can see down to earth, and see one's own family (1.26);
(g) Lucian returns to the sea by means of his ship (1.29).

There are obvious points of reference between Lucian and extended forms of the North American tale. However Lucian's whole work is avowedly and explicitly presented as parody, and one of the principal suspects, Antonius Diogenes, treated extensively matters connected with the north, from the Tanais to Thule, and even the environs of the moon;[9] we should at least feel the obligation to look at whether there might have been any missing links between the North American fairytale and any folklore belonging to the Old World.

There is certainly a general resemblance between several points in Lucian's fantasy dialogues and a folktale reported from Siberia long after Thompson's study of the American material.[10] It concerns a voyage by boat by a man who loses members of his crew to tree women before having his kayak taken up to heaven. After sharing with swarms of insects in the sky, he lives on the moon and sees his own family through a hole in the sky. He is sent back down to earth by the man in the sky, who shows him sacrifices arriving in the upper world and specifies what sacrifice his family needs to make in order to ensure his own safety. They refuse and he dies. The two swarms of insects are reminiscent of the opposing forces in the sky wars Lucian describes in great detail, which include whole brigades of gigantic insect warriors (1.13–16); and the demonstration of the sacrifice is reminiscent of a passage in a related fantasy by Lucian about a man who goes up to the sky and sees how sacrifices work (*Icaromenippus* 25f.), though here the man in question returns to tell the tale. What, then, might be the explanation? The most obvious 'diffusionist' explanation is that star-lore stories are very basic material of myth, and that belief in visits to the stars by mortals are rooted in an undatable old folklore shared by Siberian peoples and North American Indians. Lucian could have been aware of it either through writers dealing with the folklore of northern peoples, such as Antonius Diogenes; or indeed through his own native geographical contact with folklore of the Caucasus (he himself came from Samosata on the Euphrates). Once more we note contacts between *Verae Historiae* and Armenian stories of starmaidens handed down in medieval Armenian Epic literature (Amiran Darejaniani):[11] a knight is able to go to the land of King Asman who has stardaughters who can be won as brides.

The conclusion we should reach is that the total independence of Thompson's tales from the Old World is not proven; nor is their antiquity to be assumed to be as recent as the first collected Native American tales, in the early nineteenth century.[12] But we need a great many more missing links before the real facts of the distribution of the starmaiden tale can be known.

APPENDIX 4

AT Type 552 and the Orestes story

There is a resemblance between events in Achilles Tatius (through *AT* Types 451 and 552) and the tales surrounding Orestes, Iphigenia, Chrysothemis, Hermione and Neoptolemos. The search for the centre of the earth figures prominently in the folktale, as does some implication of predestined doom for the hero's rival, whether Neoptolemos, ambushed and murdered (= Charmides), or Thersander. In both tales there can be a shifting balance between concentration on the hero's or heroine's blood relatives (and search for lost ones) and the acquisition of a bride or groom: Achilles' novel is unusual among the romances (as is *Apollonius of Tyre*, likewise *Snow White*-based for important parts of the action) in the emphasis on family connections.

The starting-point of any investigation of ancient analogues is easiest from the most stable feature of this very flexible complex: the given fact of the brother and three sisters (with the brother often very much younger than the sisters). One thinks at once of Orestes:

> Prince Orestes has three sisters: Electra, Chrysothemis and Iphigenia (Iphianassa). Electra is married to a swineherd peasant in Euripides; and Iphigenia is associated in some way with a hind, and also with a gravedigger in the sense that Thoas among the Taurians is bent on human sacrifice (though she is not presented as his wife). Chrysothemis is usually represented by the mythographers as unmarried. He is of course assisted in tasks by the brothers-in-law and their wives: Pylades, latter-day partner of Electra, is his faithful companion throughout; and even Thoas helps him (by being duped) to escape from the Taurians with the statue of Artemis. Thereafter he has an exploit of dragon-slaying (of sorts) when he has to fight the Furies, sometimes depicted in simple snake form; he has, of course, to find the centre of the earth by going to Delphi; and he marries his cousin Hermione, daughter of Menelaus and Helen, after bringing about the death of his rival Neoptolemos, who is fated not to marry her.

This summary is a composite of the tragedians' plots drawn largely from the least conventional details of Euripides' *Electra* and *Orestes*, but there is nothing outrageous or tendentious about the result. Although there are points, clearly indicated, where the scheme is an awkward fit, it is in fact as clear and fair an approximation as many of the folktale examples are to each other. It suggests confirmation, if such were necessary, that Euripides is unlikely to have invented the details of his marriage of Electra to the swineherd, so abruptly different from her treatment in the handling of the same material by Sophocles. The folktale notably does not have anything corresponding to the murder of Clytemnestra and Aigisthus.

Once we are in a position to see that the Iphigenia-related texts belong to the same folktale complex as Achilles' novel, we are better placed to appreciate why the novels are often alleged to have a resemblance to *Iphigenia in Tauris*. It is not a matter of imitation of Euripides, any more than it is when Xenophon puts his heroine into a forced marriage with a peasant, as Euripides does in his *Electra*; the plot outline and such individual motifs belong to the same tale-type, which would have been accessible as an orally circulating folktale in the normal way.

NOTES

1 INTRODUCTION

1 Petronius *Satyrica* 77.6; 38.8, with the comments of Smith (Oxford 1975).
2 For its history in English, Opie and Opie (1974: 17f., Granda p/b edn).
3 The best general introduction to folk and fairytale remains Thompson (1946). The standard starting-point for any tale covered by the Grimms' collections is Bolte–Polivka (5 vols., 1911–1932). An *Enzyklopaedie des Maerchens* is still in progress (Ranke 1977–). For the history of printed editions of some best-known fairytales, Opie and Opie (1974). For newer trajectories in folktale research, see Dundes (1965), Georges and Jones (1995), and now Zipes (2000).
4 In Basile's *La Gatta Cenerentola* (Pentamerone 1.6), where a first stepmother is replaced by a still worse governess.
5 For children in the Graeco-Roman world, Wiedemann (1989).
6 For example, Rose (1928), 286–304 (frequently condescending towards his subject matter); Halliday (1933); Bolte–Polivka IV.41–47.
7 The objection of Wesselski (1931) that modern folktale is largely derived from literary collections from the later Middle Ages onwards is patently untenable on principle: Thompson (1946: 441); and is already confuted in practice by the increasing body of pre-medieval evidence: Jason and Kempinsky (1980).
8 The latter pair Pl. *Theaet.* 176B; *Gorg.* 527A; *Resp.* 350E; *Hipp. Min.* 286A (cf. I *Tim.* 4.7: *graodeis mythous*).
9 So with slight variation Cicero *Nat. Deor.* 3.5.12, so Hor. *Sat.* 2.6.77, cf. Tibullus 1.5.84; Quint. 1.8.9; Apuleius *Met.* 4.27; Minucius Felix *Oct.* 20.4.
10 *Div. Inst.* 3.18. Note also the implication of Tibullus 1.5.84: 'Let the attentive old woman guardian always sit by and let her relate to you little stories' (*Adsideat custos sedula semper anus/Haec tibi fabellas referat*).
11 Aristophanes *Lysistrata* 781ff.
12 For the confused and confusing sources on Meilanion, Gantz (1993: 335–339); for Timon, Lucian *Timon*, especially 40–42.
13 Plutarch *Convivium septem sapientium* 14, *Moralia* 157A.
14 Philostratus *Vita Apollonii* 5.14.
15 *Institutio Oratoria* 1.9.2.
16 Plut. *Mor.* 1040B.
17 Strabo 15.3; see also Scobie (1979), 246f.
18 *Adversus Valentinianos* 20 (from Ptolomaeus).
19 *Octavius* 20.4.
20 Philostratus *Imagines* 1.15.

NOTES

21 *Epistulae ex Ponto* 3.2.97. Compare the account in Lucian's *Toxaris* 5ff., and Appendix 4.
22 *Sat.* 2.37.
23 For example, Theocritus 13; Apollonius Rhodius 1.1172–1357.
24 *Adversus Valentinianos* 2.
25 As in a Siberian example of the obstacle flight tale, Riordan (1989: 57).
26 Aristophanes *Lysistrata* 781.
27 Plato *Leges* 887D; cf. *Respublica* 377B.
28 Julian *Oration* 7.207A; cf. Apuleius 4.27, *lepidis narrationibus.*
29 Strabo 1.8.
30 Strabo 15.3.
31 So Aelius Stilo apud Pompeius Festus (p.129,26 Mueller): ghosts with which nurses threaten small boys, *manias, quas nutrices minitantur pueris parvulis.* Note also Theocritus 15.40.
32 Plutarch *De Stoicorum repugnantiis, Moralia* 1040B, cf. Dio of Prusa 5.17 (*mormolukeia*).
33 Plutarch *Theseus* 23.
34 For this diversionary role, Arnobius *adversus gentes* 5.14: long-lived old ladies seeking diversion for gullible infants (*infantibus credulis avocamenta quaeritantes anus longaevas*).
35 Dio *Oration* 4.74.
36 *De natura deorum* 1.34: 'by the wakefulness of nurses' (*lucubratione anicularum*). This element might not be confined to children: Suetonius tells of Augustus' cure for insomnia by summoning readers or storytellers (*lectoribus aut fabulatoribus arcessitis, Augustus* 78) (but not necessarily of fairytales).
37 *Oration* 4.3.
38 Ovid *Met.* 4.39; cf. Aeacus' guests at *Met.* 7.661.
39 *Pro mimis* 19.11.
40 *Imag.* 2.15, cf. *Heroicus* 2.
41 *Ep.* 2.20.1.
42 For the evidence, see Chapter 4.
43 Tr. M. L.W. Laistner, in *Christianity and Pagan Culture in the Later Roman Empire* (New York, 1951: 102–109) (adapted).
44 Useful discussion of the very limited evidence in Scobie (1979).
45 Schol. *Plutus* 177.
46 *SHA Albinus* 12.
47 *Or.* 4.74.
48 Dio *Or.* 1.52–58.
49 So Plato *Leg.* 887D; *Resp.* 377; cf. Plut. *De liberis educandis* 5, *Moralia* 37 ; Arist. *Pol.* 7.17.
50 *Wasps* 1174ff. Excellent discussion in Edmunds (1990: 2–15 passim).
51 For the folklore of the Lamia, Scobie (1977).
52 On dwarfs in antiquity, Dasen (1993).
53 *Symp.* 189C–193A. There is a curious Indian parallel in Ramanujan (1995: 293–296), where a man insists on marrying a wife who is the other half of a split version of himself, with ominous results.
54 *Symp.* 201D–212A. Love the outcast, as bastard child of Poverty and Plenty, and attendant of Aphrodite: 203A–E.
55 *Met.* 2.21–30.
56 *Satyrica* 61ff.
57 On which see especially Tatar (1987); Zipes (1993a).

58 Cox (1893): 345 in all. The succeeding century has more than doubled the tally. For a useful sample of more recent versions, Philip (1988).

59 For a brief account, Thompson (1977: 430–448). The rationale is set forth by its original propounder in Krohn (1926), with a progress report in Krohn (1931). For an exemplary monograph undertaken by the method, Walter Anderson's *Kaiser und Abt* (1923).

60 See now Goldberg (1993) on the Turandot riddles.

61 For a salutary warning, El-Shamy (1980: 237).

62 Propp's *Morphology of the Folktale* (1968) propounded that Russian fairytales contained different combinations of the same 'functions' ('hero defeats villain', and the like) *always in the same order*. The implication would seem to be either that there is only one fairytale, from which existing tales are merely selections, or that there are so few essential components in so limited a number of logical arrangements that such an illusion is inevitable. The weakness of the method is that far too many of the 31 functions seem blatantly Procrustean, so that really quite substantially different tales would ultimately end up described under the same rubrics. See, however, D. Azzolina (1987) and H.J. Uther (1996) for the widening range of folktale indexes.

63 For a brief directory of known 'ancient' tales, Jason and Kempinski (1980).

64 See Gurney (1956) (text of *The Poor Man of Nippur*), Gurney (1972); Jason (1979). For a good classical example of the survival of an Aesopic Tale, Appendix Perrotina 16: Stinton (1979) against Henderson (1978).

65 On which see now Wiseman (1995).

66 For an extended collection of texts, Dundes (1989).

67 For collection of texts, Edmunds (1985).

68 For unsatisfactory distinction, Kirk (1974: 33f.).

69 Ovid *Metamorphoses* 8.618–724, with the invaluable discussion of Hollis (commentary, Oxford 1970).

70 'Simmer Water', Briggs (1970) Part 2.2.349, with further references.

71 Propp (1968: 19ff.).

72 For an anthology of these versions by *Précieuses*, Zipes (1989).

73 Zipes (1993: 256f.) (G. Rodari, 'Little Green Riding Hood').

74 Boulvin-Chocourzadeh (1975), no 11

75 Hansen in Edmunds (1990: 239–272).

76 Celoria is right to compare Heracles' tasks: the type, *AT* 465A, is centred on precisely that as the central motif.

77 For a very pornographic variation, Petronius on Eumolpus and the youth of Pergamum (*Sat.* 85ff.).

2 THE CINDERELLA STORY IN ANTIQUITY

1 Tr. N.M. Penzer (from Croce's Italian version, *The Pentamerone of Giambattista Basile* (London 1932: 56–63).

2 English tr. by Robert Samber in I. and P. Opie, *The Classic Fairy Tales* (London 1974: 161–166).

3 *The Types of the Folktale* (Helsinki 1961), Type 510 (after Bolte–Polivka).

4 *The Cinderella Cycle* (Rooth 1951). For a useful overview of the current state of scholarship on the tale, R. Wehse in *Enzyklopaedie des Maerchens* s.v.

5 As for example in Grimm 130.

6 As for example in Grimm 65, *Allerleirauh* ('All kinds of fur').

7 Cox (1893).

8 R.D. Jameson, *Three Lectures on Chinese Folklore* (1932: 47–85) (text of the tale most accessible in Dundes 1983: 75ff.).

9 A.K. Ramanujan: 'Hanchi: A Kannada Cinderella' (in Dundes 1983: 271f.); I read the Mahabharata version (Sambhava Adiparva LXXIV) in the anonymous Calcutta translation of 1884 (vol. I pp. 212–228).

10 Rooth 1951: 141. She also notes the parallel between the 'hero's flight' in her type C in Phrixus' flight on the Golden Ram in the Argonaut legend (p. 147).

11 Strabo 17.1.33.

12 Cox (1893: 132) (p. 130, Slavonic).

13 For popular storytelling in Herodotus, W. Aly (1921) *passim*.

14 A 'Rashin Coatie' reported by Andrew Lang in *Revue Celtique* 3 (1878), where the three rivals are the usual stepsisters.

15 Perry (1967: 79).

16 Plutarch *Artaxerxes*, 26f.; Pericles 24.

17 Ed. M. Philonenko (1968). Study from the perspective of Greek romance in S. West (1971: 70–81).

18 English version (conflating several overlapping texts) by H. Schwarz (1988: 156–62).

19 Neither extended tale pays much attention to the story in *Genesis* and elsewhere that Joseph was framed by the wife of Potiphar (*Gen.* 39.1–23); *Joseph and Asenath* tries to distinguish two different Potiphars, unconvincingly.

20 Strictly speaking, we are not entitled to assume that all the components for such a version were available before the medieval rabbinical tradition, but the role of the eagle in Strabo's version at least suggests that some of them were available much earlier. Their failure to appear in the Hellenistic Joseph and Asenath may be more a matter of taste than availability.

21 Schwartz (1988: 160).

22 See the cross section of samples of the type, nos 319–341 *passim* in Cox's collection.

23 Fr. 1 Dielz-Kranz.

24 M.L. West (1971: 15–27, 52–60).

25 Other occurrences of significant motifs of *Cinderella* might be seen as no more than traces in accounts of Io and Callisto. Rooth already noticed the existence of the 'spying' motif in the myth of Io, where the girl who has just been made the mistress of Zeus is spied upon by Hera through the agency of the hundred-eyed Argus (Rooth 1951: 162f.). One thinks of the distinctive 'One-Eyes, Two-Eyes, Three-Eyes' form of the tale in Grimm, where the two ugly sisters have one eye and three eyes, and are made to spy on the heroine. If we wish to press the resemblance and argue that Io herself is a Cinderella, we are faced with the unusual consequence that instead of being *helped* by a cow, as happens in 'One-Eye, Two-Eyes, Three-Eyes' variants, she actually *is* one before her elevation to the status of an Egyptian goddess. On the other hand, we should not leave out of account the fate of Rhodopis herself, elevated in Egypt to recognition she has not attained elsewhere; nor should we ignore the fact that some genealogies connect her to *melie*, the ash tree (Apollodorus *Bibl.* 2.1.1, Gantz 1993: 198). We should note the important medieval Western variant in Marie de France's *Lai Le Fresne*, where the girl is laid in an ash tree and recognised as a Cinderella figure in due course.

Just as Io can at least be related to the One-Eyes, Two-Eyes subtype, so the story of Callisto can be related to that of a third Grimm variety, *Allerleirauh* ('All-kinds-of-fur'). A girl called Callisto ('Most Beautiful') is loved by the king of heaven. Jealous elements have her changed into a bear and even killed by Artemis. But she is finally rescued by her lover and made to join the stars. The normal Cinderella form of this story (510B) has the heroine facing the threat of incest from her father; she asks for dresses of sun, moon and stars (or the like) and a dress of fur, pelts, lice or wood; she uses the latter as a disguise while she stays with the prince and suffers humiliations as a kitchen maid; one day her true identity is revealed when she cannot take her animal guise off in time, and marriage can then take place. There are a very large number of variants, many of them defective (especially through efforts to suppress the motif of incest at the beginning). In Callisto's case the bearskin and the setting as a constellation in combination certainly suggest this form of the fairytale, but without the incest. Callisto wins the love of Zeus; she is transformed into a bear to cover 'her' crime of pregnancy by Zeus; but when killed by Hera or Artemis she is rewarded by transformation into a constellation, or as bride of Zeus (testimonia in Gantz 1993: 725–729). There is no initial incest threat here, but some ground for suspicion: Callisto's father is the infamous Lycaon, whose crime is eating his offspring's own flesh; such a charge is sometimes symbolically expressive of incest (as quite clearly in the first oracle in *Apollonius of Tyre*). And while the usual animal guise for the girl escaping incest is the skin of some other animal or a wooden dress, it so happens that Basile 2.6 has a version where the girl swallows a piece of wood while in bed with her father *and is able to defend her honour by turning into a bear*. There is no star dress in this version, but the identity of the bear as a variation in a recognisable Cinderella is established. One notes, too, that one vase painting of Kallisto (Gantz 1993) *does* portray Callisto as sitting on a bear's skin (on the significance of the bear's skin in the Callisto story, see Dowden 1989).

26 See Chapter 15.
27 For general introduction, Kramer 1963, 1981.
28 On their changing relationship, Jacobsen (1976: 25–73).
29 Tr. S. Kramer (1963: 182ff).
30 S. Kramer, *The Sumerian Sacred Marriage Rite* (1969: 68f). For the sun as heroine's counsellor in Cinderella, Cox 132 (p. 130, Slavonic).
31 Kramer (1963: 200, 202).
32 J.B. Pritchard, *Ancient Near Eastern Texts relating to the Old Testament* (Princeton 1969: 638).
33 *ANET* 639ff.
34 A. Falkenstein and W. von Soden, *Sumerische und Akkadische Hymnen und Gebete* (Zurich/Stuttgart 1953: 68). For a mixture of 'heavenly and precious dresses', Cox (1893: 147) (p. 157, Neapolitan).
35 See the remarks in Pritchard (1969: 638).
36 See below Chapter 12.
37 On whom see Gantz (1993: 198).

3 *SNOW WHITE* AND RELATED TALES

1 Grimm 53, *Sneewittchen* (BP 1.450–463); Boeklen (1910, 1915); Jones (1983, 1990). I am grateful to Zipes for drawing my attention to the discussion in P. Chittenden and M. Kinney (1986), 579–650, and to the existence of South American as well as North American (colonial) versions. It still remains the case that the tale is less well represented in the oral tradition as so far collected than *Cinderella* or *Cupid and Psyche*; and early Disnification has fixed the public perception of it in an unfortunate way.
2 Schwartz (1988: 67–78), cited below at n. 18.
3 Boeklen (1910, 1915).
4 For revision of the classification of steps in the story, see now Jones (1990), especially pp. 20–25; the consequences for our versions are incidental.
5 P. Delarue (1975) *Le Conte populaire Français* 659 (3), Paris.
6 Boeklen 1.63 (Greek 3) (people wonder that the heroine does not have wings like angels; or she is hailed as an angel, elf or goddess).
7 Boeklen 1.72ff.

8 Boeklen 1.84–88.
9 Boeklen 1.87 (Portuguese 3).
10 Boeklen 1.35; below, n. 19.
11 For example, Boeklen 1.83–88 *passim*.
12 Boeklen 1.86 (wild man); 1.88 (night fairy).
13 Boeklen 1.90; 1.93.
14 Boeklen 1.122.
15 Boeklen 1.121f. (Kabyli); cf. Dawkins (1916: 346–350).
16 Boeklen 1.142–146 (among other variants).
17 Boeklen 1.10 (German 2).
18 'Romana', in Schwartz (1988: 67–78), from Jewish–Egyptian oral tradition.
19 Cf. also Calvino (1982) no. 50 Giricoccola (from Bologna); no. 111 (also Abruzzo). Calvino notes (p. 738) that dwarfs are almost non-existent in Italian oral tradition, and therefore the few dwarf versions in Italian tradition are likely to have acquired them from literary influence.
20 De Nino 50 (slightly adapted English translation in Calvino, no. 109).
21 For further characterisation, Jones (1990), especially pp. 20–35.
22 *Pentamerone* 5.5 (*Sun, Moon and Talia*).
23 This has not always been recognised even by folklorists of the most recent decades: e.g. I. and P. Opie (1974: 227) are non-committal: 'the tale contains elements that lie deep in European folk tradition; but it is not necessarily an old story, and has probably come under literary influence'.
24 Servius *ad Aen.* 4.250.
25 Cf. Philostratus Senior *Imag.* 1.5.
26 Philostratus ibid 1.5.
27 Apollodorus 3.199, 201; Pausanias 1.38.2; Euripides *Erechtheus* (Lycurgus *contra Leocritem* 98).
28 Plutarch *de fluminibus* 5.3.
29 Ovid *Met.* 11.301f.; Hyginus *Fabulae* 200f.; Euripides *Autolycus*.
30 Ovid *Met.* 6.147–312 (but there is much variation: see Gantz (1993) on Niobe, pp. 536–540).
31 *Met.* 11.295–345, slightly abridged.
32 As already in Basile's *Sun, Moon and Talia*, 5.5.
33 We also have a puzzling reversal of Pygmalion's role described in Ovid *Fasti* 3.545ff., where Anna, sister of Dido, and questionably identified with Anna Perenna, is relentlessly persecuted by Pygmalion on her flight to Italy. But we have a parallel in the antagonism of Oenoe/Gerana and her pygmies, as we have just seen.
34 Text and discussion in Winkler and Stephens (1995: 289–313). The affinity of the new fragment attributed to *Chione* by M. Gronewald (1979: 15–20) is not altogether certain, as W.-S. point out; but the connection with Snow White-type material seems to confirm Gronewald's suspicions.
35 It had already been recognised as a Snow White by Alfred Nutt as early as 1892.
36 Winkler and Stephens (1995: 303–313). Care must be taken not to allow circular argument here: suffice to say that this author's grounds for assigning it to a Snow White are independent from Gronewald's for joining it to the *Chione* fragments. The only problem that remains is the closeness of the two columns: see Gronewald (1979: 15–20).
37 The first of the certain fragments points to the Snow White-related *AT* Type 451, discussed at the end of this chapter.
38 Text by Papanikolaou; tr. Anderson, in Reardon (1989: 128–169).
39 For the similar status of Achilles' Tatius novel *Leucippe and Clitophon*, see Chapter 12.

40 Cf. Dawkins *MGAM* 343.
41 Dalmeyda (1926: xxvii–xxxi) ('physionomie de conte populaire', xxvii); O'Sullivan (1995) on linguistic and formulaic grounds.
42 Xen. Ephes. 2.3.3, 2.3.6 (and *passim*).
43 See above, this chapter nn. 25, 33.
44 Fluorita in the first Rumanian version, Boeklen 1.51.
45 Xen. Ephes. 1.2.5.
46 Xen. Ephes. 1.2.5.
47 Boeklen 1.63 (Norwegian 2); Xen. Ephes. 1.2.7.
48 Xen. Ephes. 1.2.5; Boeklen 1.63.
49 Boeklen, Greek 1; Xen. Ephes. 1.2.6.
50 Boeklen, Greek 3; Xen. Ephes. 1.2.7.
51 Boeklen 1.67.
52 *Apollonius of Tyre* 31.
53 Boeklen 1.72.
54 Xen. Ephes. 1.6.1.
55 Xen. Ephes. 1.6.2.
56 Boeklen 1.74 (Portuguese 1).
57 Xen. Ephes. 3.9.
58 Boeklen 1.76.
59 Xen. Ephes. 2.11 (the estate appears to be close to Tyre).
60 Boeklen 1.79.
61 Boeklen 1.82 (German 1e); 1.83 (Polish and Russian); 1.86 waelschtir. a (cf. Bolognese).
62 Boeklen 1.83f.; Xen. Ephes. 2.11.
63 Boeklen 1.84–88.
64 Boeklen 1.84 (German 1f.).
65 Boeklen 1.86; Xen. Ephes. 3.2; 5.9.
66 Boeklen 1.88; Xen. Ephes. 5.5, 5.7.
67 Xen. Ephes. 2.1.
68 Xen. Ephes. 4.6.5f.; Boeklen 1.90.
69 Xen. Ephes. 5.9.
70 Boeklen 1.96; Xen. Ephes. 5.9.
71 Boeklen 1.95.
72 Boeklen 1.99, 102f.
73 Boeklen 1.102f.; Xen. Ephes. 3.8.
74 For example, Boeklen 1.129–142.
75 For example,. Boeklen 1.112–118.
76 Boeklen 1.120; 1.122; 1.132–135.
77 Xen. Ephes. 5.1.
78 Xen. Ephes. 4.3.2 (by implication: Psammis prepares many camels, asses and transport horses).
79 Boeklen 1.121 (and 165).
80 Boeklen 1.125–129.
81 Xen. Ephes. 3.12.3f.
82 Xen. Ephes. 4.6.4–7.
83 Boeklen 1.91; cf. 101: dogs and cat fed poisoned food, thus detected.
84 Xen. Ephes. 5.4.
85 Chione col. 3.1 (the first two letters are a restoration).
86 *Met.* 11.295.
87 Now also Winkler and Stephens (1995: 277–288).
88 See above n. 24.

89 For example, Grimm (1992: 25) (seven ravens); Grimm 49 (six swans); Grimm 9 (twelve brothers); for camel's hide and knucklebones, Dawkins (1916: 346–350).

90 Dawkins, *MGAM* (1916: 347–351) offers a very elliptical and confused version, which needs comparison with West European versions before it makes much sense. But it emphasises the essential kinship between Snow White and the Search for the Lost Brothers nonetheless:

> A man's twelve sons leave home and go to the mountains. A daughter is born, finds out about the sons, and decides to pursue them. She reaches their mountain dwellings and secretly keeps house for them till she is discovered. A female neighbour menaces her, and the brothers kill the neighbour. The girl treads on a bone, is taken for dead, and the body given to some camel drivers. They remove the bone, and she recognises her brothers.

For a 'normal' *Snow White* from the same region, ibid.: 441–447, cf. 269ff.

91 See previous note.

92 Rather than the absurd 'unbedded one' (*a-lektra*) favoured in the last century.

93 For the relationship between Chione and Type 884, see the discussion of Achilles Tatius in Chapter 12.

4 *CUPID AND PSYCHE* AND *BEAUTY AND THE BEAST*

1 *Anilis Fabula*: Apuleius *Met*. 4.28–6.2; edn: E. J. Kenney (Cambridge, 1990).

2 Useful short treatment in Walsh (1970), 190–223, with summary of positions; older literature is usefully collected in Binder-Merkelbach (1968). The position of Reitzenstein (1912), arguing for Iranian myth, is unfashionable, but ought to be reconsidered in the light of the new Hittite evidence. It follows that if the position argued here is justified, the argument of Fehling (1977) deriving everything from Apuleius is untenable; all the more so when mythological analogues are taken into account. The Folklore monograph for the type is that of J.-Oe. Swahn (1955), covering some 1,100 versions and superseding the treatments by Bolte–Polivka (3.37–43) on Grimm no. 127 and by Tegethoff (1922), the latter of whom worked from only 200 versions; literary mannerisms overlaying the folktale are considered briefly by Wright (1971: 273–284).

3 Swahn (1955) ibid.

4 *Master Semolina*, Megas 27; Iron Stove, Grimm 127; *The Hoodie*, Campbell (1860); *The Daughter of the Skies, The Black Bull of Norroway*, Philip (1995: p. 16); Delarue; Basile 2.5, 4.4; Noy 58; Afanas'ev p. 200; Calvino 136, 182; Argenti-Rose 9.

5 Swahn 381 (his paraphrase).

6 Pindar *Ol*. 2.22.7; the *Homeric Hymn to Hermes* implies (allegedly erroneous) traditions of Semele herself delivering the child in the ordinary way.

7 Discussion in Gantz 476f.; Diodorus 4.25.4; Apollodorus *Bibl*. 3.5.3 ; Plut. *Mor*. 565F–566A; Paus. 2.31.2.

8 The thesis of Fehling (1977), who in essence takes up where the ill-starred efforts of Wesselski (1931) left off (on the latter, see Swahn 397).

9 Swahn 24–36, with a great deal more detailed information about the subtypes.

10 *Met*. 5.28.2–5; 5.29.1.

11 *Met*. 6.10–21.

12 *Met*. 6.23.2.

13 Hittite texts now collected in H.A. Hoffner, Jnr. (1990) *Hittite Myths*, Atlanta.

14 *Telepinus* version 1 (Hoffner 14–17).

15 *Telepinus* 9–18 (Hoffner 15f.); *Met.* 6.10.1–3; at best Venus pretends to test Psyche, but three of the tests are really 'fatal tasks'.
16 *Telepinus* 27 (Hoffner 17); *Met.* 6.16.3f.; cf. Bieler in Binder-Merkelbach (1968) 340; Walsh 214f.
17 Zukki-texts: KUB xxxiii.67 with, for example, Gueterbock in *JAOS* 84 (1964): 115.
18 *Telepinus and the Daughter of the Sea God* (Hoffner 15f.); *Met.* 4.33f.
19 *Telepinus* 1 (Hoffner 14).
20 *Met.* 5.24.2–5.
21 *Telepinus* 1 (Hoffner 14); *Met.* 5.25.1.
22 *Telepinus* 2f. (Hoffner 14f.).
23 *Met.* 5.28.5. This extract has a notable resemblance to fragments of the Hittite soul-myth (Hoffner 32f).
24 *Telepinus* 3 (Hoffner 15); *Met.* 6.3.1.
25 *Telepinus* version 2.4f. (Hoffner 18); *Met.* 5.28.2–8.
26 *Telepinus* version 2.9 (Hoffner 18).
27 *Met.* 6.13.3 – 6.16.1.
28 *Met.* 5.30.3–6.
29 *Telepinus* version 2.16, (Hoffner 19); for sifting grains, cf. Version 1.17 (Hoffner 16).
30 *Met.* 6.10.1f.
31 *Telepinus* version 1.17 (Hoffner 16).
32 *Met.* 6.11.4 – 6.12.5.
33 *Telepinus* version 2.9 (Hoffner 16).
34 *Met.* 6.13.4 – 6.16.1.
35 *Met.* 6.16.3 – 6.21.4.
36 *Telepinus* version 1.27 (Hoffner 17).
37 *Telepinus* version 1.22f. (Hoffner 16f.).
38 *Met.* 6.23.1f.
39 *Pace* Wright (1971: 281).
40 *Met.* 4.33.1 line 4 *vipereumque malum.*
41 Swahn 296–312.
42 'The Voyage of the Immortal Human Soul' 3 (Hoffner p. 33).
43 S. 11 p. 33 Hoffner.
44 Andromeda: *AT* Type 300, cf. Wright (1971: 273).
45 For the lamp, cf. the talking lamps in Lucian, *Verae Historiae* 1.29 and *Kataplous* 27 (contrast Wright 1971: 276). For riddling oracles, see now Goldberg (1993) on Turandot's Riddles; as to the river's amatory troubles (Apuleius 5.25), passing hero-ines routinely oblige natural objects, which reserve their gratitude for a return encounter, as in *AT* Type 480 (contrast Wright 1971: 277).
As to the tasks, the golden-fleeced sheep in Apuleius surely correspond to the sheep of the sun in the Hittite, and are therefore not exclusively a reference to classical mythology: they cannot be an invention of Apuleius (as Wright seems to imply, 1971: 277). Eating the food of Hades is pre-classical, whatever Apuleius may have supposed (*pace* Wright 1971: 280). The killing of the sisters has its analogue in the falling over the cliff of the sisters of Herse, and again need not be seen as literary (cf. Wright 1971: 281).
46 Wright (1971: 279) attempts distinction between literary and popular conceptions of Hades, no more successfully.
47 Swahn 1955: 244; Wright 1971: 276.
48 KUB XXXIII.67; Apuleius *Met.* 6.24, cf. 6.9, where it has been a threat of Venus to prolong Psyche's pregnancy as a punishment. The likelihood in this particular Anzili and Zukki text is that these two female deities are one and the same figure; the

direction in the text itself is that the tale be recited by the midwife, so implying a birthing incantation, as Otten's preface suggests. We thus have a myth where Zukki's adventures are, as far as we can make out, parallel to those of Telepinus; it is as if we have a Psyche story that replicates rather than complements that of Cupid; she wanders off angry, fertility suffers, she is placated and returns. In other words, Psyche would be playing a role closer to that of Venus, as a vindictive sex-goddess requiring placation by expectant mothers. If that is so, then we already have a complete Hittite Cupid and Psyche sequence after all, and Psyche = Zukki.

49 Wright 1971: 276.

5 THE OBSTACLE FLIGHT

1 On intermediate tradition, Hunter (1989: 21).
2 Ed. and tr. G. Farber-Fluegge (1973).
3 Useful discussion in Gantz (1993: 340–373).
4 Translated by G. Lewis (1974) Harmondsworth.
5 Kan Turali (Lewis 1974: 118, 122–126, 127); *Argonautica* 3.1403–6; 4.1ff.
6 *Argonautica* 3.1246ff.; 1254f.
7 Kan Turali, ibid.: 125.
8 Kan Turali, ibid.: 125f.
9 *Argonautica* 3.451–456.
10 Kan Turali, ibid.: 121.
11 Kan Turali, ibid.: 123.
12 Kan Turali, ibid.: 131.
13 Kan Turali, ibid.: 132.
14 That is certainly not to prove that Propp is right to suggest only one monomyth to which all such tales belong. Still less does it merit the superficial and impressionistic conclusion that fairy tales and romances generally shuffle the motifs like a pack of cards.
15 For example, Basile 3.8; Calvino 99, 126; Grimm 51, 71, 186, 193. Ashliman offers a wide selection of accessible texts, many published since Aarne–Thompson's check-list of 1961.
16 Briggs (1970: 1.1.290–294), summary; cf. Bruford and Macdonald (1994: 80–97).
17 Calvino no. 99, p. 363.
18 Calvino no. 99, p. 364.
19 *The Green Man of Knowledge*, Briggs 1.1.291; *Green Sleeves* (ibid.:1.1.296), the latter with the condition that the winner might ask of the loser whatever he chooses, as in the version of the episode in Theocritus 22.
20 For example, Briggs 1.1.290ff., 296.
21 Gantz (1993: 350), Apollodorus *Bibl.* 3.8.1.
22 Fr. 157 MW; for discussion of later accounts, see Gantz (1993: 350f.).
23 For example, J.F. Campbell (1860–61) *Popular Tales of the West Highlands* no.2, variants 3 and 7 (1994 repr., vol. I, pp. 128f., 132). In these a bird surviving the battle helps the hero.
24 Harpies: Gantz 353–356; birds with missile feathers, Apollonius 2.1030–89, of iron, according to the scholia.
25 For an example of cleaning a stable, see Briggs 1.1.297.
26 One interesting tailpiece concerns the 'forgotten bride' ending. It has sometimes been emphasised that Odysseus and Jason have much in common between their packages of adventures; it should be noted that Odysseus has the instance par excellence of the 'forgotten bride' motif in the person of Penelope herself. In the *Odyssey*, as in the modern fairytale, the neglected heroine employs subterfuge to stave off

suitors: they can sleep with her, but they must shut a door that never closes (cf. the loom whose work is never finished). In some cases she turns into or makes a bird to remind the hero who it is she is married to. Penelope's name would mean 'duck' or the like. An original version of such a story might have had Odysseus preparing to marry Nausicaa or stay with Calypso; the little bird would then tell him to come home, or come to disrupt the wedding (cf. Athena's changing into a bird at the scene of the carnage of the suitors).

27 Bushnaq (1986: 158–165).

28 The story, or a closely analogous one, is often included in giant-killer cycles. In such cases, however, the commonly encountered form of the trick is brought about without magic. The trickster hero puts on a false stomach full of animal gut, and pretends to 'revitalise' himself after stabbing it. The giant is then deceived into stabbing himself or his wife, but of course with fatal results.

6 THE 'INNOCENT SLANDERED MAID'

1 The tale has not received monograph treatment, but see now S.S. Jones (1993: 13–24); *AT* Types 882, 883A. For examples, Armenian: Hoogasian-Villa no. 48 (*AT* Type 883A); Greek: Dawkins (1916: 361, cf. 267); Argenti-Rose, no. 1 (incorrectly identified by its editors); Egyptian: Spitta (1883) no. 6 (Types 881 and 883A). Spanish examples are now studied by Taggart (1990: 41–58). Five Italian examples from Pitrè in Calvino nos. 157–160, 176; a single defective English example in Briggs 2.451f. For attempts at a broader classification of what amounts to an 'innocent slandered maid' genre of tale, Jones (1993); Nicolaisen (1993).

2 *Decameron* 2.9.

3 Ed. C. Brunel (1923); translation as *The Count of Ponthieu's Daughter* in P. Matarasso (1971: 113–130), Harmondsworth.

4 *Decameron* 3.7. I owe to Diego Zancani the information that Tebaldo and Tedaldo are names of etymologically separate origin; but that of course makes no difference to the ease with which they might be confused.

5 Useful recent discussion in Reardon (1982; 1992, index s.v.); apud Schmeling (1996: 309–335); Egger in Morgan and Stoneman (1994: 31–48).

6 For example, Perry (1967: 137ff.) suspecting a residual (and possibly popular) but *historical* tradition where invention is not invoked. An exception is Burrus (1987: 50), who sees Callirhoe as a literary treatment of *AT* Type 881, *Oft-proved Fidelity*.

7 Perry (ibid.: 117); Reardon (1982: 19–26).

8 Hesiod *Theogony* 288: daughter of Ocean and wife of Chrysaor ('Gold-sword'), mother of the Geryones, strongest of all men (979–982).

9 Pausanias 7.21.1.

10 Ps.-Aeschines *Ep.* 10.

11 Note in particular, Herodotus 2.113f.

12 Hesiod *Th.* 288, 351.

13 *AT* Type 612: e.g. Grimm 16, 61, 191; Calvino 179, 194.

14 Polyidus and Glaucus: Gantz (1993: 270f.); Apollodorus *Bibl.* 3.3.1f.; Hyginus *Fab.* 136.

15 Gantz (1993: 268ff.).

16 Chariton (1989: 1.1.11–15).

7 BUTCHERING GIRLS: *RED RIDING HOOD* AND *BLUEBEARD*

1 Bolte–Polivka no. 26, 1.234–237; for a useful casebook approach, Dundes (1989), the editor himself emphasising the link with *AT* type 133. Zipes (1993a) offers a

detailed survey of the major shifts in emphasis since Perrault, as well as a respectable cross-section of retellings, including those of Perrault and Grimm. See also Opie and Opie (1974: 119–121); Tatar (1999: 3–10).

2 Zipes (1993a: 18–20).
3 Text in Boulvin and Chocourzadeh (1975), no. 11.
4 Delarue 1 (1957: 373f.); tr. in Zipes (1993: 21ff.).
5 But in fact there is a French male version as well, from lower Poitou, printed by Massignon (no. 16). In this instance the grandmother sets about the wolf before the father kills him, and neither boy nor grandmother is swallowed. Note the gender differentiation in what is taken to the grandmother: girls take some kind of dainties, the boy black puddings.
6 Grimm 37, *AT* Type 700.
7 Lang, *Red Fairy Book* (1890: 215–220).
8 According to the Diegesis relating to *Aetia* fr. 98f.
9 A Pindaric scholium contributes the unusual detail that Lycus was responsible for the death of Heracles' three children (Schol. *Isthmian* 4.104f., in contrast to the general tradition that Heracles murdered them himself during his madness); Gantz (1993: 380).
10 Gantz (1993: 227).
11 At this juncture we might also note the tale of the Teumessian Fox (Antoninus Liberalis 41, cf. Apollodorus 2.4.7): it is unhuntable, and requires child sacrifice once a month from the Thebans until it too is lithified by Zeus (to prevent the problem of its being hunted by Minos' inescapable hunting dog).
12 We have, however, another flame-girl who *was* swallowed and recovered alive, though not this time from a wolf: in Hesiod, Hestia is among the offspring of the cannibal Cronos, who is swallowed alive by her father and recovered by Zeus when a stone is substituted for him in his father's belly (Hesiod *Theogony* 453–495). As she became goddess of the hearth, an association embodied in her name, she too can be claimed in some sense as a 'flame-girl'.

We should note also that there are further ramifications of Hestia and her mother Rhea in connection with a wolf and the substitution of a stone: Cronos's disgorging of his children shows at least one distinctive ingredient of the tale – the substitution of a stone for the swallowed child (in this case a single stone rather than a lethal load of them). However, coincidence does not end there: the name of Cronos's wife is Rhea, and her Latin namesake Rhea Silvia is recorded as having been frightened by a wolf in Servius Auctus (valuable assembly of testimonia in Wiseman 1995). Rhea was frightened by the wolf while attending to her business as a vestal virgin, a devotee of the Latin Hestia, Vesta. The two Rheas cannot immediately be identified, as one is a vestal under oath of celibacy and the other is a mother of several children. Or so it seems, except that Vesta herself was supposedly a virgin with the title of *mater* (R. Gordon in *OCD*, 3rd edn, s.v.), and so the objection is rather lessened. Rhea Silvia ('Rhea of the Woods') is as a vestal associated with a sacred flame and some sort of errand as well, sanctioned by Vesta.

If the two Rheas were presented as identical, then the story when reconstructed would indeed resemble ours:

There once was a girl who belonged to the wood. She used to tend the flame of the goddess Vesta, but while she was performing a task for the goddess, she was frightened by the sight of the wolf. She went home to her husband to find that he ate their children. She substituted a stone for one of them, and Gaia – Hestia's grandmother, be it noted – made him bring all the other five out alive. Her husband was punished for his crime by the son he had swallowed, and confined to Tartarus.

There is a further connection. The famous literary werewolf story in Petronius *Satyrica* 61f. has a man setting out to see his would-be lover Melissa now that her husband has died. The soldier he takes with him changes into a wolf and gets to Melissa's first, but is driven off wounded and resumes his human form the next day with the wounds still showing. Melissa and her household had driven him off themselves. What is interesting in the light of the foregoing discussion is that in one context at least the name Melissa was a cult title of Rhea (*OCD3* s.v.).

13 For the classical sources, Gantz (1993: 728f.); Ovid (*Met.* 1.199–243) as usual offers the most detail, but omits the name of the victim, who in this case is a man; cf. also Ps.-Eratosthenes 8D (Lycaon's own grandson Arkas); a child (Hesiod) fr. 163 MW = Katast. 8R *et al.*

14 Grimm 26 (*Little Redcap*).

15 Hyginus 96 furnishes the critical detail of Achilles' pseudonym among the girls; for other sources, Gantz (1993: 581). A further instance of rape of a wolf's daughter occurs in the story of Sisyphus and Autolycus, where Sisyphus seduces Mr Wolfself's daughter in revenge for the stealing of his cattle. I suspect that the ancient and difficult to etymologize Sisyphus is really a simplification of Xisouthros, an oriental name for the Greek Deucalion (cf. Sumerian Ziusudra). If that is indeed the case, then *both* Deucalion and Pyrrha had a victory over the wolf-figure. And of course both have a key adventure with reconstituting the human race out of stones – yet another way of paraphrasing the idea that stones can be used to procure regeneration (put stones in the wolf's belly, and you can take swallowed children out alive; throw them over your shoulder, and they turn into people).

16 Zipes (1993: 229), from James Thurber (1939) 'The Girl and the Wolf', in *Fables for Our Time and Famous Poems* (New York).

17 Horace, *Ars Poetica* 340, with Brink's commentary *ad loc.*.

18 De Nino 12 (= Calvino 116).

19 Longus 3.15–18.

20 Longus 1.20f., 29f.

21 Ps.-Theocritus 27.42, 49–59.

22 In Zipes (1993: 95f.).

23 Other elements of wolf-lore may be relevant to details of Red Riding Hood. We might recall some of the oddities of the Lupercalia where young men, dressed in goatskin capes, strike women with a strip of hide to make them fertile (discussion in Wiseman 1995: 80–87). The two Luperci run by different routes, as do Red Riding Hood and wolf through the wood, but otherwise it is not easy to fit our random assortment of ancient wolf-lore to the contours of our story. For further treatment of lykanthropy, W. Burkert, *Homo Necans* (1983: 84–90); R. Buxton in J. Bremmer (1987: 60–79); also *OCD3* s.v. Lycaon. For the possibility of temporary wolf-men, cf. Marie de France's *Lai Bisclavret*.

24 There may be a symbolism of incest in the idea of a father devouring his own daughter, cf. the incest riddle in *Apollonius of Tyre* 4.

25 Bluebeard: Grimm 46 (Fitcher's Fowl); Bolte and Polivka 1.398–412; Opie and Opie (1974: 133–141) with R. Samber's first printed English version (1729: 137–141).

26 A possible euphemism for loss of virginity, as modern fairytale scholarship has not been slow to argue: for strong reservation, Tatar (1999: 141).

27 For St Tryphine and Commorre, Opie and Opie (1974: 136).

28 For this account, Apollodorus 3.15.1; Antoninus Liberalis 41; cf. Palaiphatos 2. The detailed form of the story in Antoninus is that he ejaculates snakes, scorpions and millipedes into his partners, rather than that he executes his wives.

29 For discussion, Gantz (1993: 270) (Apollodorus 3.3.1f.; Hyginus *Fab.* 136).

30 That is, (P)eriboiia, as in Bacchylides 17.

31 At any rate in Aeschylus' version, *Choephori* 612–622; and evidently implied in the Ps.-Virgilian *Ciris* 187; Ovid has him refusing the lock in horror, *Met.* 8.95f.

32 *Met.* 8.33f.; *The Uncommercial Traveller* (Dickens) ch.15. Note that modern Bluebeards often have the heroine helped by a dog: here Scylla's own name means 'puppy'.

33 For this episode in the tradition hostile to Minos, Diodorus 4.79.1ff.; Apollodorus, *Epitome* 1.14f.; and Gantz (1993: 275).

34 Bluebeard can be naturally related to the title *caeruleus*, appropriate to sea deities (Poseidon, Triton, Nereus, Proteus, or the like: *caeruleos habet unda deos*, Ovid *Met.* 2.8).

35 For the sources, Gantz (1993: 238f.). Hermes, with his underworld associations, might be no less obvious than Deion himself in this context.

36 Opie and Opie (1974: 133).

37 Epimetheus, the husband of Pandora, would as a Titan have spent a period of imprisonment underground after the revolt against Zeus, and might therefore qualify for devil as well as mortal status. (On Epimetheus, Gantz (1993: 154): Hesiod's *Theogony* leaves any role of Prometheus and his brother in the Titanomachy unexplained). But the story as offered in Hesiod is presented as a misogynist tale: the beautiful woman brings destruction on mankind by breaking the taboo of the forbidden jar, and no punishment is offered for opening it. If the story of Pandora is a 'Bluebeard's wife' story, we do not have the whole of it here.

38 For the sources, Gantz (1993: 242f.): Euripides' *Erechtheus*, fr. 360N2; Demosthenes 60.27; Apollodorus, *Bibl.* 3.15.1; Hyginus *Fab.* 46, 238; Suda (with a variety of details).

39 Sources, Ovid *Met.* 7.672–862; Antoninus Liberalis 41; cf. Hyginus *Fab.* 160, 189; Gantz (1993: 238). (In general there are attempts to distinguish between Cephalus, son of Deion, and Cephalus, son of Hermes, but occasional conflation). It should also be noted that the name Deion/Deioneus has overtones of 'destroyer', while Hermes himself has his own underworld associations as escort of souls to the nether world. There is a prominent role for fox and dog in the Cephalus story; English Bluebeards sometimes carry the title 'Mr Fox'.

40 A similar range of daughters of another early Athenian king, Cecrops, are taboo breakers as well: all are given a casket of snakes by Athena and told not to open it, which they do (sources in Gantz (1993: 235–239)). I am grateful to my colleague Jim Neville for drawing this parallel to my attention.

41 On whom see further C. Sourvinou-Inwood, *Reading Greek culture* 147–88. For the analogy between Bluebeard's consort and Persephone, Krappe (1930: 5).

42 Ovid *Met.* 5.533–50; Apollodorus *Bibl.* 1.5.3, 2.5.12; for other accounts, Gantz (1993: 64–68).

43 We might think also of the scene in *Cupid and Psyche* where the heroine has to take a 'Pandora's box' from the Underworld and opens it to find a fateful sleeping drug instead, Apuleius *Met.* 6.20f.

44 Text in Heidel (1949: 97ff.) (a great variety of taboos relating to clothing and actions, but curiously not about food).

45 Sumerian: Jacobsen (1976: 55–63); cf. *AT* Type 312C.

46 For example, burning of infants: *Homeric Hymn to Demeter*; Ovid *Fasti* 4.502–560; as mare: Pausanias 8.25.5. Note, too, the apparent conflation of Pandora and

Persephone mythology in scenes depicting satyrs beating the ground, or Epimetheus depicted with a hammer, as Pandora/Persephone comes out of the ground: 'there is clearly something here that we do not understand', Gantz (1993: 68). The rescue of a Bluebeard victim who has just broken the taboo seems eminently plausible.

47 Spanish oral tradition in Taggart (1990: 60ff.).
48 Ibid.: 68.
49 Ibid.: 73.

8 MAGICIANS AND THEIR ALLIES

1 Christiansen (1958: 3020), motif A1; Philip (1995: 379).
2 Philip (1992: 309–401); cf. the Scottish version in Philip (1995: 379–383), which has a box rather than a book.
3 Glassie, no. 99, Cromwell's Bible (1985: 214f.).
4 For Lucian's use of folktale themes in the *Philopseudes* Bompaire (1958: 457–460), suggesting use of handbooks of popular material, cf. Anderson (1976: 24–30), noting possible literary retouching.
5 Philip (1995: 380).
6 *Philopseudes 33.*
7 So Philip (1995: 381); Christiansen (1958), Type 3020.
8 Lichtheim III (1980: 128–132) (Setne I.3f.).
9 *Exodus* 14.21–29; Westcar Papyrus 6.1–15 (Djadja-em-ankh), 9.15–20 (Djedi); Lichtheim I (1973: 217, 219).
10 Diodorus 4.52.1f.; Apollodorus 1.9.27; Ovid *Met.* 7.297–321; Hyginus *Fab.* 24; Gantz (1993: 366f.).
11 Two good versions in Crane (1885: 221–227) (around the rogue Beppo Pipetta).
12 El-Shamy, no. 17 (1980: 117–121).
13 Gantz (1993: 174) (Pherekydes 3F119); El-Shamy (1980: 119).
14 Sisyphus, Gantz (1993: 173f.).
15 Gantz (1993: 91f.); Plato *Resp.* 408 BC; Apollodorus *Bibl.* 3.10.3.
16 *AT* 560/561; Aarne (1908) *Vergleichende Maerchenforschungen*, Helsingfors.
17 On Galland, see now Irwin (1994: 14–18 and *passim*).
18 The Kurdistani tale 'The Magic Flute of Asmodeus', in Schwartz (1983) has no fewer than six such objects.
19 Plato *Respublica* 359C–360B.
20 Nicolaus of Damascus (Jacoby FGrH90F44).
21 We should note traces of *AT* Type 314 in the horse motif: see especially Delarue's survey of French versions 1 (1957: 242–263).
22 As summarised by Ashliman at *AT* 715.
23 Ranke (1966), no. 70.
24 And has long been recognised to have at least some features belonging to folklore: Helm (1906: 332f.). But the tale as a whole has not been identified, hence the erroneous speculations of Marcovitch (1976) on the reasons for the choice of a cock.
25 So Dawkins (1916: 523).
26 *MGAM* (1916: 521f.). A different version of what is really the same basic tale at pp. 401f., and variants summarised pp. 243f.
27 Cf. Opie and Opie (1974: 38).
28 Gurney (1956).
29 Gurney (1972: 149–158).
30 Cosquin (1912), somewhat vitiated by an obsolete thesis on the origins of the tale; cf. Thompson (1946: 69); *AT* Type 325 (sometimes combined with *AT* 1525); related to Christiansen *ML* 3020; good annotation in El-Shamy (1980: 247f.). For

further examples, Briggs 1.1.162, 1.1.347; Bushnaq (1986: 166); Calvino 128; Dawkins *MGF* (1955: 24); Grimm 68.

31 *Setne Khamwas and Si-Osire* (Setne II.2–7) in M. Lichtheim III (1980: 142–151): for this defining game of counter-magic, pp. 149f.

32 Fr. 33a.12–19 M-W.

33 Ovid *Met.* 8.873f., with Hollis (1970) *ad loc.* The girl already has a long history, with puzzling allusion in the *E Hoiai*, fr. 43a MW; for brief outline, Gantz (1993: 68f., 174f.).

34 El-Shamy (1980: 41).

35 Schol. Ar. *Nub.* 889; discussion in the edn by K.J. Dover (1968: xc–xci).

36 Ar. *Nub.* 768–772.

37 Ar. *Nub.* 226; Georgian, Wardrop no. 1; Egyptian: El-Shamy no. 6 (1980: 40f.).

38 Weinreich (1988: 74).

39 Socrates' *daimon* is still a matter for philosophical speculation as late as Plutarch's *de genio Socratis* (*Moralia* 575A–598E).

40 We can look to the other end of antiquity for a quasi-historical report of events similar to those of the tale. We have an account of the philosopher Sosipatra from the sophist Eunapius (*VS* 466–469) in the late fourth century AD. Once more elements of the folktale loom large in an obviously inflated and idealised account:

> Two men arrive at Sosipatra's father's estate, and demonstrate an amazing increase in the vintage. They may be heroes or demons, or still higher powers. On the strength of this, they take the five-year-old Sosipatra off for instruction; on the strength of her progress she goes off with them for another five years. Her evil kinsman Philometor tries to entice her into his powers and gain control of her (for amorous purposes); she engages the theurgist Maximus of Ephesus to counter his magic with Maximus' own, and so defeats Philometor; with her clairvoyance she is able to note that Philometor has been injured when his chariot overturned.

Eunapius is anxious to see the whole episode in the most creditable terms, but his presentation obscures the natural thrust of the story. Sosipatra has been trained by self-confessed Chaldaeans; she foils an attempt through her own magician on the part of an evil party to gain control of her, and almost as soon as his misdemeanours are detected, he meets with a potentially serious road accident, the details of which she knows exactly as it happens. Eunapius refuses to see the episode as it would most naturally have been interpreted in the climate of his time: that Sosipatra's superior powers have *caused* her opponent's misfortune. The only minor difference between the ancient anecdote and the modern folktale is that there is a change of magicians halfway through; it is *not* one of her own teachers, but another magical practitioner who is trying to get the better of her and comes to a suitably unfortunate end. Of course we can have nothing of Sosipatra's changing into a horse as such, any more than we can with Pheidippides, but *both* instances of clairvoyance noted concern detailed perception of the movement of horse-drawn vehicles.

9 BETWEEN LIVING AND DEAD

1 Briggs 1.1.159; for other versions see Briggs' index s.v. 326A (p. 38).

2 A very full example is that of 'Laying Wild Harris' Ghost', with its hero, Revd Mr Polkinghorne of St Ives (Briggs 2.1.518–522).

3 Cf. 'Laying Wild Harris's Ghost', Briggs 2.1.518–522, *passim*. Here the exorcist has to lay troublesome black spirits (*Bukkha-dhu*), while performing the normal laying

services for the persistently haunting ghost. Cf. also 'The Roaring Bull o' Bagbury', Briggs 2.1.560f.
4 Briggs 2.1.520.
5 Occasioned by the exorcist in 'The Pool of the Black Hound', where Knowles the Weaver's ghost is changed into 'a spectral hound as black as pitch' (Briggs 2.1.17.) The ghost takes the form of a bull in the laying of the Roaring Bull o' Bagbury (Briggs 2.1.561). I know no example of the ghost as a lion, but this too is at least conceivable in the tradition area drawn on by Lucian.
6 See especially the examples listed by Briggs under *ML* 4021.
7 For example, 'The Golden Arm', Briggs 1.2.530; 'Peggy with the Wooden Leggy' (ibid.: 1.2.555); 'Saddaedda', Crane no. 73; 'The Bone', Briggs 1.2.512, cf. 'Teeny-Tiny' I and II (ibid.: 1.2.561ff.); 'The Liver' (ibid.: 541). Briggs classifies what is really a version of this tale as a migratory legend of the 'difficult exorcism' type (Christiansen *ML* 4021): the second husband of Madam Vernon steals the pot of money she has laid up for the children of the second family; the dead wife haunts the property till the ghost is laid (Briggs 2.1.532f.).
8 *Philopseudes* 27.
9 Lichtheim 3 (1980: 128–137) (Setne I.3f.)
10 Grimm 44; Bolte and Polivka 1.381.
11 *Verae Historiae* 1.34. This is highly unlikely to have been the *source* of the popular version, *pace* Krappe (1930: 23); Lucian claims to be parodying 'straight' literary works throughout this text. For its relationship to the 'Star Maiden' tale, see Appendix 3.
12 *Philopseudes* 25.
13 Trenkner (1958: 69f.) (in line with the popular origins of a wide cross-section of Euripidean themes).
14 Tr. G. Lewis (1974 (no. 5): 108–116).
15 This is the key to the myth of *Inanna's Descent*: she too has to find a victim to take her place, in this case her unwilling husband Dumuzi: see Jacobsen (1976: 59).
16 Apollo had helped him to yoke a boar and a lion to a chariot, Apollodorus *Bibl.*, 1.9.15; Hyginus *Fab.* 50f. For other Greek sources, Gantz (1993: 195f.).
17 Gantz (1993: 195), citing *Symposium* 179B (cf. Apollodorus 1.9.15).
18 Megas, *Laographia* 25 (1967: 158–191).
19 Downing (1972: 10–13) (*The Power of Love*).
20 H. Schwartz (1993: 162–164).
21 Schwartz (1993: 163).
22 El-Shamy (1980 (no. 60): 224f.) (Goha joke).
23 Commentary in Hansen (1998: 68–85), with previous bibliography.
24 Hansen (1998: 79–85) (links with *AT* Type 425J 'Service in Hell to release Enchanted Husband').
25 Ranke (1966: 207).
26 For example, 'The Legend of Sister Hylda' (Briggs 2.1.522f.); 'The Whitehaven Ghosts' (ibid.: 601f.); 'Madam Piggott' 1 (ibid.: 530f.).
27 The ghost is apparently bottled, but still capable of being 'uncorked' (Briggs 2.1.579).
28 Briggs 2.1.580f..
29 Grimm 133; Bolte and Polivka 3.78–84.
30 Afanas'ev (1945: 224).
31 Opie and Opie (1974: 247).
32 Gantz (1993: 312f.): in particular Hesiod Frr. 131f., fr. 37MW; Pherekydes 3F114; Bacchylides 11.53–58, 92–95; Herodotus 9.34 (an indefinite number of Argive

women); Apollodorus *Bibl.* 2.2.2.(26–29); Aelian *VH* 3.42. Location of the cave: Pausanias 8.18.7.

33 For the tangle of sources, Gantz 335–339. I suspect that he is probably wrong to try to distinguish two entirely separate Atalantas that have become partly fused, rather than local variants of a single story.

34 Ovid *Met.* 10.647–651.

35 *Aen.* 6.77–80 (prophetic possession); 137–141 and *passim* (bough).

36 Grimm no. 12; *AT* 310; Bolte and Polivka (1913: 1.97–99).

37 Lichtheim 2 (1976: 200–203).

38 As noted by G. Posener (1953: 107).

39 Massignon, *Fabula* 6 (1963: 53–67).

40 For the Greek Protesilaus tradition, Gantz (1993: 592f.), especially schol. Eurip. *Protesilaus* (p. 563N2).

41 Hyginus 103f.; Ovid *Heroides* 13; Catullus 68.73–130; *LIMC* 7.1 (1994: 554–60).

10 TWO HOMERIC TALES: *THE CYCLOPS* AND *ARES AND APHRODITE*

1 The question was effectively answered by Wilhelm Grimm (1857: 23f.), not convincingly refuted by Meuli (1921: 70) the conjunction of blinding and No-man stories should have persisted in oral tradition if the Homeric episode were the original of all others. See further Page (1955: 1–20), following Hackman (1904); cf. Thompson (1946: 200) in the general context of deception stories.

2 Hackman (1904: 9–106 (group A), 107–154 (groups B/C)).

3 Gilgamesh I.2–4 (Dalley 1989: 53–56). The creature is trapped in a manner similar to the trapping of satyrs (though with sex rather than wine as the bait).

4 For example, Downing (1971: 168–175), a version from Armenia where such a trait is very typical.

5 *Od.* 9.105–566; Sindbad's Third Voyage.

6 Ovid *Met.* 13.740–897; cf. Theocr. 11.

7 For example, Virgil *Georg.* 4.170–175 (metal-workers); Cyclopes as builders: Bacchylides 11.77–81; Pausanias 2.16.5.

8 The Cyclops also possesses a treasure-trove in *The Book of Dede Korkut*, see below.

9 *AT* Type 300.

10 Convenient short run of examples in Frazer's Apollodorus 2 (1921: 404–455), whose numbering of examples I have followed; more substantial cataloguing in Hackman (1904: 9–154); Thompson (1961) *AT* 1137; and finally Glenn (1971).

11 For example, Frazer (1921: 31), also from the *Arabian Nights* (Story of Seyf El-Mulook); Frazer (ibid.: 29) (Syriac), actually a tale in which the hero recovers the giant's lost eyes.

12 Hackman (1904: 179–188).

13 Scottish, Frazer 2 (1921: 412).

14 Hackman (1904: 160f., 174–179), found in relation to Type A.

15 Cf. Martin Smith (1975) on *Satyrica* 48.7: *aut de Ulixe fabulam, quemadmodum illi Cyclops pollicem †porricino† extorsit. Solebam haec ego puer apud Homerum legere.*

16 *Od.* 9.504f.

17 For example, in a Basque version, Frazer 5; and a Roumanian, Frazer 6.

18 Tr. in Lewis (1974: 140–150). Discussion: C.S. Mundy (1956: 278–302); and now J. Glenn (1971).

19 *Od.* 9.432–435; sheepskin versions: e.g. Frazer (1921: 22–23, 25, 27), from Sicily, Greece and Albania.

20 Apollodorus 3.10.4.

21 Frazer (1921: 4).
22 Hence Page can hardly be right in asserting: 'these two stories have so little in common that they could not have less without ceasing to have anything' (1955: 5); he says nothing about the context of fire in the No-man tale.
23 *Od.* 8.266–366; Egyptian text translated in Parkinson (1997: 106–109).

11 SOME MORAL PARABLES: *THE PIED PIPER, THE THREE WISHES, RUMPELSTILTSKIN, THE SINGING BONE*

1 For a brief discussion, see Zipes (1995: 119–136), usefully citing the Grimms' version of 1816, not included in his translation of the 1857 edition, from which the tale was omitted.
2 As evidenced by his cult title Smintheus (*Iliad* 1.39); for the anecdote, Strabo 13.1.48. I am grateful to an anonymous referee for drawing my attention to Fontenrose (1983), who compares the tradition on Laomedon's Troy with the Norse myth concerning the walls of Asgard.
3 Tr. Ryder (1925: 449–453, 'Slow, the Weaver').
4 Useful remarks in Rose (1928: 299).
5 Ovid *Met.* 11.90–145.
6 *Met.* 11.146–194.
7 'The Seventh Sage's Tale' in *The Book of Sindbad* offers a sexual variant, where the first wish is for a longer member, with other developments accordingly.
8 For the Tithonus tradition, *Homeric Hymn to Aphrodite* 218–238 (ending in inaudible babble), and Hellanicus 4F140 (change to cicada or grasshopper); Gantz (1993: 36f.).
9 Tr. K.F. Kilburn. Similar examples in Lucian's *Gallus* init., *Navig.* 11. Cf. also Aelian's tale of Thrasyllus, the fool who thinks he owns all the ships who come into the Peiraeus, *Varia Historia* 4.25 (from Heraclides Ponticus, according to Athenaeus).
10 Briggs 1.1.217–220.
11 Von Sydow (1909, 1943); I have relied on Thompson's report (1946: 48).
12 For the Samothracian mysteries and the Cabiri, Burkert (1985: 281–285), pointing out the absence of specific dedication to these gods, i.e. that they are unnamed in inscriptions, doubtless a factor in the instability of their equation with Greek deities. For our purposes, it is sufficient that some authors, including Herodotus 2.51, were prepared to offer the identification. The element of drollery surrounding the cult is also important and appropriate for connection with 'our' tale: vase paintings from the sanctuary emphasise 'grotesque caricature...Pygmy or negroid figures abound, with distorted faces, fat bellies and dangling genitals' (Burkert ibid.: 282). The senior of the Cabiri can be represented as a bearded Dionysus, with children's spinning tops and other toys dedicated to his junior Kad- or Kas-milos.
13 Brunner-Traut (1948: 115–120); accessible paraphrase in R. Nye, *Classic Folktales from around the World* (1996: 258f.).
14 The tale-type associated with Meleager himself (*AT* Type 1187) concerns a separate adventure.
15 On which see further Kakrides (1949: 127–148).
16 Crane no. 8.
17 One notes, too, that Bata's analogue Peleus has killed one man (at least) during a hunting accident, hence the need for purification by Acastus: there may be more to the chequered career of a Meleager, Bata or Peleus type than at first meets the eye.
18 Kakrides (1949: 132f.) (third Turkish variant).
19 Mackensen (1923).

20 Thompson (1977: 136).
21 See further Chapter 13.

12 FAIRYTALE INTO ROMANCE

1 For example, Cox, hero-tales nos. 336, 338 (= 511A, Little Red Ox); other examples between 319 and 341 help define the type; Longus (1987: 1.29f.; 2.13–15; 3.33f.).
2 Philip (1988: 91–94); Longus (1987: 2.33–37).
3 In both cases the girl has difficult parentage (in Sakuntala she is the love-child of a nymph and a mortal, and so has to be fostered; in Heliodorus (4.8) she is wrongly suspected of being a royal bastard). She performs sacred functions at a shrine. We might also compare the medieval Western *Fresne* tale on both counts. The couple in Sakuntala and Heliodorus are cursed with the need for further adventure by a spirit accidentally offended (the ghost of Odysseus in Heliodorus, 5.22); and there is a failure in recognition between the couple (Heliodorus 7.7).
4 For characterisation, Kortekaas (1984: 3ff.); Archibald (1991); Schmeling (1996: 540–550).
5 *Apollonius of Tyre* 28–50. It is illuminating to look at *Cupid and Psyche* from this perspective. Here Venus acts as the jealous rival and goddess, persecuting the heroine in several murder attempts (Apuleius *Met.* 6.10–21), and using supernatural surveillance (a talking bird) (*Met.* 5.28.2f.). She nearly succeeds when she sends the heroine to fetch a box from Hades, which Psyche then opens and falls into a near fatal sleep (*Met.* 6.16.3 – 6.21.2). She goes initially to a deserted palace where a place is set for her and a bed, as Snow White finds the vacant place at her hut (*Met.* 5.1.2 – 5.3.3, but with invisible servants and disembodied voices). But this time the lover is Cupid – himself so often depicted as a tiny boy. If this, too, is seen as a mythical version of *Snow White*, we have an explanation for the episode of the dogs to be fed: she has to feed Cerberus on her underworld journey to find the waters of life.
6 Most surprising is that the second task matches one of Achilles' more unusual digressions: we are told that Libyan women can extract gold from a lake of pitch (*AT* 2.14).
7 A number of other folktale variants occur of the attempts to establish the heroine's role as a woman: she sleeps with the hero, but does not yield to his embraces ('A maid I came, a maid I departed' (*AT* Type 884B), or there may be a whole sequence of sex tests in which she defies attempts to identify her as a woman.
8 Megas 34, a form of the tale that steers very close to the situation of the *Twelve Dancing Princesses*, when the centre of the earth is felt to be underground, and gold, silver and jewelled branches have to be brought to prove the hero has found it. For good short treatment, Megas' note (ibid.) and Dawkins (1951: no. 12), a Dodekanese version.
9 I have drawn particularly on the overlapping versions in Afanas'ev, *Maria Morevna*, 553–562; Basile, 4.3; Dawkins, 379 and (1951) no. 12; Crane, no. 13; Calvino, nos 100, 133; Grimm 197, 228 (Zipes' numbering).
10 Dawkins (1951: 163).
11 Dawkins (1951: 165).
12 In Achilles, the phoenix episode is detached from the heroine's coma and actually occurs slightly before it, at the end of Book 3.
13 And some of the minor secondary details offer very distinctive correspondences between Achilles and the folktale: in particular, the phoenix, so apparently irrelevant in Achilles (3.25), has a function in the folktale; even the motif of water drinkers tossing their drink and catching it in their mouths (4.18) has a counterpart in it (this detail is actually irrelevant in both).

There are also other pieces of the jigsaw: the search for the lost brother-in-law has a good deal of overlap with the search for the lost sister, Type 451, and the latter in turn with the Snow White core of Achilles; note also the overlap of the Leucippe folktale (sex change, sister, and magic white horse).

14 Achilles 3.8; Afanas'ev p. 555.
15 Achilles 3.7; Grimm no. 228 (1992: 676f.).
16 Achilles 1.17; Dawkins (1951: 175).
17 See Chapter 3 n. 29.
18 Achilles Tatius 1.4, already anticipated in the painting of Europa, 1.1 (white chiton, red robe).
19 We should not lose sight of the fact either that the last Snow White romance we noticed, Xenophon's *Ephesiaca*, has the hero giving in, or about to give in, to a woman named Kyno (Bitch); Achilles' hero Clitophon yields eventually to Leucippe's rival Melite ('Maltese lapdog').
20 Achilles 2.13; 5.17.
21 For the relationship of Achilles' novel to Type 552 and the Orestes story, see Appendix 4.

13 FOLKTALES AND SOCIETY: SOME REFLECTIONS ON ANCIENT EVIDENCE

1 For the constantly fluctuating relationship of classics and anthropology, P. Cartledge (1995: 17–28).
2 See now especially Ong (1982), especially 16–30.
3 For a good cross-section of interdisciplinary approaches to classical myth, Edmunds (1990).
4 For sample readings in the competing methodologies in Folkloristics, Dundes (1999), and still more usefully in his folklore casebooks on *Cinderella*, *Oedipus* and *Red Riding Hood* (1982, 1985, 1989); Georges and Owen Jones (1995), notably 31–57 (as a historical study of an evolutionary process), 231–268 (as an inbuilt psychological mechanism). Warner (1994, 1999) shows, in contrast to many, a broad chronological range, but this is of relatively limited use unless one also accesses oral tale-type evidence in the traditional way. And many of the clues to ancient mythological analogues unfortunately turn up in the least accessible sources.
5 I am currently completing an anthology of texts, which I hope will provide practitioners in traditionally separate disciplines with the means to explore this often inaccessible material for themselves.
6 Note especially Lieberman (1972); Rowe (1979); Zipes (1986).
7 For example, von Franz in Dundes (1982: 207); Hallett and Karasek (2nd edn, 1996: 51 among much).
8 See Verdier (1978: 17–55), accepted by Zipes (1993a: 24f.).
9 Zipes (ibid.: 54f.), translating a version of Ulrich Link which appeared in the Muenchner Neueste Nachrichten in 1937 (as counter-Nazi parody).
10 Brownmiller (1976: 243f.); Zipes (1993: 350f.).
11 Zipes (1993: 350–379).
12 See Chapter 7, nn. 3 and 17.
13 Pausanias 6.6.7–11.
14 Zipes (1993: 379).
15 Cf. Zipes (1979: 173): 'the ideological and psychological pattern and message of Cinderella do nothing more than reinforce sexist values and a Puritan ethos that serves a society which fosters competition and achievement for survival.'
16 Bourboulis (1953: 40–52) reproduced in Dundes (1983: 98–109).

NOTES

17 See Chapter 2, n. 29.
18 *Joseph and Asenath* 19.
19 Aelian, *Varia Historia* 12.1.
20 Cf. Dowden (1991), on Greek women's rituals.
21 For the problems of the matriarchy in antiquity, much over-emphasised early in the twentieth-century, S. Pembroke in *OCD*, 3rd edn s.v.
22 See Chapter 3, n. 31.
23 Basile 5.1 (*Sun, Moon and Talia*).
24 For example, Ovid. Met. 11.295–345; Athenaeus 9.393ef; Antonius Liberalis 16.
25 Bettelheim (1976: 291–295).
26 See above, Chapter 4, n.48.
27 Livy I. 57ff. Cf. now Nicolaisen (1993: 61–71) ('Why tell stories about innocent, persecuted heroines?').
28 For example, *Chaereas and Callirhoe* 6.5ff. (the heroine resists the eunuch's combination of threats and blandishments offered on behalf of the King of Persia).
29 Cf. Swann Jones (1993); Nicolaisen (1993).
30 For the strange case of Perpetua, see now Salisbury (1997).
31 For the variation in the handling of the classical Medea, see now Clauss and Johnston (1997).
32 Bettelheim (1976: 300f.).
33 For recent discussion, Tatar (1987: 156–171, 178f.) (hard on most previous interpretation).
34 See above, Chapter 7, n. 28.
35 Krappe (1930: 5).
36 For a whole reader on the debate, see now Segal (1998).
37 See above, Chapter 4, n. 48.
38 *Joseph and Asenath* 16f.
39 Dowden (1989: 9–16).
40 For 'false bride' rituals in folk practice in modern Europe, Roehrich (1991: 101ff.); cf. Roheim in Dundes (1999: 215ff.), with reservations on his 'Oedipal' reading of the origins of the custom, p. 230.
41 Cf. Kirk (1962: 40–43).
42 For the ambiguous nature of trickster folklore, Radin (1956: *passim*).
43 *Met.* 8.437–525 with Hollis (1970: *ad loc.*).
44 Bettelheim (1976: 71f.) is not one of them, focusing very oddly on the story as a tale for children when, by his own admission, the fantasies attached to it are normally those of adults.
45 For the dead in the archaic and classical Greek religious world-view, see Sourvinou-Inwood (1996).
46 This has been the continuing focus of much of Zipes' work in particular, for example, (1979), (1997), (1999), working towards a social history of folktale.
47 Zipes (1995: 119–123).
48 See Verdier (1978).
49 Zipes (1993b: 43–60).
50 Zipes (1995: 122f.).
51 See above, Chapter 2, n. 29.
52 For a very proper dismissal of Bettelheim's ultra-speculative methods, Zipes (1979: 160–195). The whole book reads like a description of psychoanalytical practice couched in the metaphor of fairytales, rather than a serious discussion of fairytale coloured by psychoanalytical practice; see also Dundes (1991: 74–83). The word 'abuse' figures ominously in the titles of both these long reviews. For a scarcely less bizarre approach, see Rubinstein in Dundes (1982: 221–228).

NOTES

53 Despite Bettelheim (1976: 248). It is to his credit that he has recognised, however, that Zezolla's desire to get rid of her mother in Basile's version, so frequently expurgated from later versions, is an obverse to the explicitly incestuous designs of her father in the *Cap o' Rushes* form of the tale.
54 For example, Bettelheim (1976: 266, 271f.).
55 So Mills, in Dundes (1982: 169–192).
56 For example, Dégh (1969); Falassi (1980: 55–68) in Dundes (1982: 276–293).
57 Edmunds (1985: 128).

14 CONCLUSIONS

1 See Appendix 1.
2 See now especially Tatar (1987).
3 Unfortunately continuing into the third edition of the Oxford Classical Dictionary, s.v. Folktale, where Aarne–Thompson is *still* unmentioned, and the Stith Thompson motif-index is dismissed as 'atomistic'. Of course it is, but it presupposes complementary use of the whole-tale index.
4 See Appendix 1.
5 In a personal communication.
6 Perry (1967: 11–15).
7 Philip (1992), from *Have with you to Saffron Walden*.

APPENDIX 1 SOME DIFFICULT CASES

1 *AT* 545B; Bolte–Polivka 3.487. Note especially Straparola, 2.1; Basile 2.4 (*Gagliuso*); Perrault, *Le Chat Botté*; Grimm 216 (Zipes' numbering); Dawkins *MGAM* 455ff.; Argenti–Rose, no. 23, *The Vixen and the Golden Frumety*; Crane nos. 33f.; Calvino 185; Thompson stresses the literary nature of Perrault's version, and notes the degree of deviation from it outside Western Europe in genuine oral versions.
2 *EA* 10016/1. Good reproduction in Rawson (1977: v).
3 The modern tale does have at least one example where the Fox at least *pretends* that the hero of the tale is her son (Argenti–Rose 1948: 23).
4 Although not reported as such in Aarne–Thompson.
5 Cf. Argenti–Rose 23.
6 Grimm no. 1: BP 1.1–9.
7 For example, Briggs 1.1.443 (from R. Chambers (1870) *Popular Rhymes of Scotland*, p. 87, as told to Charles Sharpe by his nurse *c.* 1784).
8 The expression goes back at least as far as *The Complaynt of Scotland* (1549), as a tale told among a group of shepherds: Opie and Opie (1974: 239); Walter Scott knew this destination, mentioned in an allusion to the 'Prince Paddock' known to him as a child, in a letter cited by Edgar Taylor in Gammer Grethel (1839: 344); see also Briggs 1.1.563f. (abridged from Jacobs 215).
9 Briggs 1.1.267f. (two versions) belonging to type *AT* 1180 (440 without the marriage promise); 1.1.563 (complete).
10 Briggs 1.1.563f.; cf. Briggs 1.1.258, a combination of Types 440 and 480.
11 'The Frog Sweetheart', Briggs 1.260f.
12 The bogle in an elaborate variant, 'The Maiden Fair and the Fountain Fairy', Briggs 1.1.397–400, from N. and W. Montgomerie, *The Well at the World's End* (1956: 23–28).
13 In the light of the other versions, we might expect a tailpiece in which the dog should appear in due course to become the disenchanted prince; a similarly truncated version is found with 'two robinets': Briggs 1.1.267f.

NOTES

14 This is the form of the earliest modern version, Straparola's *The Pig Prince*.
15 *BP* 1, p. 4.
16 Apollodorus 2.1.4; Hyginus *Fab.* 259/259A.
17 Hyginus *Fab.* 170.5: Rose marks the name as corrupt.
18 *Dialogi Marini* 8.
19 Again, Lucian's sketch has Poseidon led to the spot by a Triton, who might be seen as an alternative to the satyr.
20 This is the picture presented in Aeschylus' *Supplices* (174f., 750–753, 757–759), from the trilogy to which his satyr-play *Amymone* belonged.
21 Hyginus 160.5.
22 For brief discussion, Sutton (1980: 14–17). Marriage is raised in fr. 13R, but it is not clear whether by Poseidon or the satyr, or indeed in a context applicable to either.
23 Roberts (1958). Previous treatments: on Grimm 24, *Frau Holle*, Bolte–Polivka 1.207–227.
24 Standard Commentaries on the Greek text (among many): Handley (1965); Gomme and Sandbach (1973); neither considers the folktale dimension, and of course Trenkner's monograph, which did deal in some detail with popular elements in Menander's plots, was likewise too early to be able to relate the *Dyskolos* to this dimension.
25 Roberts (1958: 162ff.) for a sketch of geographical spread.
26 Roberts (1958: 85f.): oven, IV.E.1; tree shaken or picked, IV.D.1; escape with encounters, IV.U.
27 Fourteenth-century Latino-Czech MS known to Polivka, Roberts p. 14; Basile 4.7, 5.2; Perrault, *Les Fées*; further early versions, Roberts (1958: 13f.).
28 For earlier literary variants of this motif, cf. the inset exempla in the *Barlaam and Iosaphat* Cycle, e.g. *Balavariani* 2.12 (tr. D.M. Lang (1966) *The Balavariani: A Tale from the Christian East*, London, p. 75f.
29 Gantz (1993: 235–238); Euripides *Ion* 9–26, 260–282; Ovid *Met.* 2.552–561; Apollodorus *Bibl.* 3.14.6; Pausanias 1.18.2; Hyginus *Fab.* 166; *Astr.* 2.13 (with considerable variation in the details). Note that the English version *Three Heads in the Well* has the girls as the three daughters of the King of Colchester, a correspondingly 'early' English traditional monarch.
30 Dawkins (1916: 346); cf. also p. 334.
31 The story of Minos and Procris gives a sexual version of the girl's lap given snakes and the like. Modern versions have a more modest orifice – the mouth – discharging the gold and the snakes.
32 *Dyskolos* 120f.
33 Roberts (1958: 82) (sheep sheared, IV.A.3).
34 Roberts (1958: 99) (VIII.B.2).
35 *Dyskolos* 472, 480.
36 *Dyskolos* 828–831.
37 So Trenkner (1958: 142–146).
38 For example, *Dyskolos* 5–10.

APPENDIX 2 TWO ANCIENT HERO TALES

1 Frazer (1921: 2.385) (relationship of Thetis to Swan-maiden type).
2 Lichtheim *AEL* 2 (1976: 203–210).
3 Basile 1.7.
4 Ranke 29.
5 For the latter, Crane no. 6.
6 Megas no. 21.

7 Dawkins, *MGAM* p. 489.
8 See Chapter 7.
9 For example, El-Shamy no. 3; Megas no. 30.
10 Gantz (1993: 228–231). Some modern comparative materials in Frazer's Apollodorus 2 (1921: 383–388).
11 Variants of Peleus and Thetis discussed by Gantz (1993: 225–232).
12 With considerable discrepancy in the details: cf. Gantz (1993: 222f.).
13 *Two Brothers* also incorporates an important Cinderella motif, the tracing of the lock of hair by the king: on its position in the two tales, Rooth (1951: 140ff.) (good comparison between Egyptian *Two Brothers* and a modern Socotran Arab version first noted by D.H. Mueller).
14 Gantz (1993: 229f.).
15 Opie and Opie (1974: 211f.).
16 Tr. A. George (1999: 1182f.).
17 Opie and Opie (1974: 217).

APPENDIX 3 *THRUSHBEARD* AND *THE STARMAIDENS*

1 Philippson (1923).
2 Ed. H. Behrens (1978).
3 In Dundes (1965: 414–474).
4 Apuleius *Met.* 5.9f.; 5.27.
5 Swahn (1955: 296–312); see also Chapter 4.
6 Schol. Apollonius Rhodes 4.57f.; Gantz (1993: 35).
7 Thompson in Dundes (1965: 438).
8 Thompson in Dundes (1965: 448).
9 I am not convinced by the refreshing arguments of J.R. Morgan (1985) that Antonius was not one of Lucian's targets despite Photius' avowal or assumption that he was (Cod. 166.111b); see Schmeling (1966: 556ff.). But either way there can scarcely be any doubt of his access to some strata of popular storytelling; cf. above Chapters 8 and 9 *passim*.
10 J. Riordan (1989: 129; 135).
11 Stevenson (1958: 66–90).
12 Cf. Thompson in Dundes (1965: 457).

BIBLIOGRAPHY

I Texts and anthologies

(Items placed in this section may often contain elaborate commentary or prefatory material as well as texts.)

Achilles Tatius, *Leucippe and Clitophon*, (ed.) J.-Ph. Garnaud (1991) Paris.

Aelian, *Historical Miscellany (Varia Historia)*. (ed.) N.J. Wilson (1997) Cambridge, MA.

Apollodorus, *The Library* (Bibliotheca), (ed.) J.G. Frazer (1921) vols I–II, London.

Apollonius of Tyre: Historia Apollonii Regis Tyrii, (ed.) G.A.A. Kortekaas (1984) Groningen.

Apuleius, *Cupid and Psyche*, (ed.) E.J. Kenney (1990) Cambridge.

—— *Metamorphoses*, (ed.) D.S. Robertson, (tr.) P. Vallette (1940–1945) Paris.

—— (as *The Golden Ass*) (tr.) P.G. Walsh (1994) Oxford.

Argenti, P. and Rose, H.J. (1948) *The Folklore of Chios* vols I–II, Cambridge.

Basile, G. (1932) *The Pentamerone of Giambattista Basile*, (tr.) N.M. Penzer (from Benedetto Croce's Italian version), London.

Book of Dede Korkut, The, (tr.) G. Lewis (1974) Harmondsworth, Middx.

Briggs, K. (1970) *A Dictionary of British Folktales in the English Language*, vols I–II, London.

Bruford, A.J. and Macdonald, D.A. (1994) *Scottish Traditional Tales*, Edinburgh.

Bushnaq, I. (1986) *Arab Folk Tales*, Harmondsworth, Middx.

Calvino, I. (1982), *Italian Folk Tales*, Harmondsworth, Middx.

Campbell, J.F. (1860–1861) *Popular Tales of the West Highlands*, vols I–II, Edinburgh.

—— (1940, 1960) *More West Highland Tales*, vols I–II, Edinburgh.

Celoria, F. (1992) *The Metamorphoses of Antoninus Liberalis: A Translation with a Commentary*, London.

Chariton, *(Chaereas and) Callirhoe*, (ed.) G.P. Goold (1989) Cambridge, MA.

Count of Ponthieu's Daughter, The, (ed.) C. Brunel (1923) Paris.

—— (tr.) P. Matarasso (1971) Harmondsworth, Middx.

Crane, T.F. (1885) *Italian Popular Tales*, Boston.

Dalley, S. (1989) *Myths from Mesopotamia*, Oxford.

Dawkins, R.M. (1916) *Modern Greek in Asia Minor*, Cambridge.

—— (1951) *Forty-Five Tales from the Dodekanese*, Cambridge.

—— (1953) *Modern Greek Folktales*, Oxford.

—— (1955) *More Greek Folktales*, Oxford.

Delarue, P. (1957–1976) *Le conte populaire français*, vols I–IV (latter two volumes with M.-L. Tenèze), Paris.

Downing, C. (1972) *Armenian Folk Tales*, New York.

El-Shamy, H. (1980) *Folktales of Egypt*, Chicago.

Enlil and Ninlil, (ed.) H. Behrens (1978) Rome.

Farber-Fluegge, G. (1973) *Der Mythos 'Inanna und Enki'*, Rome.

Grimm, J. and Grimm W. (1857) *The Complete Fairy Tales of the Brothers Grimm*, (tr.) J. Zipes (1992) (the 1857 collection, with forty additional tales), New York.

Hallett, M. and Karasek, B. (1996) *Folk and Fairy Tales*, 2nd edn, Peterborough, Ontario.

Hansen, W. (1998) *Anthology of Ancient Greek Popular Literature*, Bloomington, IN.

Heliodorus, *Aethiopica*, (eds) Rattenbury, R.M. and Lumb, T.J., (tr.) J. Maillon (1935–1943) Paris.

Hesiod, Fragments (eds) R. Merkelbach and M.L. West (1967), Oxford.

Heidel, A. (1949) *The Gilgamesh Epic and Old Testament Parallels*, Chicago.

Hollis, A.S. (1970) *Ovid: Metamorphoses Book VIII*, Oxford.

Hoogasian-Villa, S. (1966) *100 Armenian Folktales*, Chicago.

Hunter, R.L. (1989) *Apollonius of Rhodes: Argonautica Book III*, Cambridge.

Hyginus, *Fabulae*, (ed.) H.J. Rose (1933) Leiden.

Joseph and Asenath, (ed.) M. Philonenko (1968) Leiden.

Kramer, S.N. (1942) *Gilgamesh and the Huluppu Tree*, Bloomington, IN.

Lang, A. (ed.) (1890) *The Red Fairy Book*, London.

Lewis, G. (1974) *The Book of Dede Korkut*, Harmondsworth, Middx.

Lichtheim, M. (1973–1980) *Ancient Egyptian Literature*, vols I–III, Berkeley, CA.

Longus, *Daphnis and Chloe*, (ed.) M.D. Reeve (1987) Leipzig.

Lucian, (ed.) M.D. Macleod, vols I–IV (1972–87) Oxford.

Megas, G. (1970) *Folktales of Greece*, Chicago.

Nye, R. (1998) *Classic Folktales from around the World*, London.

Parkinson, R.B. (1997) *The Tale of Sinuhe and Other Ancient Egyptian Poems, 1940–1640 BC*, Oxford.

Perrault, C. (1957) *The Fairy Tales of Charles Perrault*, (tr.) G. Brereton, Harmondsworth, Middx.

Philip, N. (1989) *The Cinderella Story*, Harmondsworth, Middx.

—— (1992) *The Penguin Book of English Folktales*, Harmondsworth, Middx.

—— (1995) *The Penguin Book of Scottish Folktales*, Harmondsworth, Middx.

Philonenko, M. (1968) *Joseph et Aséneth*, Leiden.

Philostratus Senior, (tr.) A. Fairbanks (1931) Cambridge, MA.

—— (eds) K. Kalinka and O. Schoenberger (1968) Munich.

Phlegon of Tralles, *Book of Marvels*, (tr.) W. Hansen (1996) Exeter.

Pritchard, J.B. (1969) *Ancient Near Eastern Text relating to the Old Testament*, Princeton, NJ.

Ranke, K. (1966) *Folktales of Germany*, (tr.) L. Baumann, Chicago.

Rawson, Jessica (1977) *Animals in Art*, London.

Reardon, B.P. (1989) *Collected Ancient Greek Novels*, Berkeley, CA.

Schwartz, H. (1987) *Elijah's Violin and Other Jewish Folktales*, Harmondsworth, Middx.

—— (1988) *Miriam's Tambourine, Jewish Folktales from around the World*, Oxford.

—— (1993) *Gabriel's Palace: Jewish Mystical Tales*, New York.

Seki, K. (1963) *Folktales of Japan*, Chicago.

Stephens, S. and Winkler, J.J. (1995) *Ancient Greek Novels: The Fragments*, Princeton, NJ.

Straparola, G. F. (1894) *The Nights of Straparola*, vols I–II, (tr.) W.G. Waters, London.

Weinreich, B.S. (1988) *Yiddish Folktales*, New York.

Xenophon of Ephesus, *Ephesiaca*, (ed.) A.D. Papanikolaou (1978), Leipzig.

Zipes, J. (1986) *Don't Bet on the Prince: Contemporary Fairy Tales in North America and England*, New York.

—— (1989) *Beauties, Beasts and Enchantment: Classic French Fairy Tales*, New York.

—— (1991) *The Penguin Book of Western Fairy Tales*, New York.

II Secondary Literature

Aarne, A. (1908) *Vergleichende Maerchenforschungen*, Helsingfors.

Aarne, A. and Thompson, S. (1961) *The Types of the Folktale*, Helsinki.

Afanas'ev, A. (1945) *Russian Fairy Tales* (tr. N. Guterman), New York.

Aly, W. (1921) *Volksmaerchen, Sage und Novelle bei Herodot und seinem Zeitgenossen*, Goettingen.

Anderson, G. (1976) *Studies in Lucian's Comic Fiction*, Leiden.

—— (1986) *Philostratus*, London.

Aptowitzer, V. (1924) 'Asenath, the wife of Joseph: a Haggadic literary-historical study', *Hebrew Union College Annual* 1: 239–306.

Archibald, E. (1991) *Apollonius of Tyre: Medieval and Renaissance Themes and Variations*, Cambridge.

Ashliman, D.L.(1987) *A Guide to Folktales in the English Language*, New York.

Azzolina, D. (1987) *Tale-Type and Motif-Indexes: An Annotated Bibliography*, New York.

Behrens, H. (1978) *Enlil und Ninlil: Ein Sumerischer Mythos aus Nippur*, Rome.

Bettelheim, B. (1976) *The Uses of Enchantment*, London.

Binder, G. and Merkelbach, R. (eds) (1968) *Amor und Psyche*, Darmstadt.

Boeklen, E. (1910, 1915) *Sneewittchenstudien*, vols I–II, Leipzig.

Boggs, R.S. (1933) *The Half-Chick Tale in Spain and France* (FFC 111), Helsinki.

Bolte, J. and Polivka, G. (1913–1932) *Anmerkungen zu den Kinder- und Hausmaerchen der Brueder Grimm*, vols I–V, Leipzig.

Bompaire, J. (1958) *Lucien écrivain*, Paris.

Bottigheimer, R.B. (1986) *Fairy Tales and Society: Illusion, Allusion and Paradigm*, Philadelphia.

Boulvin, P. and Chocourzadeh, N. (1975) *Contes populaires persans du Khorassan*, Vols I–II, Paris.

Bourboulis, P.P. (1953) *Studies in the History of Modern Greek Story-Motives*, Thessalonica.

Bremmer, J. (1987) *Interpretations of Greek Mythology*, London.

Brockington, M. (1995) 'The Indic version of *The Two Brothers* and its relationship to the *Ramayana*', *Fabula* 36: 259–272.

Brownmiller, S. (1976) *Against Our Will: Men, Women, and Rape*, New York.

Brunner-Traut, E. (1989) *Altaegyptische Maerchen*, 8th edn, Duesseldorf.

Burkert, W. (1983) *Homo Necans* (tr. P. Bing), Berkeley, CA.

—— (1985) *Greek Religion* (tr. J. Raffan), Oxford: Basil Blackwell.

Burrus, V. (1987) *Chastity as Autonomy: Women in the Stories of the Apocryphal Acts*, Lewiston, NY.

Cartledge, P. (1995) 'The Greeks and anthropology', *Classics Ireland* 2: 17–28.

Chittenden, P. and Kiniry, M. (1986) *Making Connections Across the Curriculum* (on *Snow White*, pp. 579–650), New York.

Christiansen, R. (1958) *The Migratory Legends* (*FFC* 175), Helsinki.

Clauss, J.J. and Johnston, S.I. (1997) *Medea*, New Jersey.

Clodd, E. (1898) *Tom Tit Tot*, London.

Cosquin, E. (1913) *Les Mongols et leur prétendu rôle dans la transmission des contes Indiens vers l'occident Européen*, Paris.

Cox, M.R. (1893) *Cinderella*, London.

Dalmeyda, G. (1926) *Xenophon d'Éphèse*, Paris.

Dasen (1993) *Dwarfs in Classical Antiquity*, Oxford.

Dégh, Linda (1969) *Folktales and Society: Storytelling in a Hungarian Peasant Community*, Bloomington, IN.

Dover, K.J. (1968) *Aristophanes' Clouds*, Oxford.

Dowden, K. (1989) *Death and the Maiden: Girls' Initiation Rites in Greek Mythology*, London.

—— (1991) *The Uses of Greek Mythology*, London.

Dundes, A. (1965) *The Study of Folklore*, New Jersey.

—— (1982) *Cinderella: A Casebook*, New York.

—— (1989a) *Little Red Riding Hood: A Casebook*, New York.

—— (1989b) *The Flood Myth*, Berkeley, CA.

—— (1999) *International Folkloristics*, Lanham, Maryland.

Dundes, A. and Edmunds, L. (1995) *Oedipus: A Folklore Casebook*, 2nd edn, Wisconsin.

Edmunds, L. (1985) *Oedipus: The Ancient Legend and its Analogues*, Baltimore.

—— (1990) *Approaches to Greek Myth*, Baltimore.

Falassi, A. (1980) 'Cinderella in Tuscany', in Dundes (1982), pp. 276–293.

Franz, M.-L. von (1972) *Problems of the Feminine in Fairy Tales*, Irving, TX.

—— (1974) *Shadow and Evil in Fairy Tales*, New York

Fehling, D. (1977) *Amor und Psyche*, Wiesbaden.

Fontenrose, J. (1983) 'The building of the city walls: Troy and Asgard', *Journal of American Folklore* 96: 53–63.

Gantz, G. (1993) *Early Greek Myth: A Guide to Literary and Visual Sources*, Baltimore.

George, A. (1999) *The Epic of Gilgamesh: A New Translation*, London.

Georges, R.A. and Jones, M.O. (1995) *Folkloristics: An Introduction*, Bloomington, IN.

Glassie, H. (1985) *Irish Folk Tales*, New York.

Glenn, J. (1971) 'The Polyphemus Folktale and Homer's *Kyklopeia*', *TAPhA* 102: 133–181.

Goldberg, C. (1984) 'The Historic-Geographic Method: Past and Future', *Journal of Folklore Research* 21: 1–18.

—— (1992) 'The Forgotten Bride' (*AT* 313C), *Fabula* 33: 39–54.

—— (1993) *Turandot's Sisters: A Study of the Folktale AT 851*, Bloomington, IN.

Gomme, A. and Sandbach, F. (1973) *Menander: A Commentary*, Oxford.

Gronewald, M. (1979) 'Ein neues Fragment zu einem Roman', *ZPE* 35: 15–20.

Gurney, O. (1972) 'The Sultanpepe Tablets V: *The Tale of the Poor Man of Nippur*', *Anatolian Studies* 6: 150–159.

Hackman, O. (1904) *Die Polyphemsage in der Volksueberlieferung*, Helsinki.

Haliday, W.R. (1993) *Greek and Roman Folklore*, New York.

Handley, E. (1965) *The Dyskolos of Menander*, London.

Helm, R. (1906) *Lucian und Menipp*, Leipzig.

Hoffner, H.A., Jnr. (1990) *Hittite Myths*, Atlanta.

Hoogasian-Villa, S. (1966) *100 Armenian Tales*, Detroit.

Irwin, R. (1994) *The Arabian Nights: A Companion*, Harmondsworth, Middx.

Jacobsen, Th. (1976) *Treasures of Darkness*, New Haven, CT.

Jameson, R.D. (1932) *Three Lectures on Chinese Folklore*, Peking.

Jason, H. and Kempinsky, A. (1981), 'How Old Are Folktales?', *Fabula* 22: 1–27.

Jones, S.S. (1983) 'The Structure of Snowwhite', *Fabula* 24: 56–71.

—— (1990) *The New Comparative Method: Structural and Symbolic Analysis of the Allomotifs of 'Snowwhite'* (FFC 247), Helsinki.

—— (1993) 'The innocent persecuted heroine genre: an analysis of its structure and themes', *Western Folklore* 52: 13–41.

Kakrides, J. (1949) *Homeric Researches*, Lund.

Kirk, G.S. (1962) *The Songs of Homer*, Cambridge.

—— (1974) *The Nature of Greek Myths*, Harmondsworth, Middx.

Kortekaas, G.A.A. (1984) *Historia Apollonii Regis Tyri*, Gronigen.

Kramer, S.H. (1963) *The Sumerians, their History, Culture and Character*, Chicago.

—— (1969) *The Sumerian Sacred Marriage Rite*, Bloomington, IN.

—— (1981) *History Begins at Sumer*, Philadelphia.

Kramer, S.H. and Maier, J. (1989) *Myths of Enki, The Crafty God*, New York.

Krappe, A.H. (1930) *The Science of Folk-Lore*, London.

Krohn, K. (1926) *Die folkloristische Arbeitsmethode*, Oslo.

—— (1931) *Uebersicht ueber einige Resultate der Maerchenforschung*, (FFC 96) Helsinki.

Laistner, M.L.W. (1951) *Christian and Pagan Culture in the Last Century of the Roman Empire*, New York.

Lieberman, M. (1972) 'Some Day My Prince Will Come: female acculturation through the fairy tale', *College English* 34: 383–395.

Luethi, M. (1976) *Once Upon a Time: On the Nature of Fairy Tales*, Bloomington, IN.

Mackensen, L. (1923) *Der singende Knochen* (FFC 49), Helsinki.

Marcovich, M. (1976) 'Pythagoras as Cock', *American Journal of Philology* 97: 331–335.

Massignon, G. (1963) 'L'enfant qui devait être pendu à l'age d'homme', *Fabula* 5: 53–67.

Matarasso, P. (1973) *The Quest of the Holy Grail*, Harmondsworth, Middx.

Megas, G. (1967) 'Die Sage von Alkestis', *Laographia* 25: 158–191.

—— (1970) *Folktales of Greece*, Chicago.

Meuli, K. (1921) *Odyssee und Argonautika*, Berlin.

Mills, M.A. (1982) 'A Cinderella variant in the context of a Muslim woman's ritual', in Dundes (1982), pp.180–192.

Morgan, J.R. (1985) 'Lucian's True Histories and the Wonders beyond Thule of Antonios Diogenes', *CQ* n.s. 35: 475–490.

Morgan, J.R. and Stoneman, R. (1994) *Greek Fiction*, London.

Mundy, C.S. (1956) 'Polyphemus and Tepegoez', *BSOAS* 18: 279–302.

Nicolaisen, W.F.H. (1993) 'Why tell stories about innocent persecuted heroines?', *Western Folklore* 52: 61–71.

Nutt, A. (1892) 'The Lai of Eliduc and the maerchen of Little Snow White', *Folk-Lore* 3: 26–48.

Ong, W. (1982) *Orality and Literacy*, London.

O'Sullivan, J.N. (1995) *Xenophon of Ephesus: His Compositional Technique and the Birth of the Novel*, Berlin.

Opie, P. and Opie I. (1974) *The Classic Fairy Tales*, London. (Note: citations are from the Granada p/b edn.)

Page, D.L. (1955) *The Homeric Odyssey*, Oxford.

Pantajja, E. (1993) 'Going up in the world: class in *Cinderella*', *Western Folklore* 52: 85–104.

Perco, D. (1993) 'Female initiation in northern Italian versions of *Cinderella*', *Western Folklore* 52: 73–84.

Perry, B.E. (1952) *Aesopica*, Urbana, IL.

—— (1967) *The Ancient Romances*, Berkeley, CA.

Philip, N. (1989) *The Cinderella Story*, Harmondsworth, Middx.

Philippson, E. (1923) *Der Maerchentypus von Koenig Drosselbart* (*FFC* 50), Greifswald.

Posener, G. (1953) 'On the tale of the Doomed Prince', *JEA* 39: 107.

Propp, V. (1968) *Morphology of the Folktale*, Austin, TX.

—— (1984), *Theory and History of Folklore*, Minneapolis.

Radin, P. (1956) *The Trickster*, New York.

Ramanujan, A.K. (1983) 'Hanchi: A Kannada Cinderella' in A. Dundes *Cinderella: A Casebook*, New York, pp. 293–296.

—— (1995) *Folktales from India*, New York.

Ranke, K. (1934) *Die Zwei Brueder: eine Studie zur vergleichenden Maerchenforschung* (FFC 114), Helsinki.

—— (1977–) *Enzyklopaedie des Maerchens*, (9 volumes published to date), Berlin.

Reardon, B.P. (1982) 'Theme, structure and narrative in Chariton', *YCS* 27: 1–27.

—— (1992) *The Form of Greek Romance*, Berkeley, CA.

Reitzenstein, R. (1912) *Das Maerchen von Amor und Psyche bei Apuleius*, Leipzig.

Riordan, J. (1989) *The Sun Maiden and the Crescent Moon: Siberian Folk Tales*, Edinburgh.

Roberts, W.E. (1958) *The Tale of the Kind and the Unkind Girls*, Berlin.

Roehrich, L. (1962) 'Die mittelalterlichen Redaktionen des Polyphem-Maerchens (*AT* 1137) und ihr Verhaeltnis zur ausserhomerischen Tradition', *Fabula* 5: 48–71.

—— (1991) *Folktales and Reality* (tr. P. Tokofsky), Bloomington, IN.

Rooth, A.B. (1951) *The Cinderella Cycle*, Lund.

Rose, H.J. (1928) *A Handbook of Greek Mythology*, London.

Rowe, K.E. (1979) 'Feminism and fairy tales', *Women's Studies: An Interdisciplinary Journal* 6: 237–257.

Ryder, A.W. (1925) *The Panchatantra*, Chicago.

Salisbury, J.E. (1997) *Perpetua's Passion*, London.

Schmeling, G. (ed.) (1996) *The Novel in the Ancient World*, Leiden.

Schwartz, H. (1983) *Elijah's Violin and Other Jewish Folktales*, New York.

—— (1988) *Miriam's Tambourine: Jewish Folktales from Around the World*, New York.

Scobie, A. (1977) 'Some folktales in Graeco-Roman and Far Eastern sources', *Philologus* 121: 7–10.

—— (1979) 'Storytellers, storytelling and the novel in Graeco-Roman antiquity', *RhM* 122: 229–259.

—— (1983) *Apuleius and Folklore*, London.

Smith, M.S. (1975) *Petronius, Cena Trimalchionis*, Oxford.

Sourvinou-Inwood, C. (1996) *Reading Greek Death*, Oxford.

Spitta, W. (1883) *Contes arabes modernes*, Leiden.

Stevenson, R.H. (1958) *Amiran-Darejaniani: A Cycle of Medieval Georgian Tales*, Oxford.

Sutton, D.F. (1980) *The Greek Satyr Play*, Meisenheim.

Swahn, J.-Oe. (1955) *The Tale of Cupid and Psyche*, Lund.

Sydow, C.W. von (1909) *Två spinnsagor: en studie i jaemfoerande folksagoforskning*, Stockholm.

—— (1943) *Finsk metod och modern sagoforskning*, Lund.

Taggart, J.M. (1990) *Enchanted Maidens*, Manchester.

Tatar, M. (1987) *The Hard Facts of the Grimms' Fairy Tales*, Princeton, NJ.

—— (1999) *The Classic Fairy Tales*, New York.

Tegethoff, E. (1922) *Studien zum Maerchentypus von Amor und Psyche*, Bonn.

Thompson, S. (1946) *The Folktale*, Bloomington, IN.

—— (1953) 'The Star Husband tale' in *Studia Septentrionalia* 4: 93–163 (reprinted in Dundes (1965: 414–474)).

—— (1955–1958) *Motif-Index of Folk Literature*, vols I–VI, Bloomington, IN.

—— (1977) *The Folktale*, Berkeley, CA.

Trenkner, S. (1958) *The Greek Novella in the Classical Period*, Cambridge.

Uther, H.-J. (1996) 'Type and motif-indices 1980–1995: an inventory', *Asian Folklore Studies* 55: 299–317.

Verdier, Y. (1978) 'Grands-mères, si vous saviez: le Petit Chaperon Rouge dans la Tradition Orale', *Cahiers de Littérature Orale* 4: 17–55.

Walsh, P.G. (1970) *The Roman Novel*, Cambridge.

Warner, M. (1994) *From the Beast to the Blonde*, London.

—— (1999) *No Go the Bogeyman*, London.

Wesselski, A. (1931) *Versuch einer Theorie des Maerchens*, Reichenberg.

West, M.L. (1971) *Greek Philosophy and the Orient*, Oxford.

—— (1997) *The East Face of Helicon*, London.

West, S. (1974) '*Joseph and Asenath*: A Neglected Greek Romance', *CQ* NS 24: 70–81.

Wiedemann, T.H. (1989) *Adults and Children in the Roman Empire*, London.

Wiseman, T.P. (1995) *Remus: A Roman Myth*, Cambridge.

Wright, J.R.G. (1971) 'Folktale and literary technique in *Cupid and Psyche*', *CQ* NS 21: 273–284.

Zipes, J. (1979) *Breaking the Magic Spell: Radical Theories of Folk and Fairy Tales*, Austin, TX.

—— (1983) *Fairy Tales and the Art of Subversion: The Classical Genre for Children and the Process of Civilisation*, New York.

—— (1993a) *The Trials and Tribulations of Little Red Riding Hood*, New York.

—— (1993b) 'Spinning with Fate: Rumpelstiltskin and the Decline of Female Productivity', *Western Folklore* 52: 43–60.

—— (1995) *Creative Storytelling*, New York.

—— (1997) *Happily Ever After: Fairy Tales, Children, and the Culture Industry*, New York.

—— (1999) *When Dreams Came True: Classical Fairy Tales and Their Tradition*, New York.

—— (2000) (ed.) *The Oxford Companion to Fairy Tales*, Oxford.

INDEX OF FOLKTALE TYPES

AT Type Titles are generally those of Aarne-Thompson (1961). Where I have used an obviously different label, the *AT* title follows in brackets. Subdivisions of individual numberings (510A, 884B, etc.) are sometimes less stable in their boundaries than the numerical classifications themselves.

GENERAL INDEX

Note: bold numbers indicate comparison tables

Turkish tales 74–7, 125; 'Brother Cock'
109
Twelve Dancing Princesses, The (*AT* Type
306) 119–22, 167; comparison table
120–1
Two Brothers, The (*AT* Type 303) 91,
143–4, 170, 183–5, 186
Two Brothers–Peleus, comparison table
184

Ubainer 131–2
underworld 38, 119, 164; motifs 67, 177;
taboos 100; tales 122

Varia Historia (Aelian) 29, 31–2, 33
Venus 64
Verae Historiae 192
Villeneuve, Madame de G.–S. 70
Virgil (*Aeneid*) 120
Voluptas 69
Von Sydow, Carl 139

'wager on wife's chastity' tales 83, 85,
156, 161
Wasps (Aristophanes) 4, 10
water: drawn from a well 176, 180–1; in
tasks 176–7; *see also* sea; well motifs
water nymphs 88, 184

well motifs 58, 84, 101, 178, 179, 180–1;
drawing water from 176, 180–1; 'well
at world's end' 176, 182
Whitman, Cedric 19–20
Wild Harris's Ghost 114
wisdom tales 15, 133, 164
wishes 136–7, 138, 164
witch-hunting 103
witches 16, 17, 45, 54, 94, 162, 170, 179,
183, 184, 185
wolves and wolf tales 18, 92–7, 121
women's rituals 163
Wonder-working Doll, The (Straparola) 109
Worn-out Shoes, The 119–22

Xantheus 27, 28
Xenophon of Ephesus 145, 147, 148, 156

'youth doomed to be hanged, the' 122

Zeus 38, 61–2, 89, 184, 186; and *Beauty
and the Beast* 70; and Chione variant
47; and Semele myth 61; and
Thrushbeard 190
Zipes, Jack 159, 172; and *Red Riding
Hood* 92–3; and sociology of fairytales
164–5

Printed in the United States
38571LVS00004BA/33-66

9 780415 237031